Sacrifice and Moral Philosophy

The aim of this book is to foster a more explicit and direct discussion of the concept of sacrifice and its importance in moral philosophy.

Acts of self-sacrifice have a special place in our moral lives. We admire and celebrate those who give up their lives so that others may live. Despite this important role that sacrifice plays in our moral thinking, moral philosophers have had surprisingly little to say about the nature of sacrifice. This lack of attention to the nature of sacrifice is particularly important given that sacrifice also has an important role to play in several key debates in moral philosophy. The chapters in this volume make an important contribution to our understanding of sacrifice in three areas. The first part of the book investigates the nature of sacrifice. The next group of chapters investigates the role of sacrifice in moral philosophy. Three of these pieces investigate the role of sacrifice in our moral lives generally, while two investigate the role of sacrifice in relation to particular moral theories. The final two chapters investigate the value of sacrifice in relation to political and theological issues.

The chapters in this book were originally published as a special issue of the *International Journal of Philosophical Studies*.

Marcel van Ackeren is an External Investigator at Freiburg's Centre for Integrative Biological Signalling Studies, a Research Associate at Oxford's Uehiro Centre for Practical Ethics and Associate Member of the Faculty of Philosophy in Oxford, UK. He has held visiting positions at Cambridge, Berne and Milan, was a fellow at the Institute for Advanced Studies (Wissenschaftskolleg) in Greifswald and was a fellow and researcher at the Institute for Advanced Studies in Bioethics at Münster University. He works in ethics, history of philosophy and methodology.

Alfred Archer is an Assistant Professor of Philosophy in the Department of Philosophy and at the Tilburg Center for Logic, Ethics and Philosophy of Science at Tilburg University, the Netherlands. His primary research is in moral philosophy, particularly supererogation (acts beyond the call of duty) and the nature and ethics of admiration. He also has research interests in political philosophy, applied ethics, philosophy of emotion and the philosophy of sport.

Sacrifice and Moral Philosophy

Edited by
Marcel van Ackeren and Alfred Archer

LONDON AND NEW YORK

First published 2020
by Routledge
2 Park Square, Milton Park, Abingdon, Oxon, OX14 4RN

and by Routledge
52 Vanderbilt Avenue, New York, NY 10017

Routledge is an imprint of the Taylor & Francis Group, an informa business

Except Chapter 9 © 2020 Taylor & Francis

Chapter 9 © 2018 Amanda Cawston and Alfred Archer. Originally published as Open Access.

With the exception of Chapter 9, no part of this book may be reprinted or reproduced or utilised in any form or by any electronic, mechanical, or other means, now known or hereafter invented, including photocopying and recording, or in any information storage or retrieval system, without permission in writing from the publishers. For details on the rights for Chapters 9, please see the chapter's Open Access footnote.

Trademark notice: Product or corporate names may be trademarks or registered trademarks, and are used only for identification and explanation without intent to infringe.

Publisher's Note
The publisher accepts responsibility for any inconsistencies that may have arisen during the conversion of this book from journal articles to book chapters, namely the inclusion of journal terminology.

Disclaimer
Every effort has been made to contact copyright holders for their permission to reprint material in this book. The publishers would be grateful to hear from any copyright holder who is not here acknowledged and will undertake to rectify any errors or omissions in future editions of this book.

British Library Cataloguing in Publication Data
A catalogue record for this book is available from the British Library

ISBN13: 978-0-367-50859-3

Typeset in Minion
by Newgen Publishing UK

Contents

	Citation Information	vii
	Notes on Contributors	ix
	Introduction: Self-Sacrifice and Moral Philosophy	1
	Marcel van Ackeren and Alfred Archer	
1	On the Moral Significance of Sacrifice	8
	Joseph Raz	
2	How Morality Becomes Demanding Cost vs. Difficulty and Restriction	15
	Marcel van Ackeren	
3	Sacrifice and Relational Well-Being	35
	Vanessa Carbonell	
4	When does 'Can' imply 'Ought'?	54
	Stephanie Collins	
5	Sacrificing Value	76
	Lisa Tessman	
6	The Value of Sacrifices	99
	Jörg Löschke	
7	Sentimentalist Practical Reason and Self-Sacrifice	119
	Michael Slote	
8	Demandingness and Boundaries Between Persons	137
	Edward Harcourt	

CONTENTS

9 Rehabilitating Self-Sacrifice: Care Ethics and the Politics
   of Resistance   156
   Amanda Cawston and Alfred Archer

10 The Cross   178
   Sophie-Grace Chappell

   Index   199

Citation Information

The chapters in this book were originally published in the *International Journal of Philosophical Studies*, volume 26, issue 3 (July 2018). When citing this material, please use the original page numbering for each article, as follows:

Introduction
Self-Sacrifice and Moral Philosophy
Marcel van Ackeren and Alfred Archer
International Journal of Philosophical Studies, volume 26, issue 3 (July 2018), pp. 301–307

Chapter 1
On the Moral Significance of Sacrifice
Joseph Raz
International Journal of Philosophical Studies, volume 26, issue 3 (July 2018), pp. 308–314

Chapter 2
How Morality Becomes Demanding Cost vs. Difficulty and Restriction
Marcel van Ackeren
International Journal of Philosophical Studies, volume 26, issue 3 (July 2018), pp. 315–334

Chapter 3
Sacrifice and Relational Well-Being
Vanessa Carbonell
International Journal of Philosophical Studies, volume 26, issue 3 (July 2018), pp. 335–353

Chapter 4
When does 'Can' imply 'Ought'?
Stephanie Collins
International Journal of Philosophical Studies, volume 26, issue 3 (July 2018), pp. 354–375

viii CITATION INFORMATION

Chapter 5

Sacrificing Value
Lisa Tessman
International Journal of Philosophical Studies, volume 26, issue 3 (July 2018), pp. 376–398

Chapter 6

The Value of Sacrifices
Jörg Löschke
International Journal of Philosophical Studies, volume 26, issue 3 (July 2018), pp. 399–418

Chapter 7

Sentimentalist Practical Reason and Self-Sacrifice
Michael Slote
International Journal of Philosophical Studies, volume 26, issue 3 (July 2018), pp. 419–436

Chapter 8

Demandingness and Boundaries Between Persons
Edward Harcourt
International Journal of Philosophical Studies, volume 26, issue 3 (July 2018), pp. 437–455

Chapter 9

Rehabilitating Self-Sacrifice: Care Ethics and the Politics of Resistance
Amanda Cawston and Alfred Archer
International Journal of Philosophical Studies, volume 26, issue 3 (July 2018), pp. 456–477

Chapter 10

The Cross
Sophie-Grace Chappell
International Journal of Philosophical Studies, volume 26, issue 3 (July 2018), pp. 478–498

For any permission-related enquiries please visit:
www.tandfonline.com/page/help/permissions

Notes on Contributors

Marcel van Ackeren, Cluster of Excellence, University of Freiburg, Associated: Faculty of Philosophy and Uehiro Centre for Practical Ethics, University of Oxford, Oxford, UK

Alfred Archer, Department of Philosophy, University of Tilburg, Tilburg, the Netherlands

Vanessa Carbonell, Philosophy Department, University of Cincinnati, Cincinnati, OH, USA

Amanda Cawston, Department of Philosophy, University of Tilburg, Tilburg, the Netherlands

Sophie-Grace Chappell, Philosophy Department, Faculty of Arts and Social Sciences, The Open University, Milton Keynes, UK

Stephanie Collins, Institute for Religion and Critical Inquiry, Australian Catholic University, East Melbourne, Australia

Edward Harcourt, Faculty of Philosophy, University of Oxford; Keble College, Oxford, UK

Jörg Löschke, Institute of Philosophy, University of Bern, Bern, Switzerland

Joseph Raz, Faculty of Law Emeritus, University of Oxford, Oxford, UK; Columbia University, New York, NY, USA; The Dickson Poon School of Law, King's College London, London, UK

Michael Slote, Department of Philosophy, University of Miami, Coral Gables, FL, USA

Lisa Tessman, Philosophy Department, Binghamton University, Binghamton, NY, USA

Introduction: Self-Sacrifice and Moral Philosophy

Marcel van Ackeren and Alfred Archer

On 14 February 2018, Nikolaz Cruz carried out a gun attack in a Florida High School, killing 17 people. Among the victims was the 15-year-old school student and junior cadet Peter Wang, who died while holding a door open to allow other students to escape the shooting. Wang's heroic act of sacrifice prompted US Army to posthumously award him a Medal of Honor, while the military academy West Point honored Wang by admitting him into their class of 2025. Acts of self-sacrifice such as this have a special place in our moral lives. We admire and celebrate those who give up their lives so that others may live. Despite this important role that sacrifice plays in our moral thinking, moral philosophers have had surprisingly little to say about the nature of sacrifice.

This lack of attention to the nature of sacrifice is particularly important given that sacrifice also has an important role to play in several key debates in moral philosophy. The concept features most prominently in the discussion of moral demandingness. Many contributors to this debate claim that there are constraints on the amount of sacrifice that can be morally demanded of people. Following Susan Wolf's (1982) and Bernard Williams' (1979) critiques of classical modern moral theories many ethicists now argue that a moral theory that demands huge sacrifices from the addressees of the demands is faulty and must at least be altered.

Sacrifice also has a key role to play in the related discussion of supererogation. Since J.O. Urmson's (1958) influential paper on supererogation, it has been widely accepted that sacrifice is an essential feature of the concept of supererogation. As Dale Dorsey (2013, 357) describes: 'Many hold that one essential feature of the supererogatory is that supererogatory actions are supererogatory in part because they involve some non-trivial sacrifice to the agent.' But this standard account of supererogation has recently been challenged by arguments that also make use of the concept of sacrifice. It has been claimed that an act can be supererogatory even if it does not involve any sacrifice on the part of the agent (see Archer 2015, 2016; Ferry 2013; Horgan and Timmons 2010). It has also recently been observed, that sacrifice is the very concept that links these two debates on (over-)demandingess and supererogation (see Benn 2016).

Sacrifice also plays an important role in debates concerning the nature of well-being. It has been claimed that Desire Fulfilment Theory (the view that it is only the fulfilment of desires that is non-instrumentally valuable) should be rejected because it has the absurd implication that self-sacrifice is impossible (Overvold 1980, 117). One response that has been made to this criticism is that it mistakenly assumes that an act of self-sacrifice cannot advance the agent's self-interest. Connie Rosati (2009, 314) argues against this assumption, claiming 'an act can both advance a person's good and constitute an act of self-sacrifice'. Similarly, Joseph Raz (1999) has argued that self-sacrifices do not damage our well-being (see van Ackeren 2016).

Finally, sacrifice has an important role to play in the discussion of care ethics. Care ethics has been proposed as a feminist approach to ethics because it pays attention to the moral experience of women in a way that traditional moral theories do not (Jagger 1991). However, care ethics has also been criticized by feminists for encouraging women to adopt an ethics of self-sacrifice that fails to promote the interests of women (MacKinnon 1987; Hampton 1993).

Given this importance of sacrifice for some important topics in contemporary moral philosophy we might expect there to be a significant philosophical literature examining the nature of sacrifice. This is not the case. In fact, analytic philosophers have only recently started to see sacrifice as something that is worthy of sustained philosophical investigation in its own right. This debate about the nature of sacrifice remains in its infancy and there are not more than a handful papers on this topic, let alone an anthology. Thus the aim of this special issue is to foster a more explicit and direct discussion of the concept of sacrifice and its importance in moral philosophy. The papers in this volume make an important contribution to our understanding of sacrifice in three areas. The first group of papers investigates the nature of sacrifice. The next group of papers investigates the role of sacrifice in moral philosophy. Three of these papers investigate the role of sacrifice in our moral lives generally, while two investigate the role of sacrifice in relation to particular moral theories. The final two papers investigate the value of sacrifice in relation to political and theological issues.

1. The Moral Nature of Sacrifice

The first widely agreed upon feature of sacrifice is that it must involve a cost to the agent performing the act. Jonathan Dancy (1993, 118), for example, defines sacrifice as a 'cost to the agent'. This element of sacrifice has tended to be the focus of philosophical discussion, though it is perhaps a somewhat thinner notion than the everyday use of the term. As Overvold (1980, 113–114) points out, we might think that the everyday notion of sacrifice involves further features such as the action being performed intentionally or voluntarily.

However, the claim that a sacrifice involves a cost to the agent leaves a number of questions unanswered. The first concerns the relevant comparison against which an act should be considered costly. One option would be to hold that the relevant comparison is to the position the agent was in before performing the act. However, this seems to be the wrong approach, as cases where an agent opts to cut her losses and chooses the least costly option from a range of costly alternatives should not count as cases of sacrifice (Archer 2015, 108). Instead, we should view sacrifice in a counterfactual way, in which the agent is judged to have chosen a costly option over a less costly action that was available to her (Archer 2015, 2016).

The second issue is whether the cost involved in sacrifice should be understood as an overall cost to the agent's well-being or in a weaker way. Carbonnell (2012, 237) has argued that a sacrifice need not involve an overall cost to the agent. We can also be said to make a sacrifice when we endure some loss that is not compensated for, where this is understood as one that is not directly replaced without loss. For example, consider a child who dedicates her life to becoming a gymnast and so loses out on many of the pleasures of a normal childhood such as playdates, ice cream and lazy weekend mornings. According to Carbonell, the gymnast should count as making a sacrifice even if her decision to dedicate her life to gymnastics results in a net gain in well-being. This view fits most comfortably with an objective list view of well-being according to which there are a number of different sources of well-being.

The contributions in this volume extend this discussion of the moral significance of sacrifice in a number of ways. First, Joseph Raz' 'On the Moral Significance of Sacrifice' discusses great sacrifices, that is those sacrifices that make the life of the agent bad in a serious or permanent way, but do not end her life. He distinguishes various ways in which a sacrifice is of no special moral significance and then indicates different ways in which it is. He then considers the question whether a sacrifice can be morally required by presenting arguments in favour of and against that view. His discussion stresses the need for a finer-grained discussion of sacrifice and exemplifies some of the problems that a unified and systematic theory of sacrifice is facing.

Next, in 'How Morality Becomes Demanding?' Marcel van Ackeren investigates what counts as a morally required sacrifice. Most of the literature presupposes the standard account which views demandingness as a matter of costs to the agent but does not argue for it. Very recently, however, various new theories have challenged this standard account. Van Ackeren defends the standard view of demandingness against the recent challenges by presenting a new variant of it. To van Ackeren

4 SACRIFICE AND MORAL PHILOSOPHY

demandingness is only a matter of costs to the agent. First, he argues against the new difficulty view of demandingness by showing that difficulty can increase demandingness only by being costly. Second, he shows that restrictions of options can increase demandingness only by being costly. He distinguishes three ways restricting options can increase demandingness, namely by prohibiting actions that the agent wants to perform in order to promote his well-being, by limiting the development of future preferences and projects and also by making the society less open.

Vanessa Carbonell in 'Sacrifice and Relational Well-Being' starts by acknowledging that the well-being account of sacrifice is attractive. However, she then argues that sacrifices made on behalf of loved ones may be problematic for this account. She argues that 'loving sacrifices' occur in a context where the agent's well-being and the beneficiary's well-being are intertwined, and concludes that a notion of 'relational well-being', analogous to 'relational autonomy', can help account for loving sacrifices without rejecting the well-being theory of sacrifice. This discussion not only highlights the intricate relation of sacrifice and well-being but also stresses the relational character of sacrifice.

2. Sacrifice and Ethical Theory

As we have already discussed, one of the main debates in which sacrifice plays an important role is the discussion of moral demandingness. Key to this discussion is the question of how much sacrifice to their own well-being can be morally demanded of people. The papers in this volume extend this discussion in several important ways.

Stephanie Collins' 'When Does Can Imply Ought' investigates an intuitively plausible moral principle that she calls 'The Assistance Principle'. According to this principle, if we have the opportunity to fulfil important interests at not too high a cost then we have a duty to do so. Collins investigates how the concept of sacrifice should inform our understanding and implementation of this principle. She argues that we need to accept a tripartite conception of sacrifice that includes agent-relative, recipient-relative, and ideal-relative sacrifice in interpreting and applying the assistance principle. In doing so, she provides a more nuanced and informative account of the assistance principle than can be found in the existing literature on the topic.

In 'Sacrificing Value' Lisa Tessman discusses sacrifice in relation to a conflict of values. She argues that some conflicts of values are genuine dilemmas, so that no resolution is morally clean. In cases of conflict in which self-sacrifice is one of the options, ambivalence may be particularly appropriate. There may be in such cases special sources of plurality and incommensurability of values, because in part the conflict is likely to be between something that is valued by a social group, and something that is valued particularly by an individual who has to consider self-sacrificing. And in part it is because individuals may have trouble balancing self-regarding and other-regarding concerns in the process of value construction. Tessmann provides a rich elaboration of these complications, and presents cases in which we might suspect that someone has self-sacrificed too much or too little.

Jörg Löschke's 'The Value of Sacrifices' provides a fruitful new perspective on the value of sacrifice by investigating an unexplored aspect of sacrifice. Löschke argues that there are cases in which the sacrifice of person A can have an impact on the practical reasons of person B, either by generating practical reasons for B to act in certain ways or by intensifying existing reasons of B for specific courses of action. Löschke argues that sacrifices can have other-regarding normative impact because sacrifices can be intrinsically good. The intrinsic value of sacrifices is explained by the recursive account of value: sacrifices are intrinsically good if and because they are appropriate responses to intrinsic values, and appropriate responses to intrinsic values are themselves intrinsically good. Furthermore, sacrifices are difficult to make, and successful pursuit in difficult activities can also be intrinsically good.

The second group of papers in this section discusses sacrifices with regard to one distinct normative moral theory. In 'Sentimentalist Practical Reason and Self-Sacrifice' Michael Slote further develops his own sentimentalist approach to morality by showing that the sentimentalist can seek to reduce practical to sentimentalist considerations. Slote starts by observing that sentimentalists are hesitant to offer accounts of moral reasons for action. Slote argues that prudential reasons can be identified with the normal emotional/motivational responses people feel in situations that threaten them or offer them opportunities to attain what they need. And in the most basic cases altruistic/moral reasons involve the empathic transfer of one person's prudential reasons and emotions to another person or persons who can help them. Practical/moral reasons for self-sacrifice also depend on empathic transfer and can vary in strength with the strength of the transfer.

Consequentialism is the normative ethical view that is most often objected to for the level of sacrifices it requires from people. In 'Demandingness and Boundaries Between Persons' Edward Harcourt advances this discussion by providing a novel demandingness objection to consequentialism. He starts by arguing that many arguments in the debate concerning the stranger/special other distinction are in error thanks to assumptions they share about our relations with special others, which focus entirely on what we pleasurably sacrifice to special others (see Carbonell's contribution) and not at all on what we properly withhold from them. He then argues that boundaries between ourselves and our special others are a common feature of our relations with special others but also a good-making feature of them. He concludes that demandingness objections that rely on the argument in question fail. But he claims that the same observations about our relations with special others can give rise to a more plausible objection according to which there are demands strangers may not properly make on us.

3. Sacrifice and Protest

The final two papers in the volume consider, in different ways, the role that sacrifice can play in political protest. Amanda Cawston and Alfred Archer's 'Rehabilitating Self-Sacrifice: Care Ethics and the Politics of Resistance' investigates how feminists should view acts of self-sacrifice performed by women. According to a prominent feminist critique of care ethics, such acts may run counter to feminist aims. Feminist critics of care ethics claim that this approach to morality encourages women to engage in acts of self-sacrifice rather than to promote their own well-being and development. Care ethicists have responded to this critique by identifying limits on the level, form or scope of self-sacrifice that work to restrict its role in their theories. Cawston and Archer argue that these responses fail to appreciate the positive value that self-sacrifice can play in combatting patriarchal oppression. They then provide a new response to the critique of care ethics by exploring these positive roles for self-sacrifice and thereby rehabilitate its standing with feminists.

The final paper in the volume is Sophie-Grace Chappell's 'The Cross'. Chappell explores the nature of sacrifice through a detailed investigation of the Christian conception of sacrifice. Chappell explores this conception through a rich and detailed investigation of what the New Testament tells us about what Jesus was doing in allowing himself to be crucified. There are two groups of meanings of this sacrifice, political and personal. The political element of this sacrifice stems from the fact that Jesus' public proclamations of his teachings were in defiance of the authorities of the time and he knew that his execution was the inevitable consequence of this defiance. The personal aspect has to be seen, according to Chappell, in the terms of Levitical ritual sacrifice. However, it is a ritual sacrifice that transcends, consummates and abolishes ritual sacrifice. As well as providing a fresh perspective on how sacrifice in general should be understood, Chappell makes a convincing case that in order to understand Christ's sacrifice we need to pay more attention to how The Bible explains it.

References

Archer, A. 2015. "Saints, Heroes and Moral Necessity." *Royal Institute of Philosophy Supplementary* 77: 105–124. doi:10.1017/S1358246115000223.

Archer, A. 2016. "Supererogation, Sacrifice, and the Limits of Duty." *The Southern Journal of Philosophy* 54 (3): 333–354. doi:10.1111/sjp.2016.54.issue-3.

Benn, C. 2016. "Overdemandingness Objections and Supererogation." In *The Limits of Moral Obligation*, edited by M. van Ackeren and M. Kuehler. London: Routledge.

Bernard, W. 1979. *Utililitarianism. For and Against. (With J.J.C. Smart)*. Cambridge: Cambridge University Press.

Carbonnell, V. 2012. "The Ratcheting-Up Effect." *Pacific Philosophical Quarterly* 93: 228–254. doi:10.1111/j.1468-0114.2012.01425.x.

Dancy, J. 1993. *Moral Reasons*. Oxford: Blackwell.

Dorsey, D. 2013. "The Supererogatory, and How to Accommodate It." *Utilitas* 25: 355–382. doi:10.1017/S095382081200060X.

Ferry, M. 2013. "Does Morality Demand Our Very Best? Moral Prescriptions and the Line of Duty." *Philosophical Studies* 165: 573–589. doi:10.1007/s11098-012-9968-6.

Hampton, J. 1993. "Feminist Contractarianism." In *A Mind Of One's Own: Feminist Essays on Reason and Objectivity*, edited by L. M. Antony and C. Witt. Boulder: Westview Press).

Horgan, T., and M. Timmons. 2010. "Untying a Knot from the inside Out: Reflections on the "Paradox of Supererogation." *Social Philosophy and Policy* 27: 29–63. doi:10.1017/S026505250999015X.

Jagger, A. M. 1991. "Feminist Ethics Projects, Problems, Prospects." In *Feminist Ethics*, edited by C. Card. Lawrence: University Press of Kansas.

MacKinnon, C. 1987. *Feminism Unmodified*. Cambridge, MA: Harvard University Press.

Overvold, M. C. 1980. "Self-Interest and the Concept of Self-Sacrifice." *Canadian Journal of Philosophy* 10: 105–118. doi:10.1080/00455091.1980.10716285.

Raz, J. 1999. *Engaging Reason: On the Theory of Value and Action*. Oxford: Oxford University Press.

Rosati, C. S. 2009. "Self-interest and Self-sacrifice." *Proceedings of the Aristotelian Society* 109: 311–325. doi:10.1111/pash.2009.109.issue-1pt3.

Urmson, J. O. 1958. "Saints and Heroes." In *Moral Concepts*, edited by J. Feinberg. Oxford: Oxford University Press, 1969.

van Ackeren, M. 2016. "Putting the Central Conflict to Rest? Raz on Morality and Well-Being." In *The Limits of Moral Obligation. Moral Demandingness and Ought Implies Can*, edited by M. van Ackeren and M. Kühler, 51–67. New York: Routledge.

Wolf, S. 1982. "Moral Saints." *The Journal of Philosophy* 79: 419–439. doi:10.2307/2026228.

On the Moral Significance of Sacrifice

Joseph Raz

ABSTRACT

The paper offers a few reflections on moral implications of making sacrifices and on possible duties to make sacrifices. It does not provide an exhaustive or a systematic account of the subject. There are too many disparate questions, and too many different perspectives from which to examine them to allow for a systematic let alone an exhaustive account, and too many factual issues that I am not aware of. Needless to say, the observations that follow are in part stimulated by the popularity of some views that are mistaken. I will not however examine any specific view or account of these matters. The aim is to provide some pointers that will be helpful when considering specific issues regarding the moral significance of sacrifice.

I take 'making a sacrifice' to mean knowingly giving up something, of such value to the agent that foregoing it would be deprivation or a hardship, for the sake of something or someone that one values, other than oneself or one's interests. In the long run, a sacrifice could turn out to enhance one's interests etc., but if it was done in order to enhance one's interests, it would not be a sacrifice. Benefits from a sacrifice can of course happen accidentally or unforeseeably. But they can be foreseeable. I may make a sacrifice in order to save my child's life, and his life's eventual richness and happiness may greatly enrich my life. So long as in no way did I do it in order to avoid a disaster *for my life* it was a sacrifice. Needless to say, as with anything that depends on the agent's intention, there will be many cases regarding which it will be hard or impossible to determine whether they involve a sacrifice or not. What is clear is that a gift or any self- deprivation undertaken in order to be given an honour or a benefit is not a sacrifice even if the benefit does not come – it was just a bad deal.

My interest is in the moral significance of making a great sacrifice. Needless to say, sacrifices may take many different shapes and forms, and also be of different degrees. So I will use 'a great sacrifice' stipulatively to include ones that seriously and permanently impair one's health or render one seriously disabled, and those that prevent one from carrying on with the life one has. By 'the life one has' I mean the sort of life one is embarked on, where that sort is identified by the features that are of central importance to the person whose life it is: so, if both Abe and Bob are hospital nurses, it could be that being a nurse is (part of) the life of one of them and not of the other, if one of them cherishes being a nurse whereas the other does not care about it in any way other than as a source of income. I will not discuss the sacrifice or the giving up of one's life, even though it is commonly thought to be the supreme sacrifice. I believe with Epicurus that death is nothing to us, that is, nothing to the person who is dying, or at least that that is generally the case. Therefore, generally giving up one's life is a sacrifice only when it is a hardship or deprivation for people or causes dear to the person who is giving up his life. Given that this is not the occasion to consider this view about the value of staying alive,[1] I will avoid discussing this kind of sacrifice.

Sacrifices can be or fail to be virtuous, obligatory, something one has reason to do and much else. To simplify matters I will often refer to them as being or not being moral requirements. I use the term to fudge the question of the precise moral status involved, saying something like: if a great sacrifice is morally required it has one of the possible moral statuses, namely it is virtuous, obligatory, supererogatory etc., and it does not matter for current purposes which status it has.

From the point of view of individuals involved there is a big difference between actions that risk ending up with a large sacrifice for the agent, e.g. loss of limb or being kidnapped, and actions that essentially involve making a sacrifice, such as resigning an irreplaceable job, or where the sacrifice is a virtually certain side effect of the action intended. Where there is a known significant risk of a sacrifice which does not materialise no sacrifice occurred, though the agent was ready and willing to make a sacrifice. Where there was a known risk and the risk materialised, so that the agent suffered a significant loss and hardship, we do correctly say that the agent made a big sacrifice. In spite of the considerable differences between the different cases much of the time I will lump them together. This is not to deny the importance of the felt differences for agents, and the consequential policy differences when designing or controlling circumstances that call for sacrifices. Yes, it is preferable to ask people to run the risk of a sacrifice than to make a sacrifice outright etc. But much of the time the differences would not matter to the discussion of the paper.

Generally speaking, making a sacrifice is not in itself morally significant. Of course, we sometimes refer to sacrifices made as an indication of how much one values the cause or person. But this is just an instance of the general way of assessing how much one cares or values something by how much one is willing to do to secure it or to avoid losing it etc. As one among several indicators it serves well, but there is nothing special in mentioning a sacrifice in that way.

Is it wrong to make some sacrifices? Yes, but that is not specific to sacrifices either. It is wrong to make silly sacrifices or badly judged ones, or those that are irresponsible towards oneself or another (one's child).

Is the making of a justified, well-judged sacrifice saintly? Not necessarily; not even if it was one's duty to make the sacrifice, and not even if one made it for the right reasons, say abandoning one's career and moving to another town to look after an aged parent, when there is no satisfactory alternative. One may resent having to make the sacrifice, hate the parent whose need made it necessary, hate oneself for not being able to do better etc. And in such cases there is nothing saintly about the sacrifice.[2]

The manner in which one makes the sacrifice and the web of beliefs and attitudes surrounding it determine what it implies regarding one's moral dispositions and one's moral character. But that is so for any of one's actions and omissions. Again, there is nothing special about sacrifice here. But is not the making of a sacrifice necessary for the action to be anything like saintly? This question requires a broad ranging examination of the degree to which and the ways in which acts, activities and omissions reflect on or manifest established dispositions and character traits. It cannot be undertaken here. I for one do not think that even extreme moral virtue can only be manifested by making a sacrifice. But I will not argue for that view here.

Is one ever morally required to make a sacrifice, or to make a serious sacrifice, say to sacrifice the life one has?

Clearly, common opinion allows that sacrificing the life one has can be one's moral duty. After all, common opinion has it that people have a moral duty to volunteer for military service under certain circumstances, even though doing so regularly forces people to abandon the life they have, without a secure prospect of being able to resume it later on.

I mentioned that the very act of joining the armed forces is often a major sacrifice. Needless to say, in the course of serving in the armed forces one may be required to sacrifice health, limbs or life. The same is true of people who join the armed services without conscription, or extend their membership after conscription, as well as of police officers, fire brigade officers and some others.

These are instructive illustrations for several reasons. First, analogical reasoning relying on some such cases makes a plausible case for there being a moral duty to make serious sacrifices in some cases. In many of these cases, the moral duty follows the imposition of a legal duty. That is, there are circumstances where there is no moral duty to join the armed forces, except that once there is such a legal duty, that becomes also a moral duty. In other cases, there is a moral duty to do something, even if it involves making serious sacrifices, a duty that is independent of any legal or other institutional duty. But let us consider first the cases where a legal or institutional duty comes first.

First, to clarify the obvious: it is not my contention that whatever the law requires becomes, as a result, a moral duty; only that sometimes this is the case. Second, there is no denying that sometimes when the law's requirements involve making serious sacrifices, that very fact engenders resentment and grudging obedience, as well as a tendency to evade or simply break the law. But often enough it does not. Rather, most people join in the belief that the requirement is justified, being a civic duty or something of the kind. They know that life involves duties to others, and duties to the community, and that they personally bear their share of the burden of such duties. I do not mention these facts to suggest that these attitudes are self-verifying, that people have these duties because they believe that they have them. My sole point is that these facts remind us that the thought that morality cannot require serious sacrifices because making them is more than can be expected of ordinary human beings, that making them without resentment, or making them at all, can be expected only of saintly people, is simply empirically false.

It seems not too difficult to understand how the making of sacrifices can become part of the fabric of life. Here is part of the story: In principle we all know or can know when sacrifices will be expected of us. We know that if a fire breaks out in the next door building we may have to run into a burning building to try to save trapped people. But we don't know if and when such a fire will break out. One difference with conscription, when it is part of the regular law so that all people who meet certain conditions are liable to a predefined period of conscription when they reach a certain age, is that people know or can know of the sacrifice expected of them years ahead of time. A second difference is that while the folklore of heroism and sacrifice typically concerns individuals acting singly or in small groups (though not always: remember the Battle of Thermopylae) conscription and other legally required sacrifices affect large segments of the population, selected or determined in a fair way (at least they could be so determined). A third important difference is that the legal requirements are, as we say, backed by sanctions, formal and informal.

The sanctions make it easier for people to make the required sacrifices, and this for at least two reasons. First, they can see or come to believe that they have no choice: the sanctions, formal such as fines or community service or imprisonment, and the informal ones, loss of reputation, adverse social reactions, loss of face, not to say loss of one's job etc., mean that in many of these cases one has, or feels one has no choice but to make the required sacrifice. Besides, the fact that the requirement is enforced, as we say, by law, assures people that they are not taken advantage of by shirkers who benefit from their sacrifices, while not sacrificing anything themselves. The law, when functioning properly, solves the assurance problem, making it psychologically easier for people to carry the burdens allocated to them.

The fact that conscription and other legally enforced sacrifices apply to large sections of the population also makes sacrifice easier, as it is easier to act as part of a similarly oriented body of people. One derives strength and support from sharing the conditions one is in with others. The advantages of the first difference are also obvious. Knowing in advance of the sacrifice and its general character makes it possible to take it into account when thinking about and planning one's future. It may even enable one to change its character as a sacrifice. For example, one may decide on a military career. As a result the period during which one is conscripted is no longer a sacrifice of the life one has. It becomes the life one has. Many people find less dramatic solutions: while their time in the armed services is a disruption of their normal life as it was and as it will be, they try to use the time in the military to acquire some skills that interest them for their own sake, or for future use, etc. Even when no such avenues to lessen the sacrifice are available, it is easier to bear when its place in one's life is predictable.

Could it be that one may be morally required to make big sacrifices only if there is a legal or other institutional requirement to that effect? One reason to doubt this possibility is that so far as the three differences listed above are concerned, the differences they mark are a matter of degree. Almost universally people's moral views are shared among large groups. So that whether or not they are institutionally enshrined they are known and understood by whole groups of people, thus having a public definition even when they are not legally defined. That definition eases the burden of decisions about when is a sacrifice required, and means that people's conduct in making required sacrifices is socially supported and failure to make them is socially disapproved. Without denying that conditions are different when the moral duties are legally enshrined, one has to admit that there are many similarities between the social recognition and the legal recognition of moral duties, similarities that make compliance with those duties easier for individuals, partly by enabling them to incorporate the duties into the parts of their lives that provide meaning and a sense of fulfilment, and partly by providing a background of support for compliance and pressure against violations of moral requirements.

That great sacrifice is sometimes morally required leaves open the possibility that it cannot be something one has a strict duty to do, or that if there is a strict duty to make a great sacrifice, failure to fulfil that duty is excusable, and if not altogether excusable then at least any blame attached to the failure is mitigated by the fact that it is a failure to make a great sacrifice. Various considerations can tempt people into such views. One of them relies on some thoughts about the relations between motivation and sacrifice. But what thoughts?

One assumption is that there is a reverse correlation between degree of sacrifice and degree of motivation: the greater a sacrifice the less willing one is to make it. It can be given a form which makes it close to true. For example, it may be taken to say that if one can achieve a goal one is set on either by doing A or by doing B, and the agent believes that the only difference between them is that A involves a smaller sacrifice on his part than B, then the agent will choose to realise his goal by doing A rather than by doing B. Most of the time agents will have that preference, but not always. Sometimes an agent will pursue his goal by doing B because (a) that will enable him to feel more confident that he has done all he could have done, or because (b) he would feel that his (greater) sacrifice would expiate his guilt for being in a condition where he has to pursue that goal etc. Sometimes the failure of the assumption may be attributable to an irrationality in the agent (as perhaps in case (a) above), but that is not always so (a sense of expiation through sacrifice is not necessarily irrational).

Once we develop the assumption to make it true it turns out to be nothing more than (a direct derivation from) the truism that there is no case for incurring greater disadvantages than would likely suffice to secure one's goal. It does not tell us anything about the connection between sacrifice and motivation.

What some people have in mind is (among other variants on this thought) something like this: suppose that people who are C have a duty to achieve goal G. Doing so may require different things of those people. Some of them could achieve the goal only if they make a great sacrifice. But normally people cannot be expected to make great sacrifices. Human nature is such that one can rarely and/or with great difficulty be motivated to make a great sacrifice. Therefore, either that moral duty does not apply to them, or they are excused if they do not fulfil it etc. However, many of the earlier reflections aimed to show that that assumption, that view of the connection between great sacrifice and motivation is mistaken. Hence the questions about the scope of moral duties and the grounds for excuses are not affected by such views about sacrifice.

We need to understand when is the making of great sacrifices particularly difficult to motivate. It is likely that what makes great sacrifices difficult also makes compliance with moral duties in other cases difficult. Not surprisingly, it turns out that many factors affect the motivation to comply with moral requirements. We gain some understanding of their nature by examining the conditions, like those surveyed above, which help with complying with demanding moral duties: the ability to predict when one may encounter them, and to find ways of integrating them into one's life; the support one gains from the common opinion of one's community, and of course of one's friends, etc. The absence of such factors creates the emotional, and therefore the motivational difficulty of facing up to one's obligations. These, however, are the conditions of a wholesome life in general: if one is at peace with oneself one can find that complying with moral requirements enables one to affirm one's sense of self-respect and self-worth. Being consumed with self-doubt, self-loathing or guilt makes one more conflicted, more inclined to self-destructive behaviour including immoral conduct (or what one takes to be immoral). Being at odds with the society one lives in breeds alienation and negative-destructive attitudes, and drives one to extremes of defiance or of capitulation to demands that are not understood, and compliance with which increases the negative attitudes rather than infusing one with a sense that one's life has a meaning. One can go on and detail the conditions that best sustain moral life – 'best sustain' because there is no suggestion here that one cannot lead a morally exemplary life without them; however, there is no point in adding details. The general picture is fairly clear. The moral life is best sustained when moral requirements and people's attitudes towards them are integrated in what I will call a broadly understood support network of psychological and social factors encompassing all other aspects of life. It is a mistake to try to understand moral attitudes and moral life as an autonomous sphere, detached from all the rest.

One has to be lucky to find oneself at home in oneself and to be in a society that is moral and to which one feels an unconflicted sense of belonging. Saying that is no more than saying that the moral life is a social life, and that one is not assured of living in conditions that support both wholesomeness and morality. Of course, even the best support networks leave one struggling with oneself on occasion. There are no conditions, however perfect, in which one can avoid solitary struggle with one's conscience and emotions. These struggles may be occasioned when facing the demand to make a sacrifice, but they are as or more likely to occur when confronting misfortunes that, as it were, inflict sacrifices (losses that would have been sacrifices had they been the results of one's intentional action), or other circumstances that cast the success and direction of one's life in doubt.

Notes

1. I argued for it in Raz, *Value, Respect and Attachment*. Cambridge: Cambridge University Press, 2001, ch. 3.
2. I am not referring to cases in which one overcomes negative attitudes of this kind, but rather to occasions in which one succumbs to them in thought and feelings.

Disclosure Statement

No potential conflict of interest was reported by the author.

How Morality Becomes Demanding Cost vs. Difficulty and Restriction

Marcel van Ackeren

ABSTRACT

The standard view of demandingness understands demandingness exclusively as a matter of costs to the agent. The paper discusses whether the standard view must be given up because we should think of demandingness as a matter of difficulty or restriction of options. I will argue that difficulty can indeed increase demandingness, but only insofar as it leads to further costs. As to restrictions of options, I will show that confinement can become costly and thus increase demandingness in three ways, by prohibiting actions that the agent wants to perform in order to promote his well-being, by limiting the development of future preferences and projects and also by making the society less open. The paper thus defends a new variant of the standard view by arguing that difficulty and restrictions of options can increase the demandingness of morality on grounds of being costly.

1. Sacrifice and the Debate On (Over-)Demandingness

According to the *Oxford English Dictionary*, 'sacrifice' is mainly used in religious texts and contexts. However, it can also, more generally, refer to the 'destruction or surrender of something valued or desired for the sake of something having, or regarded as having, a higher or a more pressing claim; the loss entailed by devotion to some other interest; also, the thing so devoted or surrendered' (OED). Many ethical theories view morality as having such higher value and its requirements as being more pressing and authoritative than the agent's well-being.[1] Accordingly, agents should give up their own well-being or interests, happiness and desires . Such an act is called *self-sacrifice* (OED). There is widespread agreement that a normative ethical theory can require agents to perform such acts, but two current debates hotly discuss the limits of morally required self-sacrifice, namely the debate on supererogation and that on (over-) demandingness.[2] In what follows, I will focus on the latter.

At least since Peter Singer's article 'Famine, Affluence and Morality', so-called *overdemandingness* objections have become fashionable. Some label these objections a 'typical modern perversion of truth' (Raz 1993, 1297), while others argue that overdemanding theories 'strike just about everyone as absurd' (Murphy 2000, 6).[3] This debate focuses on two aspects. On the one hand, according to the *opinio communis*, overdemandingness objections reacted to consequentialism, especially impartial act-consequentialism (see Raz 1993, 1297; Hooker 2009, 148).[4] On the other hand, many have discussed only the demandingness of beneficence in combination with world poverty as its context (for example, Unger 1996; Cullity 2004). Recent studies expanded the scope of the debate by discussing theories other than consequentialism, for example, contractualism (for example, Ashford 2003; Hills 2010), virtue ethics (Swanton 2009) and deontology, especially Kant's moral theory (for example, van Ackeren and Sticker 2015; Pinheiro Walla 2015). As to the possible sources of overdemandingness, the debate now discusses – besides beneficence and world poverty – moral demands rooted in the rights or well-being of future generations (Mulgan 2006) or those related to climate change (Mulgan 2011), animal rights (Hills 2010) or refugees (Owen 2016).

Despite the absence of a taxonomy of the different overdemandingness objections (valuable starting points can be found in Hooker 2009; Benn 2016), it is safe to assume that, at least for a long time, the basic and common idea of overdemandingness objections is to argue that a moral theory which is overly demanding must be given up or at least altered (see, for example, Wolf 1982; Railton 1984; Scheffler 1992).[5] Given the importance of the debate on overdemandingness, we might expect that there is significant literature on its fundamental concept, namely demandingness. At least three reasons speak in favor of a study of demandingness.

First, demandingness is the fundamental concept of the debate on over-demandingness, because every position in favor of some overdemanding-ness objection (for example, Scheffler 1992) or against it (for example, Goodin 2009) has, at least implicitly, some conception of demandingness. For demandingness is the very thing that the first group considers to be a problem if it intensifies too much, while the latter group believes that demandingness cannot rise to such a level that it necessitates changing the theory or demand in question. Thus, we need an account of demand-ingness in order to understand what we are talking about when arguing in favor of or against overdemandingness and objections to obligations and theories. In many cases saying that something is 'too x' or 'overly x' is unproblematic. When we, for example, say that 'this shoe is too big', we can be confident that there is sufficient convergence concerning measuring shoe sizes and the idea of a fitting shoe. But with normative moral theories it is anything but clear which characteristics we refer to when arguing for or against the claim that a theory is "too demanding".

Second, the idea of overdemandingness is important because the assumption that there is a demarcation line between acceptable demandingness and unacceptable overdemandingness has ramifications for debates in meta-ethics and normative ethics. Also, establishing where the line is actually to be drawn would be of great significance for quite a number of practical issues. *Third*, a clear notion of demandingness is not only necessary for debating overdemandingness. Recent studies on supererogation (Dorsey 2011; Benn 2016; Archer and Ridge 2015) point out that most accounts of supererogation, like Urmson's (1969) classical one, are based on the notion of demandingness or self-sacrifice by arguing that actions which are overly demanding become supererogatory instead of obligatory. There might, however, be the problem of small supererogatory acts, which are supererogatory although they are not highly demanding; nonetheless, it seems that we tend to link supererogation with high demandingness.

Those three claims concerning the importance of demandingness are the background assumptions of this paper, which aims at elucidating demandingness by answering the question in which terms demandingness should be understood. This question was answered by the standard account of demandingness, which has rather been implicitly presupposed than explicitly defended. The standard view understands demandingness exclusively in terms of costs to the agent as the addressee of the demand.[6] In Shelly Kagan's (1989, 21) famous phrasing, demandingness objections are an 'appeal to cost'. This standard view was so dominant that many literature on demandingness more or less presupposed it rather than discussed alternative views.[7] But we now have two challenging and competing views, according to which we should understand demandingness in terms of difficulty or restriction of options (confinement). These challenges call for a new discussion of the concept of demandingness. In what follows, I will defend a new variant of the standard view by giving a finer-grained account of demandingness. As to difficulty (section 2), I will discuss two variants that recently challengers of the standard account of demandingness: McElwee has proposed a hybrid view of demandingness by arguing that we should understand demandingness as a matter of costs *and* also difficulty. He argues that difficulty, even if completely detached from costs, can increase demandingness (McElwee 2016). The more radical challenge is the willpower 'view according to which moral demands are understood exclusively in terms of difficulty' (Chappell 2017, 5).

I will defend the standard view by arguing that difficulty can indeed increase demandingness, but only insofar as it comes in the form of extra costs. But I will not argue that difficulty is always costly and show that cases in which difficulty is not costly are irrelevant for the discussion of the demandingness of morality.

As to the restriction of options (section 3), I will argue that restrictions can increase demandingness by being costly in three ways. Prohibitions can become costly by not allowing an action that the agent wants to perform for prudential reasons, and they also can reduce the agents' well-being by limiting their development of preferences and projects and also make their society less open.

Hence, my strategy is to show that the standard view is correct because it can explain how difficulty and the restriction of options increase the demandingness of morality when they become costly.

2. Difficulty

Recently, difficulty has received new or more attention because it was argued that degrees of blameworthiness and praiseworthiness can depend in part on degrees of difficulty (; Nelkin 2016). In line with this view, McElwee (2016) proposed a *hybrid view*, claiming that we should understand demandingness in terms of costs *and* difficulty because difficulty can lead to demandingness as an independent factor, meaning that even if difficulty is completely separated from costs, it can increase demandingness. A more radical positon, namely the willpower approach, claims that demandingness is to be understood only as a matter of difficulty (Chappell 2017) which, in turn, is understood only as willpower or effort. These two recent challenges call for a new discussion of demandingness and its relation to difficulty. For larger parts of my argumentation I will not distinguish between these two accounts because my aim is to show that difficulty can increase demandingness only if being costly; and if that is correct, it would mean that both new and challenging views are mistaken.

Difficulty is not a well-established concept. According to our widespread and intuitive use, difficulty comes in degrees. Also, difficulty can come in the form of willpower, effort, required skills and costs. There has been an attempt to provide a more unifying account of difficulty and its degrees by arguing that calling something *more difficult* for an agent

> is to say that in the relevant sense, the world in which she does so is less *accessible* from the actual world. Of course, what makes worlds more or less accessible is a matter of comparative similarity. (Coates and Swenson 2013, 638)

It has been doubted that this account exhausts the meaning of difficulty or even provides an indicator or test that captures the aspects, skills, effort and costs of our intuitions about difficulty (see Nelkin 2016, 366–378). But even if we understand difficulty in terms of accessibility or distance of worlds as a general account, there is good reason for continuing to understand difficulty in terms of required skills, effort and costs, at least for the present purpose, that is, for discussing the influence of difficulty on demandingness when complying with a moral obligation. First, the idea of accessibility or distance of worlds needs to be spelled out. The question is in which 'relevant sense' the world is more or less accessible. According to our intuition, the relevant sense can appeal to either skills, effort (willpower) or costs. Also, even if accessibility is the fundamental and unifying concept of difficulty, it seems rather unclear how difficulty, conceived as accessibility, or the distance of a world should be related to demandingness. Again, we would need to refer to the aspects of skills, effort and costs, in order to say something about the relations between accessibility and demandingness. In sum, even if required skills, effort and costs are not the only or most fundamental aspects that characterize difficulty, examining them is the best or even only way to say something about the impact of difficulty on demandingness related to moral obligations.

Let us turn to the central question whether difficulty can increase demandingness and, if so, how. I will try to answer the question in three steps and each will deal with one of the following subclasses of difficult action:

(i) difficult actions that are also costly because of the difficulty;
(ii) difficult actions that are difficult because they are also costly;
(iii) difficult actions that are beneficial.

Let us start with the clear-cut cases (i) in which the difficulty of an action is costly. These cases are clear-cut cases in the sense that, here, difficulty increases demandingness on grounds of being costly. Cases (quoted from McElwee 2016, 25–26) in which difficulty is costly include:

(ia) acts that are physically painful because they are difficult, for instance, when we are practicing a difficult cello piece and our fingers ache because they have to be stretched very often in a new and unfamiliar way;

(ib) actions that can lead to unpleasant feelings of insecurity and to frustration because the more difficult an action is, the more likely it becomes that the agent does not succeed in reaching the goal;

(ic) actions that might lead to opportunity costs because, due to the difficulty of the action, it might take more time or simply require more of the agent's attention, thus leaving the agent with less time or fewer other resources to pursue other actions promoting their well-being.

I have taken these cases from McElwee, who has suggested the hybrid view in order to stress that the existence of cases in which difficulty leads to costs is not disputed. In other words, there is agreement that this first class of difficult actions does not give us any reason to give up the standard view, that is, the view that demandingness is nothing but costs, because the cases (i) are about difficulty adding to demandingness on grounds of being costly.

However, paying attention to difficulty allows us to refine the standard account by distinguishing various forms of costs, one source of which might be difficulty. A refined picture also acknowledges that the relation of difficulty and costliness captured in (ia)-(ic) is highly relative. It seems clear that to different agents, or to the same agent in different situations, an identical difficulty can lead to varying costs in the form of pain, anxiety, or opportunity costs.

Thus, difficulty can lead to costs. But this is not the only direction in which these two can relate to each other, because costliness can also lead to difficulty. This is the second subclass of difficult actions (ii).

A costly action might require effort, because it can be difficult to motivate oneself to impose costs on oneself. Again, there is no fixed proportion between cost and difficulty. On the one hand, Urmson's soldier who makes the ultimate sacrifice by throwing himself on a grenade in order to save the life of his comrades might do so without great effort because he decides to do it in a spilt second. On the other hand, a very rich but equally miserly person might experience considerable psychological distress because he is morally obliged to donate only a small amount of money. Thus, effort and costs can come apart (see Nelkin 2016, 357). However, it is important to note that the two aspects can do more than influence their magnitude, because they can also cause each other. Imposing costs on oneself can lead to psychological difficulty in the process.

My discussion of the second group of difficult actions, in which the costliness of the action makes the action also difficult, will, again, refer to a case that McElwee (2016) takes from Ralston (2005): An agent has to cut off her arm without anesthetic in order to save her life.

Despite its extremeness, there are three reasons why the example fits the present discussion. First, it is obvious that the action is costly because of the pain and the loss of an arm. Second, the action surely is difficult, because even if we assume that the agent correctly believes that cutting off the arm will save her life and that this prospect, namely that the action is overall beneficial, gives the agent an extra motivation to perform the action, the action will remain very difficult. The difficulty lies in the required effort, and the effort can be spelled out as 'motivational difficulty of imposing costs upon oneself' (McElwee 2016, 25) or, more generally, in Chappell's words, as 'demands placed on our agency, executive control, or willpower' (Chappell 2017, 5). Third, the action is demanding because of the difficulty. Saving one's life without experiencing this difficulty would be less demanding.

Both the standard view on demandingness and the new challenging view agree that the action is very demanding. The only difference lies in answering the question of *how* the difficulty increases demandingness.

The new challenging theories argue that the difficulty increases demandingness as an independent factor, which means that the difficulty does so even if it is separated from costs.

My view is that the difficulty increases demandingness on grounds of being costly. I claim that the difficulty is something like an additional cost factor.

In order to decide how the difficulty affects the agent, I suggest the following.

Suppose we buy an experience machine from the Nozick Company. But we will use it for a purpose that differs from the original purpose in two ways. First, we reprogram the machine so that it does not make a person experience pleasure; we want the machine to make a person experience the difficulty of having to cut off an arm without anesthetics. But, of course, the machine will evoke only the experience of the difficulty but not the actual pain and the loss of the arm. Second, the point of this modified experience machine is not to ask if people would like to be connected to it. I take it for granted that the answer would be negative. The point is to get an answer to the question of *why* we do not want someone with an itchy trigger finger to use the machine on us.

I guess that we do not want the machine being used on us because we fear that it diminishes our well-being. Experiencing the difficulty of having to cut off our own arm makes our lives worse, even if we do not actually have to cut off an arm. The experience is very distressful, it will cost us valuable psychic resources and is even harmful or possibly traumatic. I believe a further response would be that using the machine should be prohibited. The costliness of this experience would make such a machine a good device for so-called white torture.

This is why I think that the difficulty in the example increases the demandingness as an additional cost, that is, a cost that adds to the cost of painfully losing an arm.

My strategy to defend the standard view was to argue that these cases of the second subclass are identical to the cases of the first subclass, that is, to those cases in which difficulty becomes costly.

This, however, does not mean that McElwee's or Chappell's challenges of the standard account have already failed. Chappell (2017, 4) concedes that the

> defender of a welfarist account of burdens could respond that there is at least a proximate cost [...] But it's not clear that this response always works, as there are plausibly cases of this form that do not involve even proximate net costs.

Thus, I will now turn to the third subclass of difficult actions, namely those which are not costly (iii).

Let us consider two sets of cases in which the difficulty is not based on costs and does not lead to further costs. The first will be about difficulties that we prefer and choose because we want to increase our well-being. The second cases will about the difficulty of motivating oneself even when one knows the action is in one's best interests.

So, first, there are cases of preferred difficulty, that is, cases in which we choose a level of difficulty that is higher than necessary because we take the action to be more beneficial because of the difficulty.

Suppose that Sophie, who is an experienced hiker, considers different routes leading to the top of the mountain. She may not opt for the least difficult one, because she is justified in expecting that a more difficult route will result in greater benefits for her. She will enjoy hiking the more difficult tour more and also profit from the enhanced training and the greater admiration this would arouse.

These cases are important because defenders of a difficulty-based view of demandingness refer to these kind of cases when arguing that there is a significant difference between costs and difficulty:

> Indeed many of our most satisfying experiences are doing things which are very difficult, but which we achieve only by applying skill or effort. Our preferred level of difficulty for tasks is not always as-easy-as-possible. A really easy crossword is no fun at all [...] By contrast, our preferred level of costliness is almost always as-uncostly-as-possible. (McElwee 2016, 26)

Second, there are other cases in which the difficulty does not seem to be related to costs. The second set of cases concerns the difficulty to motivate oneself even if one knows that the activity is enjoyable and the act beneficial. In the case of the person who needs to cut off her arm, we have assumed that the motivational difficulty is the difficulty to motivate oneself to impose costs on oneself. But now I want to consider cases in which agents experience motivational difficulty, although they know the action will be beneficial, both while acting and because of the consequences:

> For example, a lazy person might be reluctant to exercise even if they know full well that they will feel better – even in the moment – if they do it. We may imagine that the only "unpleasantness" here is in the prospect of bringing themselves to actually do it. Perhaps there can be some inherent unpleasantness in the experience of exerting willpower. But the welfare cost of exerting effort in this way is not plausibly great enough to explain the sense of burden that accompanies prudential demands (especially if this slight cost is soon outweighed by the greater benefits). Going to the effort of taking decent care of yourself simply isn't that bad for you, in terms of prudential value. But it may nonetheless be difficult, or require significant effort. (Chappell 2017, 4)

In both cases, the difficult action is beneficial for the agent, because she enjoys the activity and will profit from the beneficial consequences. The cases differ because, in the first case, the preferred difficulty motivates the agent to perform the action to a greater extent, whereas in the second case the agent finds it hard to motivate herself to perform the action despite knowing that she will enjoy the action and the beneficial consequences.

With these two classes of cases, that is, cases of preferred difficulty and motivational difficulty regarding beneficial actions, we really seem to have found difficulty that is not costly.

I will not defend the standard view of demandingness by doubting that this kind of difficulty plays an important role in our lives. But I do doubt that this difficulty is relevant when debating the demandingness of moral theories. My claim is rather that this kind of difficulty, which is indeed separated from costs, is only relevant with regard to actions and considerations that concern our well-being. At least, it is striking that both cases presented by defenders of the difficulty view do *not* concern difficulty that is related to a moral demand. Chappell (2017, 4) makes clear that the examples refer to 'prudential demands', but he still draws conclusions about moral requirements.

In the case of preferred difficulty, I argue that if an agent chooses a level of difficulty that is higher than necessary in order to profit from the level of difficulty she chooses, it might be perfectly fine to say that this agent did choose the more "demanding" action, for instance, the more demanding hiking route or crossword puzzle. But this difficulty or demandingness is not something unwanted or something that the agent can complain about. The difficulty and demandingness of the not so easy route up the mountain is welcomed by the agent because it contributes to her well-being. Thus, the higher level of difficulty is not a reason that speaks against taking the route, it speaks in favor of it.

I doubt that there are cases of demandingness connected to a moral obligation in which we speak of demandingness in the same way. Demandingness objections presuppose that demandingness is something that, from the perspective of the agent, speaks against complying with the moral demand, not in favor of it.

Now, what about the cases in which we have difficulty to motivate ourselves to do something that we enjoy and that also has further beneficial consequences? Again, overcoming this motivational difficulty is supported by prudential reason. Because we enjoy exercising and it is also good for us, we should motivate ourselves to do so. Is this kind of difficulty demanding? Again, I see no reasons why this form of demandingness is problematic or relevant for demandingness related to moral obligations. Suppose there is a chef who will bring me the most delicious wine and food and all I need to do is let him know by pressing a single button. I might be a terribly lazy person, and I might find it too difficult to motivate myself to press the button. It does not speak against an action that is only good for the agent that we the agent is too lazy to motivate to profit from the good consequences. It speaks against the laziness and not against the action or any prudential reason in favor of it. We cannot complain that we have to motivate ourselves to live a good life. This would amount to complaining about the fact that one is an agent.

My point is that the fact that proponents of the difficulty view present cases in which actions are beneficial is misleading, because they do not concern the demandingness of morality. It seems to be me that difficulty related to prudential demands differs from demandingness related to moral demands.[8] In other words: the question of how difficult or demanding it is to make one's life go well differs from the question of how demanding morality can or should be.

In order to clarify this, I will give both types of examples – preferred difficulty and motivational difficulty in connection with beneficial actions – a moral frame.

Again, I will start with preferred difficulty. As an example of a prudential consideration, the example of the person who chooses a more difficult crossword worked fine. But let us now assume that I am morally obliged to finish a crossword of my otherwise preferred level of difficulty, and if I fail, an unknown and innocent stranger will be shot.

This changes the difficulty at hand in two ways. First, the moral duty to save the other person by finishing the crossword makes me prefer that the difficulty of the crossword is as easy as possible. Once there is a moral demand, the observation that our preferred level of difficulty might be higher than our preferred level of costliness does not hold true anymore. The difference between costs and difficulty collapses once we consider moral obligations. When a person's life depends on our action, we prefer that both the costs and difficulty of it are as low as possible. The difficulty is then nothing but an obstacle that I have to face in trying to save the person.

Second, the moral demand to save another person's life, which makes me try really hard to finish the crossword, makes the difficulty costly. Being forced to think hard in order to finish the crossword as the only means to save the stranger's life is something that is not good for me. Experiencing difficulty when someone's life is at stake is certainly a very unpleasant experience. Given the moral obligation to save the other person, the difficulty of the crossword will make the action more demanding because it makes the action costlier insofar as it causes anxiety, fear, distress and so forth. The level of difficulty becomes a risk for the life of a person, and if I fail to manage this difficulty, I will blame myself for not having been able to help the person. Hence, we want the difficulty to be as low as possible because it becomes costly.

Now, we need to consider the second class of cases, in which the agent experiences a motivational difficulty despite knowing that she will enjoy performing the action and also despite being aware of the beneficial consequences. But, again, we need to consider them in connection with a moral obligation.

Suppose that Josh is morally required to help Jim move to another town – let us say because Jim has already helped Josh move and also because they are good friends. Suppose Josh likes to do weight training but, due to the commitment of helping, it seems that he will miss one training session in the gym. But Jim has many boxes filled with books so that Josh will be able to have a proper training session and profit from the consequences of exercising while helping his friend. The action will have an extra non-moral value.

Now, what if Josh all of a sudden finds it difficult to motivate himself to do the extra training in the form of lifting Jim's boxes although he will enjoy this exercise, and he also realizes the good long-term consequences. But does it make sense to say that this difficulty increases the demandingness of the moral obligation to help his friend? The additional non-moral value of the training and the motivational difficulty to achieve this non-moral value are not part of the demandingness of the obligation to help a friend. One could say that, now, two reasons speak in favor of overcoming the motivational difficulty to help the friend, namely the reason to help a friend and the reason to enjoy and profit from exercising. We would say that the demandingness Josh faces is increased only if helping his friend means to miss one beloved training session.

The motivational difficulty to gain extra non-moral profit while complying with a moral demand does not increase the demandingness of the moral obligation. This, finally, leads me to the more radical suggestions by Chappell, according to which demandingness should be understood 'primarily' or 'exclusively' in terms of difficulty. His concept of difficulty seems to be too narrow and too weak.

First, I think it is too narrow because he considers difficulty to only be a matter of willpower or effort. But this does not capture the important aspect of skills and it's impact on effort and difficultly. As to skills and effort we would say that for a skilled person, swimming one mile is not impossible, but that it is more difficult than for a trained swimmer, because it requires more effort. Thus, an action can be very difficult in the sense that it requires high skills, but once an agent is properly trained, they can master the action of swimming one mile effortlessly. In some cases, a completely untrained agent might compensate lack of training with effort, for example, when hiking a long tour; but in other cases, effort without skills does not help, for example, when translating Homer's Iliad into Urdu. Chappell's notion of difficulty, however, captures only one of three aspects of difficulty, namely willpower or effort.

Second, I think the willpower view is too weak, and hence that it makes demandingness objections lose their meaning and force. Of course, it would require a full discussion of the meaning and force of demandingness objections against ethical theories. But, as far as I can see, demandingness objections which view demandingness as a matter of the agent's well-being have the great advantage that the target theories usually imply that well-being has major normative significance. Of course, the normative and rational significance of prudential reasons is hotly debated, especially in relation to moral reasons, but the point is that these common demandingness objections can, at least partly, refer to some basic presuppositions of the theory they target, namely that well-being is important. Chappell's shift from well-being to difficulty forfeits this advantage. How powerful is the claim that a moral requirement is asking too much and thus needs to be rejected or altered when all that normatively stands against the moral requirement is the required and very narrowly defined willpower? Can an action require so much willpower that an otherwise plausible moral requirement loses its credibility? If one answers in the affirmative, I wonder how this might be explained without referring to costs. Assume that it is argued that cutting off your own arm without anesthetics in order to rescue somebody else cannot be demanded because it requires too much willpower. But the willpower itself can only be explained in terms of the pertaining costs.

I will now turn to the restriction of options and discuss how the restriction of options can increase demandingness.

3. The Restriction of Options

If one accepts the deontic distinction between acts that are required, forbidden and permissible, it is clear that the restriction of options, or confinement, can be demanding for an agent. This form or source of demandingness has received special attention with regard to consequentialism as a target theory of demandingness objections. In the framework of a consequentialist theory, this problem of confinement arises if the theory in question holds that the action with the best possible outcome is required and all other actions are forbidden. Murphy and Benn have plausibly pointed out that confinement in the consequentialist context is problematic not because of a specific content of a prohibition but as a structural or metaethical problem (see Benn 2016, 75–80).

My discussion of restrictions will take a different route, for I will be concerned with the question of how a specific prohibition can cause demandingness, for example, when an ethical theory concerned with the rights of animals demands that Mike must not buy fur coats even though they are warm and cheap.

Also, my discussion of the demandingness of this kind of confinement will focus on the relation between the restriction of options and costs.

Samuel Scheffler (1992, 98) famously argued that the 'degree of a moral theory's demandingness is a function of a number of closely related factors' and that restrictions and costs are two that are 'especially important'. But unfortunately he does not say how these factors relate.

I will, again, defend the standard account by claiming that restrictions can increase demandingness by being costly in three ways. Restrictions can be demanding

(i) by prohibiting actions that agents want to pursue and that would increase their well-being more than other possible courses of action, in which case the prohibition is directly costly;

(ii) by limiting the scope for changing or developing our desires, preferences, intentions, projects and the like, and making our decisions about this more profound; and

(iii) by making us live in a less open society.

By 'direct' I mean actions that would be good for the agent because the agents want to perform a certain act for prudential reasons. I will distinguish costliness in this 'direct' sense from costliness in another, more indirect way, because having options to perform actions can be good for agents even if they do not want to make use of these options by performing the optional act.

To elaborate this matter, I will now discuss some cases concerning it.

Let us start with a simple case of restrictions of options involving costs which increase demandingness. Suppose Mike takes the moral demand not to steal to be plausible. On a hiking tour he gets really hungry, but he is on a huge vineyard of a stranger. To him, complying with morality means to endure the hunger until he gets to the next guesthouse or home. Martha shares the view that stealing is forbidden. She is a diabetic and hikes the same tour the other day. On the vineyard, her blood sugar level drops. Only eating the ripe grapes, which contain fast absorbing sugar, can prevent a very stressful and painful hypoglycemia and a possible coma. To her, complying with the obligation not to steal means to endure the hypoglycemia or even accept the danger of falling into a coma as well as the consequences of this.

Cases like this gave rise to ethical, theological and judicial debates[9] with differing positions concerning the question of whether, when and to what extent states of necessity turn a forbidden course of action into a permissible course of action. But except for those moral theories that deny that morality and well-being can ever conflict and hold that no moral act can ever be costly, there seems to be consensus that the restriction of options can be costly for agents. This consensus is also shared by positions in the debate that assume that what morality forbids is unchangeably forbidden by it, no matter how costly it gets for the agent, like Kant in the case of perfect duties (CpR 30).

However, it is not necessarily part of the consensus to hold the view that the restriction of options can add to demandingness only insofar as the restriction is costly. Thus, we need to ask the more difficult question whether confinement can increase demandingness without being costly. This question resembles the problem that I have discussed in the previous sections: Is there something like a restriction of options that increases demandingness without being costly for an agent?

Suppose Peter is taking the same hiking tour through the large vineyard. His backpack is stuffed with his favorite snacks and he is not hungry. Also, Peter really dislikes the taste of grapes even before he got allergic to them. It is hard to see why and how it is costly for Peter not to steal and eat the grapes. Nor is it plausible to assume that the moral demand to refrain from stealing and eating the grapes somehow makes Peter's hiking tour through the vineyards more demanding than the same tour without this prohibition. This leads to the question whether the restriction of options is only costly or demanding if the restriction does not allow the agent to perform an action that the agent wants to perform and that also contributes to their well-being.

Now suppose that an ethical theory prohibits opera or same-sex marriage, but I really dislike opera and do not even dream of going to see one, nor do I wish to marry someone of the same sex. Like Peter on his tour through the vineyard, this constellation of preferences, desires, projects or intentions on the one side and the prohibitions on the other does not seem to mean that I have to sacrifice anything, because it is not prohibited that I refrain from doing something that I would like to do. If I comply with the prohibition and do not go the opera or do not marry someone of the same sex, there are no direct costs involved and thus, seemingly, no demandingness. Thus, the case of Peter not stealing and eating grapes when walking through the vineyard and me not going to the opera both seem to indicate that restrictions of options are demanding only when they are directly costly because the agent wants to pursue the forbidden action for prudential reasons.

Nonetheless, I doubt that confinement can be costly only in this direct way. Maybe, cases like the prohibition of opera and same-sex marriage also tell another story, because prohibitions of this kind can be bad for agents without being directly costly, in the sense of prohibiting an act that the agents want to perform and which would indeed be good for them. I see two reasons for arguing that the restriction of options, despite not being directly costly for the agent, can nonetheless be costly and therefore demanding. Both arguments involve the view that having options can be good for agents even if the agents do not choose to perform any of the optional actions for prudential reasons. Both arguments are centered on the value of options as options.

First, we change our preferences, desires, projects and intentions over the course of our lives. A weaker claim holds that a prohibition is problematic because it threatens to become directly costly for an agent, namely in case they develop in such a way that they wish to perform the prohibited action for prudential reasons. This claim is weaker in the sense of linking the demandingness of the restriction of options to the likelihood of costs.

A stronger claim holds that even if we stick to something our entire life, we cherish the freedom to develop and change. The possibility of change and development, which is enabled by having options, is good for us. Thus, the option to go to the opera or marry someone of the same sex is good for me regardless of whether I actually am or ever will be an opera fan or homosexual.[10] It is not necessarily good to actually change, but it is good to have the option to change.

The stronger claim seems correct, and this means that we have found a restriction of options that is costly and increases demandingness without being costly in a direct way. Even non-desired options are good for agents because having an option, for example, the option to start listening to opera, can bring extra value to my current music preferences, by making me even more committed to listening to jazz, because I have an option that I can entertain and then make a choice. Me not buying opera tickets but rather choosing to listen to jazz is what I want after deliberating my options and not after thinking that I should comply with the prohibition of opera.[11] There might be an additional instrumental value because having these options, despite not making use of them, makes my commitment to the choices I make more profound (see Murphy 2000, 29–31). The value is additional and instrumental insofar as it enhances the commitment of my choices. But the value of making choices and being committed to them seems to be not only instrumental.

Considering options might even increase one's pleasure. Suppose you decide to spend Saturday evening with your partner at home instead of accepting a party invitation. You really enjoy cooking together and sharing a good bottle of wine. Then one of you says: 'Thank God we did not accept that party invitation. Think of the bunch of boring people there!' In this way, considering an option you did not choose might enhance the pleasure of the one you did choose. This, of course, works the other way around as well. Considering the option you did not choose might equally make you feel more miserable about the choice you made. Suppose you went to the party and really dislike it and your partner says: 'Think about the quiet evening could have had and the bottle of Grand Cru we could be enjoying right now!'

Second, in order to go one step further, we need to exclude all the benefits I have mentioned so far. Suppose that we can assume that I will never become an opera fan or never would like to marryand that will not profit from having the option to changes or thinking about my options.

Even if I am not directly affected by the prohibitions in question in the form of direct costs or a prohibition to develop and change, there are reasons for me to think that these restrictions are bad for me. Having options is intrinsically good for me. Some have called this the intrinsic benefits of 'moral autonomy' (Slote 1985, Ch. 2; Brock 1991). This phrase can be misleading (see Murphy 2000, 29–31), but part of its value is to point to political autonomy in liberal political theories. Assuming that the restrictions do not apply to me alone but also to my friends, neighbors, colleagues, fellow citizens and so on, I can consider it to be good for me that *they* have the option to go to the opera and to marry someone of the same sex. For I would like to live in an open society, where people have moral options regardless of whether I would choose any of these options. First, the well-being of my fellow human beings matters to me because if they live a good life, they can be of more instrumental value to me. Second, I think that a case can be made for the claim that the options are good for me because it is good for me to live in an open society, even if no one would like go to the opera.

To sum up the results concerning confinements, we can note that they can become costly and therefore increase demandingness in three ways, namely (i) by prohibiting actions that agents want to perform and that would increase their well-being more than other possible courses of actions, in which case the prohibition is directly costly; (ii) by limiting the scope for changing or developing our desires, preferences, intentions, projects and the like; and (iii) by making us live in a less open society.

4. Conclusions

Demandingness is highly complex. The standard account of it is essentially correct but needed some refinements. Difficulty and confinement are factors that need to be taken into account: Both can lead to additional costs, thereby increasing demandingness.

The present investigation has focused on difficulty and confinement and their relation to costs and demandingness. The findings should not be taken to provide a complete picture. The relation of costs and demandingness poses more questions. We need, for instance, to decide whose costs should count as contributing to demandingness. Suppose that Sally will die if Sam does not donate one kidney. Whose costs relate to demandingness? Sobel (2007) criticized overdemandingness objections for relying on a misconstrued concept of demandingness. According to Sobel (2007, 3–8), the mistake lies in counting only the costs of the agent and not also those of the patients as demandingness. Thus, we either need a defense of the mainstream view, according to which only the costs of agents should count as demandingness (see the plausible argument in Woollard 2016),

SACRIFICE AND MORAL PHILOSOPHY 31

or we need to object to Sobel that a wider concept of demandingness, that is, one that counts costs of agents and patients alike, does not necessarily render demandingness objections senseless.

There is thus a more substantial question: What counts as a cost? Many descriptions of cases of demandingness presuppose that the resources the agent has to 'give away' in order to comply with the moral demand are their costs and constitute the demandingness. For example, when a moral theory demands from an agent to donate a certain amount of money to charity, it is often assumed that this amount of money is the agent's cost because they have to give the money to charity and cannot use it for the pursuit of their well-being. Joseph Raz has challenged this way of talking about costs and demandingness:

> A final example is a requirement, should there be one, to give, let us say, a tenth of my income to charity. Surely, there can be no doubt that the moral requirement is essentially against my interest. It is a requirement to reduce my resources in favour of others, and reducing my resources is against my interest. Indeed so, unless what I do with my resources is not reduce them, but use them. I am not acting against my interest when I go to see a film, even though I have to buy a ticket to do so. This is not simply 'reducing' my resources. It is using them. So the description of my tithe example is already loaded. If giving (that sum) of money to charity is an act that benefits me then the fact that depletes my resources does not show that it is against my interest. It is just an ordinary case of using my resources. (Raz 1999, 309)

Note the 'if'. The problem here is that his argument might give us a better description of what agents do when they use their resources *in their interest*. But his argument works only on the condition that morality is in our interest. Are there not also cases in which this is not so? In other words: What about the cases of demandingness?

Notes

1. Anscombe (1958) infamously links the religious use of 'sacrifice' with the modern metaethical debate by suggesting that the idea of moral obligations presupposes the belief in a divine lawgiver.
2. The concept of self-sacrifice presupposes that morality and the personal well-being of the addressees of the moral demands can conflict. Ethical theories like ancient eudaimonistic theories or ethical egoism do not allow for such conflicts.
3. Note that Raz does not endorse this view.
4. Taken as a historical account, this is somewhat wanting because, although the history of overdemandingness objections has not yet been investigated, there is already sufficient evidence that it did not start after Singer's paper. Already Kant (VI: 409.13–9) criticized the Stoics for turning 'the government of virtue into tyranny'. Then, some scholars, including Habermas, took Hegel's critique of Kant to involve an overdemandingness objection (Hegel's criticism

of Kant: e.g., *Elements of the Philosophy of Right* §133, 135; *Phenomenology* V.C.c., VI.C). Also, it is important to note that Singer's argument in his paper does not presuppose act-consequentialism. Thus, the story that demandingness objections came up 50 years ago as a response to Singer's act-consequentialism is rather short-sighted.

5. A comprehensive survey of the arguments since 'Famine, Affluence and Morality' should include overdemandingness objections that use concepts like integrity, alienation, content, scope, authority and the stringency of moral demands.
6. Sobel (2007) objected to the idea that only costs for the agent count as demandingness (and not those of patients). Woollard (2016) provided a plausible defense.
7. See, for example, G. Cohen (2000, 172): 'It's of course unreasonable to ask someone to do something impossible, but it's not unreasonable to ask someone to do something difficult, provided that it does not carry too high a cost.'
8. I will not discuss whether there is a common concept of difficulty. For my argument it suffices to show that difficulty related to the compliance with a moral demand differs from the difficulty related to prudential reasons.
9. See the *locus classicus* in the Bible (Dtn. 23:25). Italy's highest appeals court ruled (Sentenza n. 18248 del 02/05/2016) that Roman Ostriakov, a homeless person, who stole a piece of cheese and a sausage (worth 4.07 Euros) from a supermarket, acted in the face of an immediate and essential need for nourishment, therefore acting in a state of need, and that he is thus not to be punished at all.
10. Apart from the obvious reason of being homosexual as a reason to marry someone of the same sex and the love of opera music as reason in favor of going to the opera, there might be other reasons. I could, for instance, wish to marry someone of the same sex in order save this person from being expelled from the country, or I could want to go the opera because I hope to meet my superiors there and impress them before negotiating my pay rise. I thank Martin Sticker for pointing this out to me.
11. On this, see Murphy 2000, 29.

Acknowledgments

For very helpful discussion and comments I would like to thank Alfred Archer, Lee Klein, Jörg Löschke, Martin Sticker and especially Jeff McMahan and the other participants of the Moral Philosophy Seminar in Oxford.

Disclosure Statement

No potential conflict of interest was reported by the author.

References

Archer, A. 2016. "Supererogation, Sacrifice and the Limits of Duty." *The Southern Journal of Philosophy* 54: 333–354. doi:10.1111/sjp.2016.54.issue-3.

Archer, A., and M. Ridge. 2015. "The Heroism Paradox: Another Paradox of Supererogation." *Philosophical Studies* 172: 1575–1592. doi:10.1007/s11098-014-0365-1.

Ashford, E. 2003. "The Demandingness of Scanlon's Contractualism." *Ethics* 113: 273–302. doi:10.1086/342853.

Benn, C. 2016. "Over-Demandingness Objections and Supererogation." In *The Limits of Moral Obligation. Moral Demandingness and 'Ought Implies Can'*, edited by M. van Ackeren and M. Kühler, 68–83. New York: Routledge.

Brock, D. W. 1991. "Defending Moral Options." *Philosophical and Phenomenological Research* 51: 909–913. doi:10.2307/2108190.

Chappell, R. Y. 2017. "Willpower Satisficing." *Noûs*. doi:10.1111/nous.12213.

Cohen, G. A. 2000. "If You're an Egalitarian, How Come You're so Rich?" *The Journal of Ethics* 4: 1–26. doi:10.1023/A:1009836317343.

Cullity, G. 2004. *The Moral Demands of Affluence*. Oxford: Oxford University Press.

Dorsey, D. 2011. "Weak Anti-Rationalism and the Demands of Morality." *Nous* 46 (1): 1–23. doi:10.1111/j.1468-0068.2010.00777.x.

Goodin, R. E. 2009. "Demandingness as Virtue." *The Journal of Ethics* 13: 1–13. doi:10.1007/s10892-007-9025-4.

Hills, A. 2010. "Utilitarianism, Contractualism and Demandingness." *ThePhilosophical Quarterly* 60: 225–242.

Hooker, B. 2009. "The Demandingness Objection." In *The Problem of Moral Demandingness. New Philosophical Essays*, edited by T. Chappell, 148–162. London: Palgrave.

Kagan, S. 1989. *The Limits of Morality*. Oxford: Oxford University Press.

Kenny, A. 1963. *Action, Emotion and Will*. New York: Routledge.

McElwee, B. 2016. "What Is Demandingness?" In *The Limits of Moral Obligation. Moral Demandingness and 'Ought Implies Can'*, edited by M. van Ackeren and M. Kühler, 19–35. New York: Routledge.

Mulgan, T. 2006. *Future People: A Moderate Consequentialist Account of Our Obligations to Future Generations*. Oxford: Oxford University Press.

Mulgan, T. 2011. *Ethics for a Broken World: Imagining Philosophy after Catastrophe*. Montreal: Acumen.

Murphy, L. B. 2000. *Moral Demands in Nonideal Theory*. Oxford: OxfordUniversity Press.

Nelkin, D. K. 2016. "Difficulty and Degrees of Moral Praiseworthiness and Blameworthiness." *Nous* 50: 356–378. doi:10.1111/nous.12079.

Owen, D. 2016. "Refugees, Fairness and Taking up the Slack: On Justice and the International Refugee." *Moral Philosophy and Politics* 3: 141–164. doi:10.1515/mopp-2016-0001.

Pinheiro Walla, A. 2015. "Kant's Moral Theory and Demandingness." *Ethical Theory and Moral Practice* 18 (4): 731–743. doi:10.1007/s10677-015-9600-x.

Railton, P. 1984. "Alienation, Consequentialism, and the Demands of Morality." *Philosophy and Public Affairs* 13 (2): 134–171.

Ralston, A. 2005. *Between a Rock and a Hard Place*. New York: Atria.

Raz, J. 1986. *The Morality of Freedom*. Oxford: Oxford University Press.

Raz, J. 1993. "A Morality Fit for Humans." *Michigan Law Review* 91 (6): 1297–1314. doi:10.2307/1289764.

Raz, J. 1999. *Engaging Reason: On the Theory of Value and Action*. Oxford: Oxford University Press.

Scheffler, S. 1992. *Human Morality*. Oxford: Oxford University Press.

Slote, M. A. 1985. *Common Sense Morality and Consequentialism*. London: Routledge and Kegan Paul.

Sobel, D. 2007. "The Impotence of the Demandingness Objection." *Philosopher's Imprint* 7 (8): 1–17.

Swanton, C. 2009. "Virtue Ethics and the Problem of Demandingness." In *The Problem of Moral Demandingness. New Philosophical Essays*, edited by T. Chappell, 104–122. London: Palgrave.

Unger, P. 1996. *Living High and Letting Die: Our Illusion of Innocence*. NewYork: Oxford University Press.

Urmson, J. O. 1969. "Saints and Heroes." In *Moral Concepts*, edited by J. Feinberg, 60–73. Oxford: Oxford University Press.

van Ackeren, M. 2016. "Putting the Central Conflict to Rest? Raz on Morality and Well-Being." In *The Limits of Moral Obligation. Moral Demandingness and 'Ought Implies Can'*, edited by M. van Ackeren and M. Kühler, 51–67. New York: Routledge.

van Ackeren, M., and M. Sticker. 2015. "Kant and Moral Demandingness." *Ethical Theory and Moral Practice* 18: 75–89. doi:10.1007/s10677-014-9510-3.

Wolf, S. 1982. "Moral Saints." *The Journal of Philosophy* 8: 419–439. doi:10.2307/2026228.

Woollard, F. 2016. "Dimensions of Demandingness." *Proceedings of the Aristotelian Society* 116 (1): 89–106. doi:10.1093/arisoc/aow003.

Sacrifice and Relational Well-Being

Vanessa Carbonell

ABSTRACT

The well-being account of sacrifice says that sacrifices are gross losses of well-being. This account is attractive because it explains the relationship between sacrifice and moral obligation. However, sacrifices made on behalf of loved ones may cause trouble for the account. Loving sacrifices occur in a context where the agent's well-being and the beneficiary's well-being are intertwined. They present a challenge to individualism about well-being. Drawing inspiration from feminist philosophers and bioethicists, I argue that a notion of 'relational well-being', analogous to 'relational autonomy', can help account for loving sacrifices without either undermining the well-being theory of sacrifice or minimizing the very real sacrifices made in caregiving situations.

One of the victims of the tragic 2016 Pulse night club shooting in Orlando, Florida was a 49-year-old mother of 11 who was out dancing with one of her adult sons. According to witnesses, when the shots rang out, she told her son to get down and then put her body in front of his. She died of gunshot wounds. Her son managed to escape (Burke and Otis 2016).

This story of the ultimate parental sacrifice is especially moving, but many other loving relationships are also marked by willingly endured hardships. Spouses and adult children who are caregivers for persons with Alzheimer's disease and other dementias routinely take on small and large burdens, at personal cost, for the benefit of their loved one, especially when trying to avoid institutional care. For instance, to protect a spouse who wanders at night, some husbands and wives have been known to make themselves into a human alarm system. They sleep on the floor by a bedroom doorway, or even plant themselves snugly against the threshold of their house's front door, ensuring they will wake up to prevent an escape. Like the mother in the night club, they quite literally put their body between a loved one and danger.

It may not be immediately obvious why stories like these ought to be interesting to philosophers working on sacrifice. Sacrifices made on behalf of complete strangers may seem more important. After all, it is uncontroversial that love provides us with reasons for action. Even while philosophers disagree about the balance between strict impartiality and special moral obligations to loved ones, no one can deny that most people *feel* bound by such obligations. Someone who puts their body on the line for a family member thus follows a familiar script, whereas someone who acts on behalf of a stranger violates expectations. Arguably, sacrifice for strangers is more difficult, more surprising, more admirable and more likely to be supererogatory. Thus, it is where the philosophical action is. I am going to suggest, however, that the cases involving strangers are the *easy* ones.

This essay takes some tentative first steps toward highlighting what is puzzling and important about the sacrifices we make for loved ones. In particular, I examine whether we can understand these sacrifices as losses of well-being for the agent. The well-being account of sacrifice struggles to capture the complex prudential alchemy that occurs when two or more agents' interests and lives are bound up with one another. Agents may not see their own well-being as something measurable, or even conceivable, independently of their loved one's well-being, and we ought to take their perspective seriously. But must we abandon the very notion of individual losses in such cases, and thereby eliminate a whole class of sacrifices? I argue that we can better understand these sacrifices by introducing the concept of *relational well-being*, a way of thinking about well-being that acknowledges the complexity of close relationships. Relational well-being is modeled on 'relational autonomy', developed by feminist philosophers as a challenge to the individualism thought to be required for traditional accounts of autonomy. Relational well-being also resonates with some recent work in bioethics on 'relational interests'. By resisting extreme individualism about well-being, we can better understand the losses people bear on behalf of loved ones, how such losses can count as genuine sacrifices, and why agents might be ambivalent about them.

1. Sacrifice and Well-being

In this section I lay out what I take to be the most intuitive way of understanding sacrifice in the context of moral philosophy, which is as a loss of well-being. First, some notes about terminology. I use the term 'well-being' to refer to what makes an agent's life go well, for her. Synonyms are 'welfare', 'self-interest', 'best interests', 'quality of life' and 'prudential value'.

I will use the plain term, 'sacrifice', as a noun or a verb, to refer to cases where an agent gives up something for the sake of something or someone else. Trivial sacrifices, like when one friend lets another take the last slice of pizza, are not of interest in this essay. More specifically, I am interested in sacrifices that are incurred either for moral reasons, or toward moral ends, or as part of a trade-off between moral values. I do not distinguish between the sacrifices that accompany a moral *obligation* and those that accompany an action we deem *supererogatory*, although the magnitude of the sacrifice may partly determine whether an action is one or the other.[1]

I avoid the term 'self-sacrifice' except when quoting others. In the literature, some philosophers use 'self-sacrifice' to make clear that they intend to refer only to *voluntary* sacrifices (e.g. Overvold 1980), or only to those essentially implicating the agent's *self* (e.g. Rosati 2009), or, most dramatically, only to those involving loss of the agent's *life* (e.g. Weiss 1949). Confusingly, others treat 'sacrifice' and 'self-sacrifice' as synonyms (e.g. Jacobs 1987; Gelven 1988; Alexander 1996). I do not want to narrow the scope of sacrifice in any of these ways – either explicitly or by connotation – so I will stick with the weak, broad and generic term 'sacrifice'.

The well-being account of sacrifice, which I have defended elsewhere, goes like this.[2] In the context of ethics, sacrifice is best understood as a fundamentally normative notion. To say that an agent has made a sacrifice is to say that whatever has been lost has some value or significance to the agent's life. This contrasts with a merely descriptive account. For example, we could say that a sacrifice is any decrease in the agent's gross annual income in inflation-adjusted US dollars, regardless of whether such a decrease actually made the agent's life go any worse. But in that case it would not be clear why anyone should care that the person had made the sacrifice. Yet we do care. When people make moral sacrifices, we scrutinize them. We ask, was it worth it? We think, should I be giving up more myself? We worry, is this person going to be OK? We question, is there some ulterior motive? We feel admiration, concern, awe, skepticism, guilt, perhaps even pity or anger. These are not the marks of a purely descriptive concept.

Perhaps the reason we take such interest in other people's sacrifices – besides the gossip value – is that we see the role sacrifice plays in the complex transactions of the moral economy. It helps determine what we can get away with, and it tells us something about the relative weights of our values. For instance, you may be obligated to pitch in and help your community when a natural disaster strikes, unless doing so would be *too much to ask* of you – that is to say, too much of a sacrifice. As potential beneficiaries of your aid, your neighbors have an interest in making sure that what gets counted as too much of a sacrifice is reasonable and fair. The same goes for any sacrifices they may be in a position to make themselves. The criteria for sacrifice must be publicly intelligible because sacrifices sometimes excuse us from reciprocal moral obligations.[3] On this picture, what we are morally obligated to do is not a matter of some transcendent, absolute or nonnegotiable truth, but rather a dynamic and elastic phenomenon that emerges in the thrum of a social community. Perhaps after the natural disaster, minimal decency requires that you care for a neighbor's cat, but not that you take in a neighbor's fierce pet lion, though he is wet and scared in his outdoor pen. That you are not expected to sacrifice your own physical safety tells us something about the limits of moral obligation, as well as something about the balance between conflicting moral values – in this case, neighborly compassion and personal security.

For sacrifice to play this role, I have argued that it makes most sense to define it as a *gross loss of well-being*, where we make use of an agent-neutral theory of well-being, like the account given by Stephen Darwall (2002) in *Welfare and Rational Care*. On this view, the concept of well-being (or 'welfare') is whatever it is rational for us want for a person insofar as we care for her (Darwall 2002, 9). A person's well-being is thus defined independently of her own point-of-view and desires; her desires may be relevant to what is good for her, but they do not constitute or determine what is good for her, and she may be incapable of evaluating her own well-being simply by introspecting. The account is objective in the sense that a person could, in principle, be mistaken about her own well-being. This does not necessarily mean, however, that an outside observer could assess her level of well-being without speaking with her or learning about her values and concerns.

To do this sort of assessment of someone's life, we would need to pair Darwall's theory with a theory of the substantive *constituents* of well-being. The theories known as 'list theories' or 'objective list theories' provide us with a list of things that make any person's life go well (such as enjoyment, achievement and knowledge) or poorly (such as suffering, deception or exploitation). 'Hybrid theories' claim that something is good for a person if and only if it is both objectively good and she desires it (see Parfit 1984; Griffin 1986). Both Thomas Hurka's 'perfectionist' theory and Daniel Haybron's eudaimonistic 'self-fulfillment theory' would count as objective theories of well-being as well (see Bradley 2014; Hurka 1993; Haybron 2008). Although in the past I suggested that a traditional 'list' theory would be the most natural fit for the well-being theory of sacrifice, any objective theory is acceptable as far as the argument in this paper is concerned.

The account of sacrifice I am sketching is weak and broad, by design. In fact, I propose we leave out some of the conditions on sacrifice that other philosophers have taken for granted. These include that sacrifices be *voluntary*, that the losses incurred be *anticipated*, and that the losses implicate the *self* in some way.[4] Many sacrifices will have these hallmarks, perhaps especially the most praiseworthy ones. But it would be useful to have an account of sacrifice that captures even the more pedestrian hardships we bear. This account will be compatible with the intuitive thought that almost everyone makes some moral sacrifices in the course of a lifetime, not just people who end up in the news. Life is messy and gray, and sometimes we do not carefully attend to what we are getting ourselves into. A person may give up quite a bit for someone else, without anticipating the specific losses. Another person may take on losses, say in the course of caring for her children, that are not straightforwardly voluntary – perhaps because the alternative is, say, that she is charged by the state with child endangerment. Depending on the particulars, these may count as sacrifices. Here I depart from Richard Brandt, who claimed that the 'motivational' component of sacrifice is as important as the loss of well-being.[5]

Perhaps the most important feature of the framework I am proposing is that it counts all *gross* losses of well-being, rather than only 'net' losses, as sacrifices.[6] To be sure, the typical case of a moral sacrifice is an action taken for the sake of someone else that results in a net reduction in the agent's well-being. Such cases certainly remove any skepticism we may have about whether the agent has an ulterior motive. But actions and activities in the real world may result in a messy collection of consequences, some foreseen and some unforeseen, some that harm the agent and others that benefit her.

For instance, consider someone who gives up a fulfilling high-powered career to move to a rural area to undertake volunteer or mission work, or to care for a sick friend. The loss of her career is huge, but the new lifestyle unexpectedly opens up avenues of meaning and value in her life. Perhaps she can only appreciate the charms of the rural area *because* she no longer has a job to move back to – the area grows on her as a long-term resident in a way it would not on a mere visitor. She has thus gained access to a source of well-being that was not available to her *à la carte*, as it were. This need not make us suspect that she *really* gave up her career for the sake of the rural state of mind she now enjoys, rather than for the sake of the good she could do. After all, she didn't know she would benefit in this way. What is more, the fact that her new rural state of mind is intimately connected with *loss* – the loss her old life – suggests that even the positive benefits reaped from sacrificial life choices may themselves be negatively tinged. They may develop as coping mechanisms triggered by the loss. Our urban transplant may learn to appreciate rural life because she *has* to, because it's the best way to bear the loss of her high-powered career.[7] Her sacrifice brings some benefits, but they are mere side-effects of the losses.

If only *net* losses of well-being could count as sacrifices, we would need a way to determine when gains can *compensate* for losses. Although we may sometimes be able to say whether disparate goods and bads – even incommensurable goods and bads – compensate for each other, I do not think we have a reliable enough method of determining compensation to make our judgments of sacrifice hinge on a notion of 'net' reductions in well-being. I do not mean to cast doubt on *any* possibility of quantifying, commensurating, comparing or reconciling gains and losses of well-being. Granted, the whole point of using an agent-neutral, objective account of well-being is to bring a sense of mutual intelligibility and reciprocity to our claims about sacrifice, and this is normally done via accounting methods such as these. However, I would rather err on the side of overcounting sacrifices than undercounting them. Part of understanding the reach and significance of morality in our lives is to pay close attention to what agents give up in its pursuit, even when our view is obscured by the fact that the agent gets something else 'in return'.

2. Loving Sacrifices and the Well-being Framework

Do the sacrifices we make for our loved ones – loving sacrifices – present special difficulty for a well-being account of sacrifice? We have already seen that it can be complicated to determine whether an agent has incurred a loss of well-being in the course of an action done for the sake of someone else or some other moral value. One way of reducing the complexity is to insist that such losses need not be 'net' losses. What we will see now is that loving sacrifices present a related, but perhaps more vexing complication, because the well-being of the agent, and the loved-one's well-being, may be intertwined.

Recall the examples of loving sacrifices at the beginning of this essay: a mother who takes bullets in a night club shooting, in order to save her son; a spouse who sleeps on the floor by a drafty door, night after night, waiting to be stepped on by a confused spouse and prevent her escape. I take it as uncontroversial that these agents are making sacrifices. The well-being account of sacrifice would say that, in the first case, the mother has suffered an enormous loss to her own future well-being, in exchange for which her son has narrowly escaped an enormous loss. Granted, she may not have known, nor been able to predict, that she would *die* in protecting her son. Indeed, in the chaos of the moment she may have not acted consciously at all. I claimed earlier that it is not necessary for a loss to be specifically anticipated for it to count as a sacrifice. Still, she may certainly have been aware that she was taking a grave *risk* in acting as she did. So even on an account that requires a particular motive for an action to count as a sacrifice, her action would have qualified, with the degree of sacrifice being proportional to something like the product of loss's magnitude and its likelihood.

In the spousal caregiving case, the well-being account of sacrifice would say that the healthy spouse – let's suppose it is a husband – suffers several losses. He gives up his own physical comfort, his restful sleep (which has implications for health), his sense of normalcy, and his peace of mind. Granted, his peace of mind may be threatened whether he makes the sacrifice or not. If he stays in the bedroom, his peace of mind is disturbed by his worry that he may sleep through his wife's wanderings. If he moves to the drafty front door, the uncomfortable sleeping quarters may make the possibility of her escape all the more salient, transforming an ordinary routine ('turning in for the night') into a strange new project ('going on night watch duty').

Might his choice to move bring a 'net gain' in peace of mind – from a large loss to a smaller loss? I do not think it matters, because peace of mind is just one factor among many, and because it is the *gross* losses that matter, on my view. By moving to the front door, his peace of mind has been disturbed in a novel way, and this loss should be acknowledged, even if none of his viable options includes real peace of mind. Granted, if the husband were only deciding between the bedroom and the floor in order to minimize his own discomfort, we might have a case of what Overvold (1980) calls 'cutting one's losses', and it may not be a sacrifice. If that were the case, then the husband would just be making the most of a bad situation. But, importantly, the husband is not looking to find the least frustrating arrangement for himself; he is looking to do, and is in fact doing, what is best for his wife, of the relevant options, regardless of the consequences to his own well-being. In return for his sacrifice – his lost sleep, his backache, his disrupted sense of normalcy – his wife is safe. Perhaps she is able to stay at home for one year longer than she otherwise would have, before moving into a secure facility. Perhaps she avoids a catastrophic fall, a case of hypothermia, a car accident or even a preventable death.

On first pass, the well-being framework appears to handle cases like these reasonably well. In fact, an objective theory of well-being (like a list theory) handles these cases much better than a desire theory on which well-being consists in getting what one desires. If the mother desires to take the bullet for her son, and the husband desires to sleep on the floor, then on a desire theory we may be forced to say that these agents' actions do not go against their interests, or reduce their well-being, and thus we cannot count them sacrifices at all. That would be implausible.[8] Nevertheless, I do think we need to pay attention to the fact that, typically, we not only desire what is best for our loved ones, but in fact consider their well-being and our own to be intimately bound together. It is not simply that we desire that our loved ones' lives go well, nor simply that we take their lives going well to be one of the things that *makes* our lives go well (that is, one of the constituents of our own well-being). It is, rather, that we sometimes simply cannot pry apart their welfare from our own. At least, this may be the case in very close relationships, including parent-child relationships, marriages (or equivalent), some friendships and many relationships between humans and their beloved nonhuman pets.

At the time of her loving sacrifice, the mother who died in the Pulse night club shooting had presumably been shaping her life around the needs of her children for several decades. She had 11 children and had recently moved to Florida to be near some of them. Of course, *all* non-negligent parents take their children's well-being as a reason for action, as a consideration that carries weight in deliberation.

That's part of what it is to be a parent. One holds one's children's interests in trust, and acts so as to protect their current and future well-being, even at personal sacrifice. This changes somewhat as children become autonomous adults, but for many parents the attitudes forged during the years acting as trustees of their children's well-being do not simply go away. These attitudes – care, concern, love, a sense of guardianship or responsibility and perhaps even self-abnegation – persist, as does the weight the children's well-being carries in deliberation. (The phenomenon of 'helicopter parenting' lamented by university staff and faculty is no doubt a manifestation of the fact that, for better or worse, parental care and concern cannot simply be 'turned off' when a child turns 18.)

The mother from the night club illustrates the persistence of guardian-ship attitudes perhaps more than most. It is likely that her own identity was shaped by her pride over her children, and by her role in their lives. Evidently, she was disposed to play a parental role even toward other children. Her ex-husband remarked, 'She was selfless, always giving of herself. All the kids in the neighborhood were part of her extended family' (Burke and Otis 2016). One can only imagine what she gave up in the course of tending to the needs of 11 children and a bunch of neighborhood kids as well. 'Selfless' certainly seems like an apt description, and nothing in what follows should be construed as suggesting otherwise.

That said, by the time one has devoted over 20 years to acting out of concern for one's child, it is likely that the child's interests and one's own have begun to blur. There is a weak and a strong way of interpreting what 'blur' might mean in this context. On the weak reading, the child's well-being *contributes to* the parent's well-being. So, when the child's life goes better, the parent's life goes better. Just about any theory of well-being can explain how this might be the case. On a hedonistic theory, the parent would derive pleasure or happiness from the knowledge that her child's life is going well, or from directly experiencing the child's triumphs and joys. On a desire theory, one of the parent's strongest desires is that her child's life go well, so when her child's well-being is maintained or increased, she gets what she wants. On an objective list theory, the list may include, among the items which make life go well, that one be a successful parent, or that one stand in the caring relation to other people. On a perfectionist theory, we would say that excellent parenting – including the flourishing of one's children – is part of what it is to exemplify our human nature. On what have been called 'achievementist' views, a parent might have as one of her *goals* that her child's life goes well, and when we achieve our goals, our lives go better.[9]

On this weak interpretation of the blurry boundary between one's own well-being and that of a loved one, the ambivalent nature of parental sacrifice is understood as a kind of temporal trade-off. Perhaps a parent gives something up so that their child's life goes better. Consequently, the child's life does go better, and that contributes to the parent's well-being.

Since their interests are intimately connected, the parent has both lost and gained. For example, a parent may wake up at 5am every day for 12 years to drive their child to a good school that is far away. When the child graduates as a happy, flourishing, successful adult, the child's success makes the parent's life go better. The parent took a hit to her own well-being in the lost sleep, and then subsequently benefited from the child's success. Whether the benefits outweighed the costs is an interesting question, but irrelevant to whether the parent made a sacrifice, since only a gross loss is necessary for sacrifice.

Yet I do not think this weak interpretation captures the full degree of blurriness. It reduces parental well-being to a kind of bank account, where the lost sleep is a withdrawal, made as an investment in a project (the child's success), which later pays returns. Although we might sometimes think this way in our cynical moments, I do not think loving relationships are best characterized by this transactional framework. On a stronger interpretation of what happens when interests *blur*, what is going on is that it actually becomes difficult to *separate* the agent's welfare from the beneficiary's. It is not merely that the interests of two people are causally connected – as when an increase in your welfare causes an increase in mine. In that case we can still assess each person's welfare independently. The strong reading of blurred interests is rather that there may be no coherent accounting of my interests independently of yours. If we could ask the mom in the night club shooting about why she was willing to risk her own well-being, she might say, 'My own well-being? My son is part of me. His well-being *is* my well-being.' Similarly, if we praised the husband for his willingness to sacrifice his own comfort for his wife's safety, he might reply, '*My* comfort? I didn't even think of it. We've been married 40 years. We're a team. I care about her comfort more than my own.'

To be sure, these are sentimental, hypothetical reactions. I am not making an empirical claim about the prevalence of such attitudes or reactions. But we know from the literature on Holocaust rescuers that people frequently downplay their own heroism. I have argued that such denials illustrate the difference between subjective and objective assessments of sacrifice (Carbonell 2012). Just because someone denies that they are making a sacrifice, it doesn't mean that they are correct. Similarly, if someone makes a loving sacrifice and acts bewildered or nonplussed about the loss they have incurred to their individual well-being, we might dismiss them as simply confused, or we might ask whether we are bumping up against the limits of the utility of the notion of individual well-being. This is what I explore in the remaining sections. What I want to question is not whether there *are* individuals, but rather whether *individualism* about well-being is our only option. There is nothing groundbreaking or original in asking this question. Feminists, care ethicists, communitarians and others have put individualism under a microscope. Feminist philosophers in particular have examined relationships of love and dependency, and their implications for the self, with such sophistication that my discussion will pale in comparison.[10] But we must consider challenges to the notion of individual well-being, if well-being is going to play such a large role in our account of moral sacrifice. If moral obligation is itself a deeply social phenomenon, surely sacrifice is as well?

3. Relational Autonomy, Relational Interests and Relational Well-being

Feminist philosophers have challenged the coherence and importance of individual autonomy, arguing that it is premised on a masculinist ideal of self-sufficiency and an overly atomistic conception of the self as divorced from social relations. Rather than throwing autonomy out the window, contemporary scholars have proposed a range of reconceptualizations of autonomy, which fall under the umbrella term 'relational autonomy'.[11] Under this umbrella of views, at the weak end of the spectrum, the idea of relational autonomy simply denies that being autonomous requires being self-sufficient. At the strong end of the spectrum, relational autonomy denies the aforementioned metaphysical assumption of atomistic individual selfhood (Stoljar 2015). Defenders of relational autonomy argue that we need not try to erase autonomy, but rather to enrich our understanding of it, because, as Catriona Mackenzie and Natalie Stoljar (2000, 3) put it, 'the notion of autonomy is vital to feminist attempts to understand oppression, subjection, and agency'. The starting point of relational autonomy theorists is that 'persons are socially embedded and that agents' identities are formed within the context of social relationships and shaped by a complex of intersecting social determinants' (Mackenzie and Stoljar 2000, 4).

There is not space here to do justice to the rich literature on relational autonomy. What I am interested in is whether we can borrow insights from this way of thinking about autonomy and apply them to the case of well-being, thus helping to make sense of some cases of loving sacrifice. To that end, we ought to consider what it might mean to be skeptical about the individualism that supposedly underlies autonomy – and may also underlie the idea of individual well-being. Mackenzie and Stoljar helpfully lay out four accounts of metaphysical individualism, proceeding roughly from strong to weak:

> Individualism can be understood as any of the following claims: first, that agents are causally isolated from other agents; second, that agents' sense of themselves is independent of the family and community relationships in which they participate; third, that agents' essential properties (that is, their natures, or metaphysical identities) are all intrinsic and are not comprised, even in part, by the social relations in which they stand; and fourth, that agents are metaphysically separate individuals. (Mackenzie and Stoljar 2000, 7)

The first thesis, that agents are causally isolated, is obviously false.[12] I agree with Mackenzie and Stoljar that the second thesis, about self-conceptions, is likely false as well – though it would be difficult to empirically investigate given that virtually no humans develop their sense of themselves in isolation from at least *some* family or interpersonal relations. Theories of autonomy notwithstanding, I do not think any theories of *well-being* are premised on the sort of crude individualism captured by the first and second claims. (Since 'autonomy' literally translates to 'self-rule', it is perhaps not surprising that it is sometimes interpreted as involving fairly strong claims about individual selves. Such claims are less likely to be imported into our thinking about well-being.) When we ask what makes a person's life go well, we are surely aware of the fact that other people have a causal influence on that person's life and thus on how it is going. We are similarly aware that a person's 'sense of' self is influenced by other people and may even be bound up with another person or with that person's relation to them. To see this, we need look no further than the opening introductions on the long-running, somewhat insufferable American television game show, *Wheel of Fortune*. When asked to describe themselves to the audience, contestants almost always use their brief airtime to announce their marital status, as well as the names of their children if they have any.

What about the third version of individualism, that individuals' essential properties are intrinsic and not comprised by their social relations? Mackenzie and Stoljar claim that few theories of autonomy actually need to presuppose this claim, so even if it is false, autonomy is under no grave threat. Let's call its denial 'moderate relationalism about persons' – moderate because it denies a moderate version of individualism, weaker than the first two in Mackenzie and Stoljar's taxonomy, but stronger than the fourth. Borrowing Mackenzie and Stoljar's language, we can define the view thus:

> **Moderate relationalism about persons**: the view that agents' essential properties (that is, their natures, or metaphysical identities) are at least in part comprised by the social relations in which they stand.[13]

I do not know whether this view is true – a lot rides on what is meant by 'at least in part'. Perhaps only some social relations are strong enough to count as essential properties of an agent, and therefore perhaps only some people's natures are partly comprised by relations with others. The essential properties of the loner or narcissist might well be intrinsic and nonrelational, whereas those of conjoined twins might be profoundly relational. And, obviously, our social relations change over time, so on this view our essential properties would also change over time. Let us assume for the sake of argument that *moderate relationalism about persons* is true.[14] What would it mean for well-being if at least some people were somewhat comprised by their relations?

Here is one thing it might mean: in order to give a complete and accurate description of a person, one must include the significant social relations in which the person stands. So, the answer to the question, 'Who is A?' would often, perhaps typically, include facts like, 'A is B's father' or 'A stands in the father relation to B'. We might then recast the well-being question, 'What makes A's life go better?' as something more like, '*Given* A's essential properties – A's nature – what makes A's life go well?' Recall Darwall's (2002) analysis of welfare – it's whatever it would be rational to want for a person insofar as we care for him. The fact that A is B's father would therefore factor in any determination of A's welfare, at least indirectly, by being one of A's essential properties. What it is rational for those who care about A to want for him, for his own sake, is surely going to be responsive to A's essential nature. If this is right, then we might say that facts about B's welfare are not just substantive contributors to A's well-being, but in fact essential constituents of it. To illustrate this, consider the difference between, say, bowling, which is one of many potential contributors to A's well-being and may indeed contribute to it very much, and *being B's father*, without which A would not even be the same person. Being B's father does not merely contribute to A's welfare; it makes him who he is.

If *moderate relationalism about persons* is true, then we may have grounds for being open to the notion of *relational well-being*. This would not be a radical redefinition of well-being, any more than relational autonomy is a radical redefinition of autonomy. Mackenzie and Stoljar (2000, 8) suggest that the feminist critique need not undermine the notion of *individual autonomy*, only the notion of *individualistic autonomy*. Similarly, embracing the idea of relational well-being would not entail rejecting the very idea of individual well-being, so much as asking us to be extra careful not to fall into overly *individualistic* ways of thinking about well-being.

Mackenzie and Stoljar's (2000, 7) taxonomy ended with the fourth and weakest version of individualism: the claim 'that agents are metaphysically separate individuals'. To deny this would be to say that there simply is *no such thing* as an individual agent. This would entail the rejection of individual autonomy, but only trivially. (If there are no individual agents, then there is no sense asking whether they are autonomous.) It would presumably also entail the rejection of individual well-being. Like Mackenzie and Stoljar, and Louise Antony (1995), I am skeptical of this extreme version of anti-individualism. But I will not explore it here. Admittedly, its truth would probably tank the well-being theory of sacrifice, but in that case, losing our theory of sacrifice would be the least of our problems. Those of us interested in sacrifice have enough fodder in the *moderate* version of relationalism to keep us occupied.

While feminist philosophers have urged relationalism about autonomy, bioethicists have recently proposed relationalism about 'interests', often taken to be a synonym for well-being. The critique of individualism is especially relevant to pediatric bioethics, because the social embeddedness of children is an inescapable feature of every aspect of their care. Children not only lack the legal and psychological capacity to make important decisions about their own care, but they also typically have yet to develop robust independent self-conceptions and life projects outside the sphere of influence of their parents and family.

Bioethicist Erica Salter (2014, 27) has argued that 'autonomy's grip [on bioethics] is slowly loosening' because it is becoming increasingly clear that 'we are not unencumbered and primarily individuated selves'. She extends recent critiques of individualism to the case of decision-making on behalf of children. Clinicians are taught that such decisions should be made using the 'best interests standard' (BIS): the right decision is whatever option maximizes the expected net benefit to the child, accounting for risks and costs. Roughly, 'best interests' here is equivalent to individual welfare or well-being. On this standard, clinicians should consider *only* what is good for the pediatric patient herself, and not, say, what is good for her parents and siblings. Salter claims that the most prominent accounts of 'best interests' advise clinicians to ignore any interests the patient herself may have that are not 'self-regarding', including any interest the patient takes in the well-being of others (31).

Salter has helpfully pointed out for us that individualism about 'best interests' is a double-edged sword. To be sure, it protects children from potentially damaging decisions that their parents might make on their behalf. As Loretta Kopelman (2010, 23) writes,

> The best-interests standard was introduced to undercut policies that children ... were property of their guardians and to give children's interests *some* weight. ... Today, if a father wishes to treat his bacterial pneumonia with herbal tea, he is at liberty to do so, but he has no right to make this decision for his child.

But at the same time, the best interests standard, interpreted individualistically, encourages clinicians to artificially separate patients from their familial entanglements. On this view, as Salter (2014, 32) puts it, 'a child's interests should be understood as isolated and independent from the interests of others, including those of the individuals and communities that constitute some of the child's most intimate relationships'. This seems like both an epistemically and normatively impoverished way to approach the lives of children.

The individualism of the best interests standard might seem like a throwback to a different era, in light of the recent movement toward 'family-centered care' in pediatrics.[15] Indeed, some bioethicists are now taking seriously the notion that the family *itself* has interests – known as 'family interests' – which are not just the sum of the family members' individual interests. Some have argued that family interests should be considered in decision-making about pediatric patients. But the family interests model does not directly call into question the individualism of the traditional best interests standard. At most, family interests are something to be weighed against the individual's best interests, rather than something that challenges the very coherence of individual best interests.

However, a model Daniel Groll (2014) calls the 'wide interests model' comes closer to challenging individualism about interests. On the wide interests model, in certain intimate relationships, one person's good may be part of another person's good (2014, S83).[16] Sometimes this is interpreted merely as a causal claim, as when one sibling benefits psychologically from the knowledge that another sibling is doing well. But it can also be interpreted more strongly, such that one sibling's doing well *entails* that the other sibling does well. The wide interests model can be used both to argue that a sick child's best interests include their parents' interests, thus constraining what should be done for the child if it involves too much parental sacrifice, and that the parents' interests include their child's interests, such that actions that appear to be sacrificial actually are not (Groll 2014, S83). On the wide interests model, the relational nature of our interests (our well-being) could make it the case that putative sacrifices do not actually 'count' as sacrifices, especially if you count only net losses rather than gross losses. So we can see that whether one takes a relational rather than individualistic approach to thinking about interests can have implications for sacrifice.

Salter implores clinicians to do a better job looking out for children's 'relational interests', a term she seems to have coined, but not defined. In some places, 'relational interests' reads simply as the interest a child has in maintaining close family relationships; this interest is thwarted if the child's medical condition makes them unable to give or accept hugs (Salter 2014, 37). In other places, more controversial claims about the *self* are implied. Recall the first three of Mackenzie and Stoljar's versions of individualism: the causal version (agents are causally isolated from one another); the self-concept version (agents' self-concepts are independent of their relationships) and the properties version (agents' essential properties are intrinsic and independent of their relations). Salter's *relational interests* may be interpreted as entailing the rejection of any of these versions of individualism, but she musters the most evidence in challenging the self-concept version, and offers little by way of argument against the properties version.

With *relational autonomy*, *relational interests* and the *wide interests model* as inspiration, I offer up the notion of *relational well-being*. Like relational autonomy, relational well-being is an umbrella term. In this case, what falls under the umbrella is any account of well-being – or even any argument about a particular person's well-being – that presupposes *moderate relationalism about persons*.

Relational well-being: an account of what makes someone's life go well that presupposes that their essential properties – that is, their nature or self – are at least in part comprised by the social relations in which they stand.

In the next section, I briefly ask what relational well-being would mean for the account of sacrifice I defended earlier in this essay.

4. Relational Well-being and Sacrifice

I set out to examine the costs and benefits of resisting individualism in our account of well-being, and therefore in our account of sacrifice. I was worried that a more relational account of well-being would mean that many loving sacrifices do not count as sacrifices. This would be, I think, a serious worry for the well-being account of sacrifice. After all, even if the agents themselves were to insist otherwise, I think everyone would agree that the mother in the night club shooting and the husband who sleeps on the floor have given something up, something that matters. But if conditions of caretaking and dependency foster relational well-being, and if burdensome care-taking is seen as *promoting* rather reducing relational well-being, then many loving sacrifices are not sacrifices, for they do not reduce the agent's well-being (even in gross terms), when it is viewed relationally. Ironically, then, given that it is more often women than men who find themselves in such conditions of caretaking, an account inspired by feminist theorists would serve to explain away or even *eliminate* the very sacrifices that are most likely to be made by women.[17]

The key to avoiding this result is recognizing that relational well-being, like relational autonomy, is still a property of an individual. Relational well-being does not refer to the *relation's* well-being, as though we were anthropomorphizing the relation itself and asking what is good for it, or as though we were simply adding up individuals and asking how some event bears on them all, taken together. Nor does it mean swapping the agent's well-being with that of the person for the sake of whom she is acting. It is, rather, the same old notion of what is *good for someone*, except where we acknowledge that certain relationships are built into who that someone is.

In long-term loving relationships, or cases of extreme dependency like parenting, a person's goals, preferences, talents, dispositions – her very constitution – may change and adapt as a result of the relations in which she stands. In some important respects, her welfare and her loved one's welfare may merge, such that losses imposed on the loved one become losses imposed on her – not indirectly, via the disappointment she will feel, but directly. However, on my *gross losses* account, this is more likely to increase, rather than decrease, opportunities for genuine sacrifice. By taking on a loved one's goals, projects, etc., one has more to give up, more to lose, in addition to the self-regarding needs and comforts that we all stand to lose.

The caretaking husband, for instance, still needs a good night of sleep, and his loss of that counts as a sacrifice, even if the gain in safety that his wife gets in exchange also 'credits' to him in some way. Relational well-being permits a kind of 'double-counting' in the sense that your loved one's gains and losses might accrue to you, as well to the loved one. But the gross losses account of sacrifice means that this will simply allow you to count some of your loved one's losses as your own sacrifices; your loved one's gains will not cancel out your losses, because 'net' loss is not necessary for sacrifice. For the caretaking husband, because his relation to his wife has become one of his essential properties, he is in a position to incur a grave loss whenever *her* well-being is compromised. And again, her distress would accrue to him not just indirectly, as via emotional contagion, but directly.

The well-being account of sacrifice, when conjoined with a more relational understanding of well-being, explains both why the husband is making a significant sacrifice and – unlike a more individualistic picture – why he might understandably *deny* that he is. He is making a significant sacrifice because he is incurring real gross losses to his own well-being. Yet he might *feel* that his sacrifice is negligible or irrelevant, because his action makes his wife significantly better off, and he recognizes that his wife's good has become *part of his good*. Granted, gross losses are what matters for sacrifice, and the wife's gains do not directly compensate for the husband's losses (resulting in a 'net' neutral or positive outcome). However, it is common for agents to minimize the significance of sacrifices they make by focusing instead on the benefits generated. We do this when only our individual well-being is at stake, so it makes sense we would do so as well when someone else's well-being and our own have, effectively, merged. Sacrifices made on behalf of loved ones may therefore feel less burdensome.

The view I have sketched thus far is certainly tentative and incomplete. I have not argued for moderate relationalism about the self, but rather assumed it for the sake of argument, to see what it would mean for sacrifice. Nor have I examined the metaphysics of relational well-being in any detail, nor the implications for prominent theories of well-being. Much more needs to be said. Still, my preliminary conclusion is that we can expand our notion of well-being to be less individualistic, without giving up on the well-being account of sacrifice, and without eliminating or explaining away an important class of sacrifices. In fact, the relational account of well-being might help us make more sense of loving sacrifices than we could before.

Notes

1. I argue for the relationship between sacrifice and supererogation in Carbonell 2012.
2. The remainder of this section is inspired by, though not directly borrowed from, the account of sacrifice I give in Carbonell 2012. In Carbonell 2015, I concede that this account does not do a good job handling one class of sacrifices, those I call 'sacrifices of self'. But Tatiana Visak (2015) has argued that the well-being account can handle sacrifices of self just fine.
3. Some features of the economy of sacrifice are written into the legal system. For instance, whether you have a duty to aid someone, at some cost to yourself, may depend on the relation you stand in to the beneficiary. See Alexander 1996.
4. Overvold (1980) insists on the first two. Rosati (2009) specifies the 'self' condition.
5. Brandt (1991) was writing in response to Overvold (1980), and both of them use the term 'self-sacrifice' rather than 'sacrifice'. Perhaps the term 'self-sacrifice' connotes motivational baggage that mere 'sacrifice' does not.
6. Overvold (1980, 112) specifies that there must be a net loss. Rosati (2009) thinks gross losses suffice.
7. To be sure, her loss may feel like less of a sacrifice once she adapts to the new lifestyle. In contexts of oppression we call these 'adaptive preferences' (or 'deformed desires'). See Superson 2014. Relatedly, when we internalize the demands of a moral theory, complying with it may become less burdensome. See Sin 2012.
8. For more on this worry about desire theories, see Overvold 1980, Brandt 1991 and Darwall 2002. For arguments that desire theories can survive this worry, see Rosati 2009 and Heathwood 2011. Perhaps what the mother *most* desires of her current options is to take the bullet for her son. But she also desires to live to old age, and the frustration of that desire seems quite bad for her. Similarly, the husband's desire for a good night of sleep is frustrated even if his desire for his wife's safety is stronger.
9. See Portmore 2007 for the argument that goals achieved via 'self-sacrifice' contribute even more to one's well-being than those that do not involve sacrifice.
10. For a discussion of the relationship between dependency and the demandingness of morality, see Tessman 2015, especially chapter 7.
11. For an early statement of the view, see Nedeslky 1989.
12. Mackenzie and Stoljar (2000, 7) claim that, while Annette Baier has convincingly refuted this version of individualism, it does not follow that we should reject the concept of autonomy.
13. I am using Mackenzie and Stoljar's language of 'agent', but since we are interested in well-being rather than autonomy, we may be just as interested in 'patients' as 'agents'. For now, I set this distinction aside.
14. John Christman describes two versions of what I'm calling 'relationalism' and what he calls the 'social self thesis', corresponding roughly to the denial of Mackenzie and Stoljar's third and second versions of individualism, respectively. 'First, the thesis in question can be understood as a metaphysical claim, such that relations with other persons, institutions, traditions, and so on are seen as essentially part of the person (either at a time or over time). Alternatively, the social self thesis can be understood as a contingent psychological claim about a person's self-concept, value structure, emotional states, motivational set, or reflective capacities' (Christman 2004, 144).

52 SACRIFICE AND MORAL PHILOSOPHY

15. For more on family-centered care, see American Academy of Pediatrics 2012. For a skeptical view, according to which family interests are a 'myth', see Raho 2016.
16. For an earlier statement of the view from which Groll draws, see also Ross 1998.
17. Glorifying sacrifices might be just as harmful as eliminating them from our analysis. Ann Mongoven (2003) argues that the glorification of organ donation has led to the 'routinization' of a major sacrifice, which she thinks is dangerous.

Acknowledgements

I am grateful to Stephen Campbell, Amanda Roth and an anonymous referee for helpful comments. I regret not having the space to incorporate more of their valuable suggestions.

Disclosure statement

No potential conflict of interest was reported by the author.

References

Alexander, L. 1996. "Affirmative Duties and the Limits of Self-Sacrifice." *Law and Philosophy* 15 (1): 65–74. doi:10.1007/BF00143972.
American Academy of Pediatrics. 2012. "Patient- and Family-Centered Care and the Pediatrician's Role." *Pediatrics* 129: 394–404. doi:10.1542/peds.2011-3084.
Antony, L. M. 1995. "Is Psychological Individualism a Piece of Ideology?" *Hypatia* 10: 157–174. doi:10.1111/j.1527-2001.1995.tb00742.x.
Bradley, B. 2014. "Objective Theories of Well-Being." In *The Cambridge Companion to Utilitarianism*, edited by B. Eggleston and D. Miller. Cambridge, UK: Cambridge University Press.
Brandt, R. B. 1991. "Overvold on Self-Interest and Self-Sacrifice." *The Journal of Philosophical Research* 16: 353–363. doi:10.5840/jpr_1991_8.
Burke, K., and G. A. Otis. 2016. "Brooklyn Native Died Protecting Her Son in Orlando." *New York Daily News*, June 14. http://www.nydailynews.com/news/national/brooklyn-native-mother-11-died-orlando-nightclub-attack-article-1.2672514.
Carbonell, V. 2012. "The Ratcheting-Up Effect." *Pacific Philosophical Quarterly* 93 (2): 228–254. doi:10.1111/papq.2012.93.issue-2.
Carbonell, V. 2015. "Sacrifices of Self." *The Journal of Ethics* 19 (1): 53–72. doi:10.1007/s10892-014-9186-x.
Christman, J. 2004. "Relational Autonomy, Liberal Individualism, and the Social Constitution of Selves." *Philosophical Studies* 117: 143–164. doi:10.1023/B:PHIL.0000014532.56866.5c.
Darwall, S. 2002. *Welfare and Rational Care*. Princeton: Princeton University Press.
Gelven, M. 1988. "Is Sacrifice a Virtue?" *The Journal of Value Inquiry* 22: 235–252. doi:10.1007/BF00209385.
Griffin, J. 1986. *Well-Being: Its Meaning, Measurement, and Moral Importance*. Oxford, UK: Clarendon Press.
Groll, D. 2014. "Four Models of Family Interests." *Pediatrics* 134 (Supplement): SS81–SS86. doi:10.1542/peds.2014-1394C.
Haybron, D. M. 2008. *The Pursuit of Unhappiness*. Oxford, UK: Oxford University Press.

Heathwood, C. 2011. "Preferentism and Self-Sacrifice." *Pacific Philosophical Quarterly* 92: 18–38. doi:10.1111/j.1468-0114.2010.01384.x.

Hurka, T. 1993. *Perfectionism*. New York: Oxford University Press.

Jacobs, R. A. 1987. "Obligation, Supererogation and Self-Sacrifice." *Philosophy* 62: 96–101. doi:10.1017/S0031819100038638.

Kopelman, L. M. 2010. "Using the Best-Interests Standard in Treatment Decisions for Young Children." In *Pediatric Bioethics*, edited by G. Miller. Cambridge, UK: Cambridge University Press.

Mackenzie, C., and N. Stoljar. 2000. "Introduction: Autonomy Reconfigured." In *Relational Autonomy*, edited by Mackenzie and Stoljar. Oxford: Oxford University Press.

Mongoven, A. 2003. "Sharing Our Body and Blood: Organ Donation and Feminist Critiques of Sacrifice." *The Journal of Medicine and Philosophy* 28 (1): 89–114. doi:10.1076/jmep.28.1.89.14175.

Nedelsky, J. 1989. "Reconceiving Autonomy: Sources, Thoughts and Possibilities." *Yale Journal of Law and Feminism* 1: 7–36.

Overvold, M. C. 1980. "Self-Interest and the Concept of Self-Sacrifice." *Canadian Journal of Philosophy* 10 (1): 105–118. doi:10.1080/00455091.1980.10716285.

Parfit, D. 1984. *Reasons and Persons*. Oxford: Clarendon Press.

Portmore, D. W. 2007. "Welfare, Achievement, and Self-Sacrifice." *Journal of Ethics and Social Philosophy* 2 (2): 1–28. doi:10.26556/jesp.v2i2.22.

Raho, J. A. 2016. "In Whose Best Interests? Critiquing the 'Family-As-Unit' Myth in Pediatric Ethics." In *Bioethics: Medical, Ethical and Legal Perspectives*, edited by P. A. Clark. InTech. doi:10.5772/66715.

Rosati, C. S. 2009. "Self-Interest and Self-Sacrifice." *Proceedings of the Aristotelian Society* 109 (3): 311–325. doi:10.1111/j.1467-9264.2009.00269.x.

Ross, L. F. 1998. *Children, Families, and Health Care Decision-Making*. Oxford: Clarendon Press.

Salter, E. K. 2014. "Resisting the Siren Call of Individualism in Pediatric Decision-Making and the Role of Relational Interests." *The Journal of Medicine and Philosophy* 39: 26–40. doi:10.1093/jmp/jht060.

Sin, W. 2012. "Internalization and Moral Demands." *Philosophical Studies* 157: 163–175. doi:10.1007/s11098-010-9630-0.

Stoljar, N. 2015. "Feminist Perspectives on Autonomy." In *The Stanford Encyclopedia of Philosophy* edited by E. N. Zalta. Fall 2015 ed. https://plato.stanford.edu/archives/fall2015/entries/feminism-autonomy/.

Superson, A. 2014. "Feminist Moral Psychology." In *The Stanford Encyclopedia of Philosophy* edited by E. N. Zalta. Winter 2014 ed. https://plato.stanford.edu/archives/win2014/entries/feminism-moralpsych/.

Tessman, L. 2015. *Moral Failure*. New York: Oxford University Press.

Višak, T. 2015. "Sacrifices of Self are Prudential Harms: A Reply to Carbonell." *The Journal of Ethics* 19 (2): 219–229. doi:10.1007/s10892-015-9196-3.

Weiss, P. 1949. "Sacrifice and Self-Sacrifice: Their Warrant and Limits." *The Review of Metaphysics* 2: 76–98.

When does 'Can' imply 'Ought'?

Stephanie Collins

> The Assistance Principle is common currency to a wide range of moral theories. Roughly, this principle states: if you can fulfil important interests, at not too high a cost, then you have a moral duty to do so. I argue that, in determining whether the 'not too high a cost' clause of this principle is met, we must consider three distinct costs: 'agent-relative costs', 'recipient-relative costs' and 'ideal-relative costs'.

Introduction

According to Stan Lee, the author of Spiderman, 'with great power there must also come – great responsibility' (Lee 1962). In other words: 'can' implies 'ought'. Left on its own, this principle has the potential to be incredibly demanding. The natural move is to add a 'at not too high a cost' rider. Then we get something like: if you have the capacity to fulfil important interests, at not too high a cost, then you have a moral duty to do so. I will call this the 'assistance principle' and the duties it posits 'assistance duties'. The assistance principle is simple and appealing, as Singer's (1972) famous 'drowning toddler' example demonstrates.[1] Variants on this principle have been applied to issues as diverse as climate change (Caney 2010), humanitarian intervention (Pattison 2010) and, most prominently, global poverty (Singer 1972, 2009).

This paper will consider how the concept of sacrifice should feed into our interpretation, and implementation, of the assistance principle; that is, which kinds of sacrifice are relevant to answering the title question and limiting the demandingness of assistance duties. I will make two suggestions for how we should conceptualise sacrifice so that it appropriately limits the applicability of the assistance principle. Both suggestions challenge the view, implicit in much literature on sacrifice, that sacrifice is always a sacrifice of the *agent* or *duty-bearer*. Others' sacrifices, and other kinds of sacrifice, are, I argue, relevant to determining the existence and strength of assistance duties.

First, I will focus on the 'at not too high a cost' clause. I will suggest that the costs relevant to this clause are the *net costs* to both the *capacity-bearer* and the *interest-bearer* – as opposed to the gross costs, and/or the net costs to the capacity-bearer alone. That is, we should distinguish (net) 'agent-relative sacrifice' from (net) 'recipient-relative sacrifice'. For example, if I can rescue the drowning toddler at the cost of my shoes, then this is a gross cost to me. But if I will experience a warm glow of self-satisfaction, then this is a gross benefit to me. By subtracting my gross costs from my gross benefits, we arrive at the 'net agent-relative sacrifice' of my action. Likewise, if I rescue the drowning toddler, this is a gross benefit to him. But if I give him concussion while doing so, then this is a gross cost to him. By subtracting the toddler's gross costs from the toddler's gross benefits, we arrive at the 'net recipient-relative sacrifice'. I argue that both kinds of sacrifice – net agent-relative and net recipient-relative – should feed into the 'at not too high a cost' clause.[2]

Second, I will suggest that we should conceptualise sacrifice (as it is relevant to the assistance principle) such that our interest-fulfilling actions can *sacrifice* the better actions of others. I call this 'ideal-relative sacrifice': in acting to fulfil an important interest, we sometimes sacrifice the more ideal actions that others would have taken to fulfil that very interest. These actions might be 'more ideal' in the sense of (i) *imposing lower costs on the interest-bearer* (i.e. the more ideal action would fulfil the interest-bearer's important interest more fully or securely, or would fulfil other of the interest-bearer's other interests, alongside the important interest that generated the duty) or in the sense of (ii) *imposing lower costs on the agent who performs them* (compared to the costs our own interest-fulfilling actions would have imposed on us). For example, suppose my rescuing action would give the toddler concussion, but your rescuing action would not. If I then go ahead and rescue the toddler (when you would have done so had I not), then I have *sacrificed* your more ideal action. In this case, your action is 'more ideal' in the sense that it *imposes lower costs on the interest-bearer*. But your action might (instead or also) be 'more ideal' in that the sense that it imposes lower costs on its performer. For example, if you are wearing cheap gumboots, while I am wearing expensive high heels, then my rescuing action involves an 'ideal-relative sacrifice' insofar as your action imposes lower costs on the agent that performs it.

If some interest-fulfilling action will sacrifice the more ideal actions of others – that is, if the action will imply 'ideal-relative sacrifice' – then the moral reason to perform that action is weaker than it otherwise would have been. Acknowledging that our interest-fulfilling actions can involve ideal-relative sacrifice allows us to see that the assistance principle demands less from us than we might initially have thought. It also gives the attractive verdict that well-meaning but uninformed agents should not rush to 'help' in contexts where their actions are not those most needed.

In sum, then, there are three kinds of sacrifice that are relevant to assistance duties: agent-relative sacrifice; recipient-relative sacrifice; and ideal-relative sacrifice. The size of the agent-relative and recipient-relative sacrifices determines whether the 'at not too high a cost' clause is met, and thus helps determine whether there is an assistance duty at all. Assuming there is an assistance duty, the size of the ideal-relative sacrifice helps determine the strength of the duty, that is, how easily the duty can be outweighed by other, competing duties that are held by the duty-bearing agent.

I assume that a high level of sacrifice is *sufficient* to undermine, and to weaken, *assistance* duties. Importantly, this assumption is neutral on many other issues in the philosophy of sacrifice. For example, I will not assume that a high level of sacrifice (of any, or all of, the three types) is *necessary* for any duty – including any assistance duty – to be undermined or weakened. I will also not assume that a high level of sacrifice is necessary for an act to be supererogatory. Nor will I assume that a high level of sacrifice is *sufficient* to undermine or weaken duties *other than* assistance duties. After all, some highly sacrificial acts are nonetheless required by duty, and some non-sacrificial acts are not required by duty, or are supererogatory. My question is a focused one: how should we understand the ways in which sacrifice blocks, or weakens, assistance duties? My answer is that there are three kinds of sacrifice at issue. These kinds of sacrifice circumscribe the contexts in which 'can' implies 'ought'. Factors other than sacrifice might *also* circumscribe these contexts.

To make these points, I will develop two versions of the assistance principle: the well-placed principle and the best-placed principle.[3] The well-placed principle states that if you are *sufficiently* capable of fulfilling someone's important interests, at not too high a cost, then you have a moral duty to do so. The 'best-placed' principle states that if you are *most* capable of fulfilling someone's important interests, at not too high a cost, then you have a *strong* moral duty to do so. ('Strong' refers to how important a countervailing reason of yours would have to be to outweigh the duty in question.) Both these principles contain the 'at not too high a cost' clause, so I will analyse that clause in a way that applies to both principles, including explaining how both agent-relative and recipient-relative sacrifice bear on that clause.

But the two principles come apart on the question of whether, by satisfying the principle's antecedent, you sacrifice someone else's more ideal actions. If you satisfy the conditions of the 'well-placed' version, then your interest-fulfilling action might sacrifice someone else's more ideal actions (i.e. might involve ideal-relative sacrifice); if you satisfy the conditions of the 'best-placed' version, then your interest-fulfilling action does not have this sacrificial implication. I suggest that, because the best-placed version does not contain this sacrificial implication, the duties it produces are stronger than those of the well-placed principle. This suggestion accords with the common-sense idea that actions implying little sacrifice are more readily morally demanded than actions implying great sacrifice – but the sacrifice at issue here is the sacrifice *of someone else's more ideal action*, not the interests of the agent alone. Thus, the notion that we can sacrifice others' better actions through our good actions implies that the two versions of the principle are differently demanding.

The argument will take the following structure. I start by assuming that well-placed duties and best-placed duties are two species of the genus 'assistance duties'. I assume we can break down the duty-generating relation at issue in (both species of) the assistance principle into five rough components. Components 1 to 4 are the individually necessary and jointly sufficient conditions for a 'well-placed duty', while components 1 to 5 are the individually necessary and jointly sufficient conditions for a 'best-placed duty'. The first four components are: (1) there is an *important interest* that is unfulfilled; (2) someone is *sufficiently capable* of fulfilling that interest; (3) that agent's most efficacious measure for doing so is *not too costly*; (4) the agent could do *similarly in similar circumstances*. These components generate a 'well-placed duty'. For the relation to generate 'a best-placed duty', the fifth component must be added: (5) the agent's fulfilling the interest would be *as or less costly* than any other agent's doing so. In sections 1–2, I briefly explain the first two components. In section 3, I explain the third component, arguing that the relevant 'costs' are the net agent-relative *and* net recipient-relative sacrifices, and describing how the fourth component arises out of discussion of the third one. In section 4, I explain the fifth component. Here I motivate the idea that well-placed agents can make ideal-relative sacrifices – they can sacrifice the more ideal actions of other agents – and that this sacrifice is what makes well-placed duties weaker than best-placed duties. By developing components three, four and five, I will demonstrate that a broad and tripartite conception of sacrifice – one that includes agent-relative, recipient-relative and ideal-relative sacrifice – should be used in interpreting and applying the assistance principle.

1. 'An Important Interest is Unfulfilled'

First, to establish the scope of the discussion, it will help to know about the interests that are at issue in the well-placed and best-placed principles. I label these 'important interests'.[4] To picture these interests, we can imagine a continuum of interests, from trivial to important. Which interests are further towards the 'important' end of the continuum will depend on one's substantive theory of welfare, on which my formulations of these principles

58 SACRIFICE AND MORAL PHILOSOPHY

is neutral. For example, in an article outlining a variety of duty-generating principles, David Miller (2001) focuses on 'instances of deprived or suffering people – people whose basic rights to security, or subsistence or health care are not being protected, and who as a result are in no position to live minimally decent lives'. He suggests a version of the assistance principle – a version according to which 'responsibilities ought to be assigned according to the capacity of each agent to discharge them' – as one way of distributing duties to fulfil these interests. But Miller's characterisation is just one possible characterisation of important interests. Others might refer to basic rights (Shue 1996) or basic capabilities (Nussbaum 2006).

Important interests might be indexed in various ways. For example, they might be indexed to the agent who fulfils them. I might have an important interest not just in being loved, but in being loved *by my parents* (Liao 2006; Keller 2006). This will become important for the two species of the assistance principle: if my interest is in being loved by my father, then only my father is eligible for an assistance duty to fulfil that interest. This means that his duty will be grounded in the best-placed version of the principle (not merely the well-placed version), and thus that his duty is relatively strong, since his interest-fulfilling action will not sacrifice the better interest-fulfilling actions of others – or so I shall argue in section 4.[5] Thus, the possibility of interests that are indexed to a fulfiller increases how often the best-placed principle applies.

Despite all this scope for detail, when identifying assistance duties, interests should be defined as generally as possible while capturing all that is of value in them. For example, if what matters is just 'that I am fed tonight', then we should not split hairs between my interest in 'getting fed tonight by A' and my interest in 'getting fed tonight by B'. This is because assistance duties include not just duties in virtue of being *well-placed* to fulfil some interest, but also duties in virtue of being *best-placed* to fulfil some interest. And if there is no morally important difference between these interests, then our account of best-placed duties should not pointlessly say A and B each have a *best-placed duty* over these different interests, based on their respectively being best-placed those agent-indexed interests. (At least, our account should not say this if we assume full compliance – a point I will address in section 4). We can say that they each have a *well-placed* duty to do so. But if they are both well-placed to meet the non-agent-indexed interest, then we do not need agent-indexed interests in order to say this. Assuming they are not equally best-placed to fulfil my interest in *being fed tonight*, only one of them should have a duty to fulfil that interest based on being *best-placed* to do so. This prevents a situation in which *all* assistance duties are best-placed duties. If all assistance duties were best-placed duties, then we would not be able to capture the intuitive differences (on which, more below) between duties in virtue of being well-placed and duties in virtue of being best-placed.

We now have the following. Subject *S* has a well-placed or best-placed duty only if:

(1) Person *P* has an important interest, *I*, that is unfulfilled, where the interest is described in a way that includes all and only the morally relevant facts and indexes.

2. Someone is Sufficiently Capable of Fulfilling It

I will assume that assistance duties are duties to take some measure (action or omission) that has at least some likelihood of fulfilling an interest (the idea of 'important interest' will re-emerge shortly). I will use 'measure' assuming agents have full control over measures they take.

For an agent to have a duty to take a measure *in virtue of that measure's propensity to fulfil an interest*, the measure must be sufficiently likely to fulfil that interest. How likely is sufficiently likely? It seems strange to believe in a duty to take some measure – in virtue of that measure's propensity to fulfil an important interest – if the measure has only, say, a 0.0001 likelihood of succeeding. Yet in some cases – if the interest is important enough – an agent can have a duty to take measures that have only a tiny likelihood of fulfilling an interest. If the interest at stake is 'all persons' interests in being alive next week' and A could take the measure 'firing a rocket at the giant asteroid that, if not hit by a rocket, will hit Earth and kill everyone this weekend', then A might have a duty to take those measures, even if the measures are unlikely to fulfil all those interests. There are measures he can take that will *possibly* fulfil the interests, so he can have a duty to take those measures, where the duty is grounded in the importance of the relevant interests.

This suggests that we should not a precise threshold – say, 50 or 70% – for how likely the measure is to fulfil the interest. The reason for this is that any such threshold would be somewhat arbitrary and would rule out duties in 'high-stakes, low-likelihood' cases like that just described. Instead, I suggest, for an agent to have an assistance duty to take a measure, the likelihood that the measure will fulfil the interest must be *proportionate* to the importance of the interest. The less important the interest, the more likely it must be that some measure will fulfil it, if that measure's likelihood is to be proportionate to the interest's importance. Conversely, for an extremely important interest, a measure might have a low likelihood of fulfilling it (if the measure is taken), and yet it might be proportionate. Admittedly, this brings a consequentialist element into the assistance principle. As we shall see in section 3.2, though, this will not make assistance duties consequentialist through-and-through. Since my main aim in this paper is to characterise the nature of the *sacrifices* at issue in the assistance principle, I lack space to fully defend this aspect of (my characterisation of) the principle. If you would prefer to set a uniform likelihood threshold that all duty-generating interest-fulfilling measures must meet, then you can make the necessary substitutions for the rest of the paper.

For simplicity, and following earlier work (Collins 2015, 107–108), I will use 'A's likelihood' to mean 'the likelihood that the interest will be fulfilled if A takes his *most efficacious measure*'. This is the measure of A's that is most likely (of all A's measures) to fulfil the interest, if A takes it. And I'll use 'success' to mean 'the important interest is fulfilled'.

My suggestion, then, is that for A to have an assistance duty grounded in some interest, A's likelihood of success must be in the range of likelihoods that are *proportionate* to the importance of the interest, where more important interests are proportionate to a range of likelihoods whose lower bound is lower. If A's likelihood of success is proportionate to the interest (or if it meets the reader's preferred likelihood threshold), then we can say A is *sufficiently capable* of fulfilling the interest to bear an assistance duty to take the relevant measures.

Thus we have the second necessary condition for assistance duties:

(2) If: S takes measure M, where M is the most efficacious measure open to S to fulfil I; then I will be fulfilled with a likelihood that is *proportionate* to I's importance, where more important interests are proportionate to a wider range of likelihoods (with a lower bound that is lower).[6]

3. The Action is Not Too Costly

3.1. *Costliness to the agent*

It is here that the notion of sacrifice makes its first appearance in (both versions of) the assistance principle. It is typical to think there is no duty to take interest-fulfilling measures if doing so would be excessively costly *for the taker of the measure*, that is, if doing so would involve excessive *agent-relative* sacrifice (Rawls 1971, 100; Fishkin 1982, 15; Dorsey 2013, 357). Below, I will argue that a high agent-relative sacrifice is not, on its own, sufficient to cancel a duty. Nonetheless, it does feed into the 'not too costly' condition. An agent-relative sacrifice, as I will use the term, is a sacrifice that an agent makes of her own interests. The 'not too costly' clause refers, in part (but only in part), to agent-relative sacrifice. In this sub-section, I will consider how we should conceptualise agent-relative sacrifice in the context of the assistance principle. (In section 3.2, I will conceptualise *recipient-relative sacrifice*; in section 4, I will introduce *ideal-relative sacrifice*, that is, the sacrifice an agent makes by fulfilling an interest when another agent (the 'ideal' agent) could more ideally fulfil that interest.)

We can think of the agent-relative sacrifice as an opportunity cost: the agent sacrifices whatever she would do instead of taking the measures. Likewise, Overvold (1980, 108) argues that the baseline for sacrifice should not be one's position before the sacrificial act, but should be whatever one's position would have been had one not taken the sacrificial act.) Following Lewis (1973), we can frame this by asking what properties the agent would have in the 'nearest possible world' in which she did not fulfil the interest. Whatever properties she would have in that world is the agent-relative sacrifice of her taking the measure. Notice that many things might be different between the nearest measure-taking world and the nearest non-measure-taking world: the agent might have more or less health, knowledge, friendship, love, recreation time, or access to beauty in the nearest world where the agent takes the measure, as compared with the nearest world in which she does not take the measure. All kinds of intrinsic, extrinsic, final and instrumental values and disvalues to agent might count. Thus, the 'opportunity cost' framing does not reduce the range of goods that might be (agent-relatively) sacrificed; it simply provides a way of setting the baseline against which we can assess those (varied and multiple) sacrifices. Also, some opportunity 'costs' of taking the measure might in fact be benefits, if the nearest possible world in which the agent doesn't take the measure is one in which she's worse off. Again, the opportunity costs framing merely sets the baseline; it does not judge the value of that baseline. The opportunity costs might also include what Carbonell (2012) calls 'sacrifices of self': sacrifices that are not readily understandable as either costs or gains to agent, since they are part of the agent's very self. It is a tricky matter whether such sacrifices of one's very personality, values, or outlook should be understood as costs rather than benefits. Again, the point of the opportunity 'cost' framing does not settle that question; it simply sets the baseline for comparison.

However, when assessing whether a measure is *too* costly for the agent, we need to consider not just *which* world is our baseline for comparison, but also whether the goings-on within that world are *good or bad* for the agent. When assessing whether a given measure is or is not too costly, we should consider both the goods and the bads that the agent will undergo, in the measure-taking world as compared with the nearest non-measure-taking world. That is, when asking whether a measure has a high agent-relative sacrifice, we should compare the *net value* of these two worlds, vis-à-vis the agent.

This suggestion – to weigh up bads and goods to get an overall assessment of net value – runs counter to the view of Carbonell, who points out that some bads cannot be fully compensated for by the goods that come along with them. Suppose some interest-fulfilling measure would lead the agent to sacrifice some physical health, but increase her political freedoms.

Is the measure a net good or a net bad, for her? Carbonell's arguments imply that this question might not be answerable: 'gains of wellbeing in one area of one's life cannot be said to directly *compensate* for losses of wellbeing in another, in the most meaningful sense of "compensate," even if the gains are actually made possible by the losses' (Carbonell 2012, 238, emphasis in original). Thus, she suggests, the (agent-relative) sacrifices that are relevant for the 'not too costly' condition are *not* the net losses (or 'net value', as I labelled the same concept). Instead, the relevant sacrifices are the *gross* loses.

This is too heavy-handed a response to the fact that some goods and bads are incommensurable. After all, some goods and bads *are* commensurable. For these goods and bads, it makes sense that we balance them off against one another, when asking whether a measure that entails goods and bads is too costly to the agent. This is not to say that a cost that comes with accompanied benefits is *not a cost*, or is in some way *irrelevant* or *insignificant* to an overall assessment of the agent's situation (Carbonell 2012, 250 suggests that this is what a 'net' approach implies). It is just to say that when we are considering *whether a given cost can be demanded by a moral duty*, both the cost and the benefit should matter, *if* it is possible to balance them off. For example, suppose I can rescue a drowning toddler. If I did so I would receive a monetary gift from the parents. It seems reasonable to suppose that this could genuinely off-set the cost to me of muddying my shoes (assuming the shoes lack sentimental value). If so, that off-setting makes a difference to whether the rescue is too costly for me – reality of the shoe-sacrifice notwithstanding. In short, it is not *always* true that '[o]bligation is constrained by unreasonable sacrifice even when the sacrifices open doors to new sources of wellbeing' (Carbonell 2012, 238). This is because some of those new sources of wellbeing, sometimes, can completely off-set (what would otherwise be) an unreasonable sacrifice. We should not ignore this possibility by insisting that the only sacrifice that is ever relevant is the gross sacrifice. *If* losses and gains are commensurable, then net loss (i.e. net value) is the relevant metric for agent-relative sacrifice.

Moreover, even in those cases where the goods and the bads truly are incommensurable, the non-compensability runs both ways: just as the gain doesn't compensate for the loss, likewise the loss doesn't erase the gain. The gain is real, so it is not clear why an incommensurable loss should be viewed as 'too costly', such that it can erase an obligation to take a measure that entails the gain. For these reasons, we should use the 'net value' metric as the default metric for assessing the sacrifice an agent makes in taking interest-fulfilling measures.

That said, Carbonell is surely correct that, sometimes, an interest-fulfilling measure can realise a bad for the agent, where that bad is not commensurable with the goods the measure realises for the agent, and where the bad really does, on its own, render the measure too costly. But we can account for this by saying that measures that realise such bads have a 'trumping' power, such that they render the agent-relative value of the measure negative (or zero), irrespective of the goods that the measure also brings about. That is, Carbonell is correct that *some* bads (e.g. some that are very bad and are incommensurable with their accompanying goods) should have trumping power when it comes to assessing the agent-relative sacrifice of the measure. Perhaps the loss of the agent's basic civil rights, or the loss of their close family members, are like this. Such losses render the measures that entail them non-positively valuable for the agent, regardless of what benefits the measure would provide the agent. My point is that the presence of such cases should not deter us from assessing a measure's agent-relative sacrifice in a way that takes account of all the goods and all the bads, when it is possible to do so. We should ask after the overall value of a measure to an agent. Sometimes, the answer to that question will be that the value is negative in virtue of one incommensurable loss alone.

The possibility of incommensurability suggests that sometimes we will be able to say only whether the agent-relative value of some measure is positive or negative, or greater or lower than the value of some other measure open to the agent – we will rarely be able to put a precise number on the agent-relative value of a measure. Sometimes, different agent-relative values (each accruing to a measure the agent could take) will only be able to be given an ordinal ranking, not a cardinal one. Sometimes, even an ordinal ranking might be impossible – there may be no fact about which measures have greatest value. For example, if S's most efficacious measure for fulfilling an important interest would result in S's not being able to write a great novel (that S otherwise would write), while T's most efficacious measure for fulfilling that important interest would result in T's not being able to paint a great painting (that T otherwise would paint), then there might be no fact about which person's measure realises highest cost to the relevant agent – because the novel and the painting are incommensurable (Anderson 1993, ch. 3; Raz 1986, ch. 13).[7] In general, then, the idea of a measure having a 'non-negative' agent-relative value is somewhat metaphorical. However, compelling examples of assistance duties (such as easy rescue cases) suggest that this incommensurability does not always paralyse our ability to make judgments about which measures have more or less agent-relative value.

All this allows us to be ecumenical about the values that feed into the agent-relative sacrifice involved in the 'at not too high a cost' constraint (including which losses count as trump cards, by rendering the measure's agent-relative value automatically non-positive). However, there are a few issues on which it is important to take sides. The first is that agent-relative value should be understood objectively (or at least, inter-subjectively), rather than subjectively. This is because this value is to be used as an input into claims about what people owe each other: what I owe you and what you owe me. For these claims to be assessed for their relative plausibility, we must have a metric of plausibility that is common between them. A crucial part of this metric is the value (negative or positive) that would be realised if the claim were upheld. An objective (or at least, inter-subjective) theory of value is needed for this metric to be properly intelligible to all parties, thus responding to their moral agency and patiency. (Here I roughly follow Carbonell 2012, 232–234, who follows Scanlon 1975.) And, as Carbonell (2015, 235) points out, there is another reason why the value a stake here must not be subjective: as Darwall (2002, 3) puts it,

> if there were no difference between what a person valued and what benefited him, self-sacrifice would be impossible, except through weakness of will [...] it would be impossible for pursuing one's values ever to cost one *on balance*, since realizing a value would be the same thing as benefiting from it.

Agent-relative value, then, is not to be determined subjectively.

There is a second stand we should take on how to assess agent-relative values. This stand arises from the fact that assistance duties are forward-looking imperatives, not backward-looking assessments. The assistance principle (in both its versions) ought to be formulated to be operationalisable in practical reasoning. Yet we cannot know, ahead of taking a measure, what value (goods and bads) it will realise, vis-à-vis the agent. We should, therefore, weight the possible values by their (reasonably believed or reasonably believable) likelihoods. That is, since the assistance principle is an action-guiding and forward-looking imperative, the agent-relative sacrifice relevant to the 'not too costly' constraint is agent-relative *expected* value.

To summarise: the size of the agent-relative sacrifice of a given interest-fulfilling measure is *part of* what determines whether that measure is 'too costly'. The other determinate will be fleshed out in the next section. If the measure is too costly, then the assistance duty never arises to begin with. There is an agent-relative sacrifice just in case the cost to the agent is negative. The cost to the agent is negative just if the expected net value to the agent's interests (i.e. the sum of her expected interest-fulfilment minus her expected interest non-fulfilment), on a non-subjectively defined understanding of interests, is lower in the nearest world where she takes the measure, than in the nearest world where she does not take the measure. Some interests are so important that their non-fulfilment would render the expected net value to the agent's interests negative, regardless of what goods-for-the-agent come along with that non-fulfilment.

3.2. *Costliness to the recipient*

The agent is not the only one whose goods and bads are at stake in circumstances where the assistance principle applies. Most obviously, goods and bads for the interest-bearer (or 'recipient') are also at stake. As alluded to in the Introduction, a measure can be costly for the interest-bearer – either in the sense that the interest-bearer's important interest is fulfilled, but not fully or securely; or in the sense that the interest-bearer's other interests are frustrated by the measure. In short, at stake for the interest-bearer is not just whether the relevant important interest is fulfilled, but also whether it is fulfilled in the right way (that is, fully, securely, or without frustrating their other interests). To illustrate with the familiar example: if the drowning toddler is saved, but is knocked around and suffers concussion, then the value of the rescue measure, vis-à-vis the recipient, is diminished relative to rescue without concussion. If the non-concussion rescue would have happened in the absence of the concussion rescue, then this is a cost (for the recipient) of the rescue scenario with the concussion.

Should the value of a measure vis-à-vis the recipient also help determine whether an interest-fulfilling measure meets the 'not too costly' condition? That is, when others are fulfilling our interests, should the sacrifices they impose on us (by way of fulfilling our interest) have some bearing on whether they ought to fulfil our interests? Yes. Agent-relative expected value is not the only relevant sacrifice. In performing 'good deeds', well-meaning people affect those around them – and not for the best in every respect. If I am a clumsy swimmer and will cause the child to get concussion during my rescue, then, *even if my rescue is likely to be successful*, this sacrifice I impose on the child should be considered in assessing whether I should enact the rescue.

One might think that the costs to the recipient have already been taken into account in section 1: it is their important interest the action is aiming to fulfil. To count their interests as also bearing upon the 'not too costly' condition would, perhaps, be to count those interests twice. But this is not right. The only interest of theirs that was at issue in section 1 was the specific important interest that the measure aims to fulfil. In the child drowning case, this is the important interest in being rescued. But those on the 'recipient' end of the assistance principle have interests that are as numerous, varied, multifaceted and incommensurable as those on the 'agent' end of the principle. There is no reason why these other interests of the recipient should not be considered.

A slippery slope may appear to loom. If we're going to consider costs *and* benefits to agent *and* recipient, then why not insist that the interest-fulfilling measure must have non-negative value regarding *the entire world*, on pain of not fulfilling the 'not too costly' condition? Indeed, if one adheres to maximising, act, agent-neutral consequentialism, then it is natural to think the 'not too costly' condition is met if and only if the measure produces non-negative aggregate cost regarding the entire world. But if one is a maximising, act, agent-neutral consequentialist, then one will see the assistance principle as a mere 'rule of thumb'. And 'rules of thumb' should not have the same content as the fundamental principles that justify the rules of thumb (otherwise, they would not deserve the name 'rules of thumb'). So while it might seem natural to include 'the entire world' in the not-too-costly condition, this would undermine the role that the assistance principle is meant to play in one's theory. By limiting the relevant net value to the agent and recipient alone, we make the assistance principle operationalisable as a rule of thumb.

Meanwhile, if one is *not* a maximising, act, agent-neutral consequentialist, then one is likely to see the assistance principle as grounded in the claims (or rights) of the interest-bearer themselves. From this perspective, to consider interests beyond those of the agent and recipient would be to overlook the point that the assistance principle produces duties for a particular agent to fulfil a particular important interest (right, claim) of a particular recipient. It is the recipient – and the recipient alone – who would be wronged if his interests were not fulfilled. And he would be wronged by the agent. So, again, from a claim- or rights-based perspective, it again is natural to limit the relevant net value to agent and recipient.

We can, therefore, think of the 'expected value' of a measure as being equal to: the potential weighted benefits for agent and recipient, given that the measure is taken, multiplied by the benefits' likelihoods, minus the potential weighted costs for agent and recipient, given that the measure is taken, multiplied by those costs' likelihoods. If this value is non-negative, then the costs are not proportionate to the benefits, so the costs do not render the measure non-obligatory, and the 'not too costly' condition is met. That is, a necessary condition for an assistance duty is that the measure's expected value (regarding agent and recipient) is non-negative.

We have now arrived at the third necessary condition for assistance duties:

(3) S's taking the measure in (2) would realise non-negative expected value regarding S and P.

3.3. *Aggregative and iterative sacrifice*

Intuitively, when assessing the expected value of an interest-fulfilling measure, only that measure's value is relevant. But this creates problems for the assistance principle. After all, small costs add up, both across time and at one time. These aggregate costs sometimes block the duty. Perhaps any one measure I might take to fulfil one person's important interest is not prohibitively costly, but I cannot take measures that fulfil *all*, or even *many*, persons' important interests without incurring prohibitive cost. Saving any one child is easy; saving many children requires forgoing my most important life projects and relationships.

Suppose, then, that the aggregative, but not iterative, value is non-positive – that is, the measures taken in aggregate have a non-positive expected value, but taken iteratively each has a positive expected value. For example, suppose it takes you a day to save each of 20,000 lives. While it might be proportionate (i.e. have positive value) for you to spend one day saving one life, it might be that 20,000 days (i.e. almost 55 years) is too much for morality to demand of you, whatever the cause, thus rendering the value of the 55-life-saving measure non-positive. If each duty over each life-saving measure were dependent only on the expected value of *that one measure* being non-negative, then we would be unable to cite the overall non-positive expected value as blocking any one of the interest-fulfilling duties. But this cannot be right: I should be able to cite the aggregated expected costs of all these measures as disproportionate to their aggregated expected benefits, rendering the aggregate expected value non-positive.

For example, perhaps each measure that fulfils conditions (1)–(3) is compatible with certain life-enhancing goods such as friendship, personal projects and so on. But we cannot have these life-enhancing goods while taking measures in *all* circumstances where (1)–(3) hold. If life-enhancing goods should not be sacrificed at the altar of well-placed or best-placed duties, then we should take an aggregative, rather than iterative, approach to assessing whether the value of one act of beneficence is positive. In short, we should consider the value of our *policy* around assistance duties, not the value of discharging individual duties, if we are to give due credit to the value of, for example, life-enhancing goods (see similarly Cullity 2004, Part II; Hooker 1999; Kamm 2000, 660).

If aggregative value can be non-positive while iterative value is positive, this suggests assistance duties are not constrained by the expected (agent- and recipient-relative) value of each interest-fulfilling measure considered in isolation, but instead by the aggregated expected value of all such measures. For assistance duties, we should aggregate the value of measures that we could take to fulfil someone else's important interest, in all cases where (1)–(3) hold. This gives us something like the following necessary condition for an assistance duty:

(4) If S were to take measures in all circumstances where the other conditions of this principle hold between S and any individual, then S would realise positive *aggregate* expected value regarding S and all those individuals.

A problem remains. Suppose Peter is the only one capable of rescuing all of 100 children. Each of their interests is very important. It would realise positive expected (agent-relative combined with patient-relative) value for him to rescue 10 of them, but non-positive expected value for him to rescue any more than that. (Imagine that rescuing 11 or more would cause him to develop severe hyperthermia, which serves a 'trumping' function on any benefits to patients.) If (4) is necessary for an assistance duty, then Peter is off the hook *altogether*. Helping all 100 would realise negative value, so, by the lights of (4), he has no duty to help any of them.

But the right result is surely that Peter has a duty to rescue 10 children. After all, that is the threshold of positive expected value regarding himself and the recipients; the point at which the sum of Peter's costs and the recipients' costs does not lead to sacrifice. Peter should be let off the hook for not helping all 100, but *not* off the hook for helping 10 of them. A plausible method is for Peter to rank the 100 measures – one measure for saving each of the 100 children. Each measure is weighted according to the importance of the interest it is aimed at fulfilling, along with the other expected costs and benefits for Peter and the child in question. The weighted measures are then ranked. Peter's duty is to work his way down the ranked measures, taking each until he reaches the limit of positive aggregate value. There might be several measures that are in a 'tie' situation on the list: if Peter cannot take all the tied measures while realising positive value, then he is afforded discretion is choosing which of the tied measure-(s) he takes.

Condition (4) then becomes disjunctive:

> (4) Either: if S were to take measures in all circumstances where the other conditions of this principle hold between S and any individual, then S would realise positive *aggregate* expected value regarding S and all those individuals;

> Or: when the importance in (1) and value in (3) are used to weight the measures in (2), these measures rank sufficiently highly among similarly weighted measures (for which (1)–(3) also hold), such that the measures in (2), *and* all more highly-ranked measures, could be taken with positive aggregate expected value (regarding S and those whose important interests are thereby targeted).

4. The Action is the Least Costly of All Agents' Similar Actions: Ideal-Relative Sacrifice

Conditions (1)–(4) get us to well-placed duties. But they do not get us to best-placed duties, understood as duties that accrue to the agent *best-placed* to fulfil some important interest. If (1)–(4) were the end of the story, then multiple agents could bear duties to fulfil exactly the same interest, if they all met (1)–(4). Such a proliferation of well-placed duties would be an acceptable result in many instances, but sometimes we are interested in picking out one from among the many agents who are well-placed. This has a stronger duty than all the other well-placed agents. This is the agent we call on first, if it would be disastrous for all well-placed agents to act. Imagine a crowd of well-placed people, all jumping in to save the drowning child, getting in each other's way and causing further drownings. We don't want this. We want a single agent to act. Best-placed duties pick out this one agent. This agent has a stronger duty than all the other agents, even if it wouldn't be disastrous for all to act. And if it *would* be disastrous for all to act, then she has the duty in the first instance.[8]

To understand why best-placed duties are stronger than well-placed duties, it helps to develop a conception of sacrifice according to which we can *sacrifice others' actions*. The idea that an agent can sacrifice someone, or something, other than the agent of the sacrifice is familiar from the folk notion of sacrifice. The first listing for 'sacrifice' in the *Oxford English Dictionary* is '[p]rimarily, the slaughter of an animal ... as an offering to God or a deity'. Taking our cue from this, it seems we can sacrifice all sorts of things – not just our interests as agents – via our interest-fulfilling actions. In this section, I suggest that one thing that you can sacrifice when performing an interest-fulfilling action is someone else's performing a similar, but better, action. This helps to explain why best-placed duties are stronger than well-placed duties: acting on (some) well-placed duties *sacrifices* a better interest-fulfilling action (an action of a better-placed person). Discharging well-placed duties thus (sometimes) involves a higher sacrifice than discharging best-placed duties. We can therefore explain the weaker strength of those well-placed duties via the familiar idea that duties involving higher amounts of sacrifice are weaker than duties involving lower amounts of sacrifice: specifically, the sacrifice of someone else's better action.

We can call this sacrifice the 'ideal-relative sacrifice': the *merely* well-placed agent sacrifices the ideal action by discharging her duty. The ideal action can be better in the sense of imposing lower costs on *the agent* who performs it (compared to the costs the merely well-placed agent's interest-fulfilling actions would have impose on the well-placed agent), or in the sense of imposing lower costs on *the interest-bearer* (in the sense that either the interest-bearer's important interest is more fully or securely fulfilled, or the interest-bearer's other interests are also fulfilled, alongside the important interest that generated the duty).

To capture this, we need to add a condition to (1)–(4), such that (1)–(4) produce well-placed duties while (1)–(5) produce best-placed duties. A first pass of condition (5) is:

70 SACRIFICE AND MORAL PHILOSOPHY

(5) S is the agent whose measure (from (2)) is such that, if S takes that measure, S would realise no less expected value (regarding agent and recipient) than would any other agent who meets (1)–(4) if they took their measure.

That is, S's interest-fulfilling measure *would not make an ideal-relative sacrifice*. This condition is different from 'S is most capable'. The most capable agent is simply the one whose most efficacious measure is *no less likely to fulfil* the relevant interest than is any other agent's most efficacious measure. But the most capable agent might incur great agent-relative sacrifices – or impose great recipient-relative sacrifices – if she takes this measure. For this reason, we should not be concerned merely with her likelihood of success, but with other costs and benefits of her measure for her and the recipient.

But this is not quite the end of the story. The agent who is 'best-placed' (by the lights of condition (5) above) might not do what her moral duty demands. If Ash has broken his leg, perhaps his housemate, Brandy, is best-placed (according to condition (5)'s first pass) to take Ash to the hospital. Yet suppose Brandy is callous, and will not doing her duty. Brandy's unwillingness to take Ash to hospital does not affect her duty to do so. After all, agents cannot get out of doing their duties by simply not wanting to. Brandy has a best-placed duty.

But what about Cara, Ash and Brandy's next-door neighbour, who knows Brandy will callously watch television while Ash suffers, and that there is nothing anyone can do to convince Brandy otherwise? What is Cara's duty? She does not meet condition (5)'s first pass: Cara's measure would realise less value than Brandy's measure; Cara's measure would involve an *ideal-relative sacrifice* according to condition (5) above. But, given Brandy's callousness, Cara surely has a strong duty, in virtue of being (second) best-placed.

We can make sense of this by noting that, in determining whether some agent has a duty, we do not assume that others will comply with morality's demands. So, when determining whether an agent's measure would involve an ideal-relative sacrifice, we should be as realistic as we can about the expected probability that others will comply with their duties, just as we are realistic about natural events that might intervene and disrupt the attempts of the agent under consideration. By contrast, when determining whether an agent has a duty, it is irrelevant whether *she* will or won't comply with morality. Agents cannot get out of assisting others by not wanting to. When assessing Brandy's duty, then, we treat her as an agent, who cannot get out of her duty by simply not doing it. So she is best-placed, on that assumption: her measure would not involve an ideal-relative sacrifice. This gives Brandy a best-placed duty.

SACRIFICE AND MORAL PHILOSOPHY 71

When determining Cara's duty, however, we treat Brandy as a feature of the environment to be worked around. Given that Brandy will not do her duty, Cara is best-placed: her measure would not involve an ideal-relative sacrifice. Because we assume that the duty-bearer will comply, but are realistic about whether others will comply, there are sometimes two (or more) agents with best-placed duties to take different measures to fulfil the same interest. This is simply because, when we are considering the duties of the different agents, we hold different things fixed where those things are relevant to the existence of an ideal-relative sacrifice. Specifically, considering an agent's duty, what matters is not that the agent's measures are not worse than anyone else's, but that they are not worse than those of any other agent *who will do their duty if they have one*. After all, it is only if those other agents did their duty that the agent's measure would involve an ideal-relative sacrifice.

We can thus slightly refine condition (5):

> (5) Of all agents that meet (2)–(4), S's measure (from (2)) is such that, if she were to take that measure, she would realise no less expected value (regarding agent and recipient) than the expected value (regarding agent and recipient) that would be realised by any other agent *who would take measures to fulfil this interest if they had a duty to do so*.

Condition (5) says the measure 'would realise no less expected value', not that it 'would realise more expected value'. If two agents would realise equal value, then they both have best-placed duties to take their measures, since neither's measure would sacrifice the *better* actions of another agent.

5. Conclusion

We now have two –principles.

The Well-placed Principle:

If

(1)–(4)

Then

> (6a) In the absence of defeaters, S has an all-things-considered duty to take M; and

> (7a) If the ranking in the second disjunct of (4) ranks multiple measures equally, and if S could take some but not all of those equally-weighted measures and realise positive aggregate expected value (regarding S and recipients), then, in the absence of defeaters, S has a duty to take some of the tied measures, up to the threshold of positive aggregate expected value (regarding S and recipients).

72 SACRIFICE AND MORAL PHILOSOPHY

The Best-placed Principle

If

(1)–(5)

Then

> (6b) In the absence of *strong* defeaters, S has an all-things-considered duty to take M; and

> (7b) If the ranking in the second disjunct of (4) ranks multiple measures equally, and if S could take some but not all of those equally-weighted measures and realise positive aggregate expected value (regarding S and recipients), then, in the absence of *strong* defeaters, S has a duty to take some of the tied measures, up to the threshold of positive aggregate expected value (regarding S and recipients).

There are three kinds of sacrifice relevant to these principles: agent-relative sacrifice, recipient-relative sacrifice and ideal-relative sacrifice. All three of these have some bearing on whether a given agent-recipient pair meets the antecedents of the principles, in particular conditions (3) and (5). I have argued that both agent-relative and recipient-relative sacrifice should be understood as *net* sacrifice, not *gross* sacrifice. The problem of incommensurable sacrifices and benefits creates some problems for this, as Carbonell has noted. But I have suggested we can solve these problems by allowing that some sacrifices (by of either agent or recipient) can render an interest-fulfilling measure' value non-positive, without the need for that sacrifice to be traded off against the possible benefits of the measure.

The notion of ideal-relative sacrifice helps to capture why it is that well-placed duties are weaker than best-placed duties: if the agent- and recipient-relative value is held constant across two possible scenarios, but one of those scenarios contains a third party that is better-placed to fulfil the interest (and will do so if they have a duty to do so), then the agent's fulfilling the interest contains an ideal-relative sacrifice, and is thereby less valuable. This notion of ideal-relative sacrifice also helps address a possible concern that assistance duties are, by their nature, overly demanding of agents: we have relatively weak duties to take interest-fulfilling measures that imply ideal-relative sacrifices. Thus, such duties are more easily defeated by countervailing considerations. This means that, all-things-considered, they will demand action of us less often than the assistance principle perhaps implies at first glance.

Notes

1. Of course, some disagree. Jan Narveson (2003), for example, claims that you have done nothing *wrong* by defaulting in Singer's example. But even he agrees you have done something *very bad*.

SACRIFICE AND MORAL PHILOSOPHY

2. When I refer to 'agent', I mean 'the entity (individual or collective) with the duty in a particular context'. This label is always context-relative: everyone who is an agent in one context has been, and could yet be, a recipient in another context; and most entities who are recipients in one context have been, or could yet be, agents in other contexts (non-human animals aside).

3. Others have developed versions of the assistance principle (e.g. Singer 1972, 231; 2009, 15; Unger 1996, 12; Goodin 1985, 118; Scanlon 1998, 224). These authors' formulations tend to be brief – usually only a sentence long – and do not distinguish between the well-placed and best-placed versions. I developed these two principles in some detail in [omitted], but there I did not consider the implications for conceptualising sacrifice, did not separate the three kinds of sacrifice, and did not consider how the notion of sacrifice can explain the two principles' differential strength.

4. The idea of X's important interests may seem to evoke Raz's (1986, 166) idea of 'an aspect of X's well-being (his interest) [that] is a sufficient reason for holding some other person(s) under a duty'. I will suggest that an (unfulfilled) important interest is merely necessary, not sufficient, for an assistance duty: there are other necessary conditions regarding cost to the duty-bearer, the duty-bearer's capacities and so on. Assistance duties are thus perhaps what Raz (1986, 167–168) calls a 'conditional duty'. Though what I say is consistent with Raz's general account of interests, rights and duties, my account isn't meant to imply anything about non-assistance duties and the rights associated with them. It's thus more specific than Raz's (1986) account.

5. Of course, other agents might have duties to (take measures to) make my father capable of loving me. But these other people's duties would be duties to fulfil my interest in 'having parents that are capable of loving me'. This is a different interest, which might generate well-placed or best-placed duties for those people.

6. If the reader prefers to have a constant likelihood threshold – rather than varying that threshold in proportion to the interest's importance – then (2) becomes 'If: S takes measure M, where M is the most efficacious measure open to S to fulfil I; then I will be fulfilled with sufficient likelihood'. I thank an anonymous reviewer for pressing me to be neutral on this issue.

7. And as we shall see, my analysis of 'best-placed' will state that the best-placed agent is that whose most efficacious measures will *not realise less* value than any other agent – it will not require that she *realise more* value than any other agent. On this analysis, all else being equal, both the novelist and the painter would have a best-placed duty.

8. As an anonymous reviewer pointed out, there will be some situations in which it's best if a few agents help *together*, rather than one agent helping alone. I lack space to deal with such cases here, though I discuss them in Collins 2013.

Disclosure Statement

No potential conflict of interest was reported by the author.

References

Anderson, E. 1993. *Value in Ethics and Economics*. Cambridge, MA: Harvard University Press.

Caney, S. 2010. "Climate Change and the Duties of the Advantaged." *Critical Review of International Social and Political Philosophy* 13 (1): 203-228. doi:10.1080/13698230903326331.

Carbonell, V. 2012. "The Ratcheting-Up Effect." *Pacific Philosophical Quarterly* 93: 228-254. doi:10.1111/papq.2012.93.issue-2.

Carbonell, V. 2015. "Sacrifices of Self." *Journal of Ethics* 19: 53-72. doi:10.1007/s10892-014-9186-x.

Collins, S. 2013. "Collectives' Duties and Collectivization Duties." *Australasian Journal of Philosophy* 91 (2): 231–248. doi:10.1080/00048402.2012.717533.

Collins, S. 2015. *The Core of Care Ethics*. Basingstoke: Palgrave Macmillan.

Cullity, G. 2004. *The Moral Demands of Affluence*. New York: Oxford University Press.

Darwall, S. 2002. *Welfare and Rational Care*. Princeton: Princeton University Press.

Dorsey, D. 2013. "The Supererogatory, and How to Accommodate It." *Utilitas* 25 (3): 355–382. doi:10.1017/S095382081200060X.

Fishkin, J. 1982. *The Limits of Obligation*. Binghampton: Yale University Press.

Goodin, R. E. 1985. *Protecting the Vulnerable*. Chicago: University of Chicago Press.

Hooker, B. 1999. "Sacrificing for the Good of Strangers—Repeatedly." *Philosophy and Phenomenological Research* 59 (1): 177–181. doi:10.2307/2653466.

Kamm, F. M. 2000. "Does Distance Matter Morally to the Duty to Rescue?" *Law and Philosophy* 19 (6): 655–681.

Keller, S. 2006. "Four Theories of Filial Duty." *Philosophical Quarterly* 56 (223): 254–274. doi:10.1111/phiq.2006.56.issue-223.

Lee, S. 1962. *Amazing Fantasy #15*. New York: Marvel Comics.

Lewis, D. 1973. *Counterfactuals*. London: Basil Blackwell.

Liao, M. S. 2006. "The Right of Children to Be Loved." *Journal of Political Philosophy* 14 (4): 420–440. doi:10.1111/j.1467-9760.2006.00262.x.

Miller, D. 2001. "Distributing Responsibilities." *Journal of Political Philosophy* 9 (4): 453–471. doi:10.1111/1467-9760.00136.

Narveson, J. 2003. "We Don't Owe Them A Thing! A Tough-minded by Soft-hearted View of Aid to the Faraway Needy." *The Monist* 86 (3): 419-433.

Nussbaum, M. C. 2006. *Frontiers of Justice: Disability, Nationality, Species Membership*. Cambridge, MA: Belknap Press.Special Issue of

Overvold, M. C. 1980. "Self-Interest and the Concept of Self-Sacrifice." *Canadian Journal of Philosophy* 10 (1): 105-118. doi:10.1080/00455091.1980.10716285.

Pattison, J. 2010. *Humanitarian Intervention and the Responsibility to Protect: Who Should Intervene?* Oxford: Oxford University Press.

Rawls, J. 1971. *A Theory of Justice*. Cambridge, MA: Belknap Press.

Raz, J. 1986. *The Morality of Freedom*. Oxford: Oxford University Press.

Scanlon, T. M. 1975. "Preference and Urgency." *The Journal of Philosophy* 72 (19): 655–669. doi:10.2307/2024630.

Scanlon, T. M. 1998. *What We Owe to Each Other*. Cambridge, MA: Harvard University Press.

Shue, H. 1996. *Basic Rights: Subsistence, Affluence and US Foreign Policy*. 2nd ed. Princeton: Princeton University Press.

Singer, P. 1972. "Famine, Affluence, and Morality." *Philosophy &Public Affairs* 1 (3): 229–243.
Singer, P. 2009. *The Life You Can Save*. New York: Random House.
Unger, S. 1996. *Living High and Letting Die: Our Illusion of Innocence*. Oxford: Oxford University Press.

Sacrificing Value

Lisa Tessman

ABSTRACT

When is sacrifice – and particularly self-sacrifice – called for? This question turns out to be difficult to answer, for it tends to arise when values conflict, and hence the answer to it depends on how conflicts of values are to be resolved. If values are constructed, and if there is no single right way to construct them or prioritize them when they conflict, though there are identifiable ways in which the construction of values can go wrong, we may be left in a position of ambivalence about what should be sacrificed. In cases of conflict in which self-sacrifice is one of the options, ambivalence may be particularly appropriate. In part this is because there may be in such cases special sources of plurality and incommensurability of values, because the conflict is likely to be between something that is valued by a social group, and something that is valued particularly by an individual who has to consider self-sacrificing. And in part it is because individuals may have trouble balancing self-regarding and other-regarding concerns in the process of value construction. This paper elaborates these complications, and presents cases in which we might suspect that someone has self-sacrificed too much or too little.

1. Introduction

For anyone who is a value pluralist, as I am, conflicts of values present problems having to do with what is sacrificed and lost. Here I will consider cases of a particular sort: those in which one of the things that someone could do in the face of a conflict is to make a self-sacrifice.

Part of why I am a pluralist is because I am a constructionist about values and believe that human beings construct values in a variety of ways, which produce irreducibly different kinds of values. Some of this plurality explains features of value conflicts in general, but there are some kinds of plurality that are particularly relevant to conflicts involving self-sacrifice. This is because the construction of some values takes place at an individual level while there are other values that are constructed by social groups. For instance, individuals value different people through loving them, while a social group may express and protect the value of some specific version of honesty, civility or fairness by developing norms. When a value conflict is a conflict between something that is valued by a social group, and something that is valued particularly by an individual who has to consider self-sacrificing, there is an additional kind of plurality of values in play, and with it, an additional kind of incommensurability that calls for ambivalence in the question of which value should be prioritized. Thus plurality complicates questions of self-sacrifice in a special way.

There are also unique ways in which the construction of values at an individual level can go *wrong*, because of problems achieving an intra-personal balance of self and other-regarding concerns. Looking at the *process* of construction of values can reveal reasons to trust or distrust the resulting values, and this is so whether through self-reflection we examine our own individual process of coming to endorse certain values, whether in conversation with others we examine the process of a social group to which we belong, or even whether we examine – and offer criticism of – someone else's (or another group's) construction of values. In all cases, we might find either a reason to reject or to accept the appropriateness of (self-)sacrificing a value, but we might also find reason to remain ambivalent. However, because we are sometimes less transparent to ourselves than we are to others, we may be less able to identify in ourselves either a tendency to be too self-sacrificial or a tendency to fail to make self-sacrifices that we ought to.

Given all of these complexities, I find conflicts of values involving possible self-sacrifices to be particularly interesting and difficult to judge.

2. Sacrifice and self-sacrifice

To sacrifice something, as I will be using the term, is to give it up for the sake of something else. Sacrifices are thus typically called for when, because of a conflict, two valuable things cannot both be had and one must be given up for the sake of the other. The most prominent cases of sacrifice are those in which what is given up is particularly precious. However, the value of what is given up need not be significant for its loss to count as a sacrifice. Even when something of significant value is given up, it could still be something that, in a normal (rather than ideal) human life, we expect – and accept – that we might have to give up for the sake of something else.

It is thus useful to think of sacrifices, including self-sacrifices, as dividing into those in which the loss of the forsaken value is tragic and those in which the loss is not tragic. In non-tragic cases, the sacrifice may involve losses of things that we should expect in ordinary life to give up in order to pursue other things that we ourselves want, or to enable something that matters to other people. Think of the business executive who sacrifices all of their weekend recreation time in order to work extra hours and get ahead of competitors, or the teenager who sacrifices sleep to practice the trumpet for an extra hour each morning before school. In these kinds of cases there are benefits that (at least are thought to) make the costs worthwhile, and the sacrifice is simply a cost. Even in cases in which a person sacrifices something primarily for the sake of someone else, what is given up may be what Martha Nussbaum (2000, 1019) has referred to as *a cost that is to be borne* to indicate that it is a loss that we should take in stride. Think of the rural doctor who sacrifices a higher salary in order to work in the community in which they grew up; the citizen who sacrifices time, comfort and blood at the Red Cross blood drive; or the family member who sacrifices the pleasurable affinity felt at a holiday meal to intervene in a racist or sexist joke.

These are not the most interesting cases of sacrifice. The phenomenon of sacrifice captures our attention when what is sacrificed is, to use Nussbaum's (2000, 1019) contrasting phrase, *a cost that no one should have to bear.* This may include cases in which costs that are tolerable when taken singly add up to a troubling systemic pattern. I will set aside the less interesting kinds of sacrifices simply by saying that in cases that involve a cost that is to be borne – and thus in which there is also no patterned inequality in who bears the losses – sacrifice should be accepted as a normal part of life. I will focus instead on cases in which:

(1) values conflict, such that one must be sacrificed for the sake of actualizing or maintaining the other, and the sacrifice of either value is a cost that no one should have to bear; and

(2) the conflicting values are irreducibly different in kind, leaving room for ambivalence when facing the question of which takes priority over the other, that is, when facing the question of which is to be sacrificed; and

(3) at least one of the options is a *self*-sacrifice.

Cases of self-sacrifice are complicated because a person may not value their own self, or something else that matters to them, in the way that in some sense they ought to. This may lead to their self-sacrificing when they ought not, or failing to self-sacrifice when they ought to. Thus before proceeding further, it is necessary to distinguish self-sacrifices from other sacrifices.

The person who gives up something that partly constitutes their self for something else that also partly constitutes their self – allowing their leg to be amputated in order to preserve their own life – makes a sacrifice but not a self-sacrifice. Similarly, the person who gives up something that benefits their self for some greater benefit to their own self – leaving the comfort of a spacious house in order to live in a small apartment closer to work – makes a sacrifice but not a self-sacrifice. Even the person who gives up one altruistic pursuit that matters to them for the purpose of devoting themselves to another altruistic pursuit that matters to them even more – such as the dedicated volunteer who stops working at Meals On Wheels in order to spend more hours working at Habitat for Humanity – makes a sacrifice but not a self-sacrifice. In a *self*-sacrifice, what is given up must in some way be more strongly tied to the self than that for the sake of which it is given up. But there are several ways in which something might be related to the self.[1]

As I will define 'self-sacrifice', for something to count as a case of self-sacrifice:

(a) what is sacrificed must constitute, benefit or matter to the self in some stronger sense than that for the sake of whom/which it is sacrificed; and,

(b) the sacrifice must be made for the sake of someone or something else, or for the sake of a group to which the self belongs.

I have intentionally built some ambiguity into part (a) of this definition by using a disjunction between 'constitute', 'benefit' and 'matter to'.

As I am using the terms, something can be said to *constitute* someone if it is their self or is part of what is their self. A sacrifice is of something that constitutes the self if someone literally sacrifices their self by giving up their life, or if, for instance, they sacrifice something that partially constitutes their self such as their memory, their limbs or organs, their dignity, their identity, their integrity or their basic capacities. By something that *benefits* someone, I mean to refer to something that is in their narrowly understood self-interest to have or keep. For instance, someone who gives up an opportunity for a job interview, or their resources or their physical comfort, is ordinarily understood to be sacrificing something beneficial to them as an individual.

On an assumption of self-interest, we tend to think of an act as self-sacrificing if what is sacrificed is the self or is something that is in the self's narrowly understood self-interest. But we are not simply self-interested, so something should also be thought of as a self-sacrifice if what is sacrificed is something that *matters* to a self who is altruistic or who has thoroughly internalized propriety norms or impartial principles so that these also matter to them as an individual.

When I say that something *matters to* someone, I am using the term the way that Harry Frankfurt (1988b, 80) uses it in 'The Importance of What We Care About', when he points out that 'we are creatures to whom things matter'. Something matters to someone if it is something that is important to them, something that they care about, that they value, or love or are committed to. If people can have an obligation to make a certain self-sacrifice, they might be obligated to sacrifice something that matters to them; they might even be obligated to sacrifice that which is more important to them than anything else. Someone might sacrifice what matters the most to them as an individual for the sake of what benefits or matters to a collective to which they belong; this tends to happen when they feel the force of the normative expectation to act according to a social (and in some cases legal) norm that enables or facilitates cooperation. In such a situation, their self-interest, or their altruistic concern for a loved one, may be best served by *not* doing something that contributes to a cooperative project (whether they would contribute only their fair share, or would be picking up the slack of others), but they comply with the norm nevertheless. In doing so, they make a self-sacrifice, a sacrifice of what matters to them the most as an individual self.

For instance, picture someone who is both a parent and a soldier, and whose unit is called to participate in a dangerous, even life-threatening, humanitarian intervention. They love their children more than anything, but may be obligated, for the sake of the worthy goals of the intervention, to sacrifice what matters the most to them: their children's flourishing (which, let's suppose, depends on the parent's remaining alive and being present to actively parent them). The person who participates in this sort of dangerous action makes a self-sacrifice not only of their own safety and perhaps their life, but also of what matters most to them as an individual – their children's having what they need to flourish – and they make this self-sacrifice for the good of a larger collective.

What constitutes the self, or what benefits the self, might also matter to the self, *or might not*. And what matters to the self might also constitute or benefit the self, *or might not*. Even if what constitutes or benefits the self matters to the self, someone or something else might matter *more*. So the ambiguity in part (a) of the definition of 'self-sacrifice' is due to the fact that some acts will sacrifice one part of the disjunct but not another, or might sacrifice one part of the disjunct *for* another part of the disjunct. The lover whose beloved matters to them more than anything might sacrifice what is in their individual self-interest for the sake of the beloved – and this will count as a self-sacrifice, but only in the sense that they sacrifice one part of the disjunct for another. I take a sacrifice of *any* part of the disjunct to be sufficient for something to count as a self-sacrifice, as long as the sacrifice is made for the sake of someone or something else. So sometimes in sacrificing what matters the most to us we make a self-sacrifice (even if what we sacrifice is not what constitutes or benefits us) and sometimes in sacrificing what constitutes or benefits us *for the sake of* what matters the most to us we make a self-sacrifice.

If we were psychological egoists, then only our own selves (or our well-being and so on) would matter non-instrumentally to us; everything that we valued would either (partly) constitute or benefit ourselves. However, we (that is, most of us) are not psychological egoists; we typically value in both egoistic and altruistic ways. It is common to see people making sacrifices of what constitutes or benefits their self for the sake of someone else for whom they feel empathy, or whom they love or care about. Because the motivation to act according to impartial moral principles or to do our share in cooperative projects is typically more external to ourselves than either self-interested or altruistic motivations are, when we sacrifice what matters to us in a self-interested or altruistic way for what, we might say, matters to a social group to which we belong, this will typically be a form of self-sacrifice: we sacrifice what matters to the *individual* self.

This is where another ambiguity enters in. A social norm or an impartial moral principle might be internalized to a greater or lesser degree. When it is thoroughly internalized – so the motivation to comply with it is experienced as being internal to the individual's psyche – then it can be said to matter to someone as an individual self in a strong way, so there's a sense in which sacrificing for the sake of this norm or principle won't be a self-sacrifice; however, when it is less internalized, and the pressure and the motivation to conform comes from others, it can't be said to matter in the same way to someone *as an individual self*, in which case we might want to count sacrificing for the sake of this norm or principle as a self-sacrifice. There is some vagueness here, because it is not clear how much a norm must be internalized in order for an individual's abiding by it to be an *expression* of what matters to them rather than a *sacrifice* of what matters to them, for the sake of what matters to a wider social group.

To call something a self-sacrifice – as opposed to any other sacrifice of values – is neither to praise nor condemn it. Some self-sacrifices are called for and others aren't. And of course, even self-sacrifices that are called for might still be tragic.

3. Constructing plural values

We might think that an action that counts as self-sacrificial just because someone sacrifices what constitutes or benefits their self for the sake of what matters the most to them is unproblematic. After all, why *shouldn't* someone act for the sake of what matters the most to them, as long as doing so benefits someone else, or a group to which they belong? However, acting in an other-regarding way, even if that is what matters the most to someone, can still be problematic, if there is something problematic in how what matters the most to them came to matter. It is commonly recognized that if we are too egoistic we won't self-sacrifice even when in some sense we ought to. But I also want to say that if we don't value our own selves *sufficiently*, we might be prone to self-sacrifice – by sacrificing what constitutes or benefits our self – when in some sense we ought not. Or sometimes, independent of how much our individual selves matter to us, we might go wrong in how we prioritize the rest of what matters to us – too strongly prioritizing our own children over the requirements of justice, for instance, or too strongly prioritizing the needs of our professional clients over those of our own family. In these cases, we might be prone *not* to self-sacrifice – by refusing to sacrifice what we most value – when in some sense we ought to. Thus I would like to be able to say that what an individual most values is not always that which they in some sense ought to most value. What complicates my saying this is that I am a value pluralist and a constructivist about value.

Theorists who make two specific assumptions about value that I reject – the assumptions of value monism and value realism – will have a (deceptively) easy time determining when self-sacrifice is and isn't appropriate. The assumption of value monism is the assumption that all values can, despite on one level exhibiting differences of kind, nevertheless be reduced to a single kind of value; consequently, all values can be measured by a single metric. Value monism makes conflicts of values simple to resolve because, when the conflicting values are measurable by a single metric, it is always possible to compare them. Furthermore, if the conflicting values have been reduced to different quantities of some overarching value, then the overriding value can always substitute without unique loss for the overridden value. Thus, when values conflict, the loss of the overridden value can be fully compensated by the gain in the overriding value.[2]

The assumption of value realism is the assumption that there are facts about values that are independent of – not constructed out of – anyone's attitudes about what is valuable. For value realists, it is clear what can ground the claim that someone has gone wrong in what they value; someone's evaluative judgments might fail to track the facts about what is valuable. The value realist can answer questions about when self-sacrifice is required by reference to the facts about what is really valuable: when values conflict, we ought to sacrifice, or not sacrifice, depending on which action prioritizes the independently overriding value.

For instance, consider a maximizing, act consequentialist position that assumes that all values can be reduced to different quantities of the overall good (invoking the assumption of value monism) and that there are some independent facts about what is good (invoking the assumption of value realism). This sort of consequentialist can maintain that the right action is whatever action will result in the state of affairs that maximizes the overall good.[3] Given such a position, we would have criteria for determining what is valuable and for resolving any conflicts of value. In any conflict, a self-sacrificing action would be the right action just in case it is optimal, that is, just in case it maximizes what really matters: the overall good.

I won't argue here either for the rejection of the assumptions of value realism and value monist, or for the anti-realist and pluralist position that I take;[4] rather, I will explore the complications, from within the position that I take, of answering the question of when self-sacrifice is and isn't appropriate. The anti-realist position that I take is a form of constructivism about values, sometimes referred to as Humean constructivism.[5] I believe, to borrow the words of Sharon Street (2012, 40), that value 'is something conferred upon the world by valuing creatures, and it enters and exits the world with them', and furthermore that what we value, and thus what is valuable, is a contingent matter. Nevertheless, we can go wrong in what we value. Going wrong, however, does *not* mean that we are failing to track some independent moral or other evaluative facts. Rather, the judgment that we have gone wrong – valuing the wrong things or valuing things in the wrong way – is always made from some particular standpoint that is already shaped by our (other) values. This standpoint – which we can call an evaluative standpoint – might be more individual (for instance, it is primarily as an individual that I love – i.e. value – another individual person) or more collective (for instance, it takes a social group or community to develop social norms that are infused with value). Our evaluative judgments about our evaluative judgments are a kind of second-order judgment; in these second-order judgments, we might either endorse or reject one of our own first-order judgments. It is this ability to engage in second-order evaluations of our own first-order evaluative judgments that makes the construction of values possible. Otherwise we would be, as Frankfurt (1988a) has dubbed it, wantons, acting on whatever desire moved us most strongly at the moment; we would never be able to judge that we ought to value something other than what we do value. However, not just any process of making second-order judgments will do; we must be able to be critical in the process of construction, so the process must be checked for influences that are likely to distort it, such as cognitive biases, or coercion or a compromised capacity to exercise agency. Furthermore, the values we (as an individual or more socially) construct can themselves be plural and conflicting. Thus one question is what to do about such conflict.

Most constructivists, including Humean constructivists, conceive of the process of construction – in which we make second-order evaluative judgments – to be a rational process along the lines of reflective equilibrium: a process in which we try to reach a coherent set of values. When values conflict, they contend, we must for the sake of consistency determine which one is overriding and reject the overridden value; part of what may make one value overriding is its fit within our overall network of values, or its centrality to that network. For instance, as a member of a social group that accepts the normative value of fairness, I may realize that one of my particular evaluative judgments is unfair – say, my loyalty toward my friend has led me to judge that I ought to hire my friend instead of a better qualified candidate – and this inconsistency must be resolved. If the norm of fairness is stronger or more central than the norm of loyalty to what is otherwise a mostly coherent set of values, then my, or my social group's, second-order judgment is that the value of fairness overrides the value of loyalty, and I should resolve the conflict in favor of fairness. To put this differently, in this process of construction, I – or my social group – can be said to reflectively endorse the value of fairness, imbuing it with the sort of authority that is the mark of (constructed) moral values. I might still have such a strong first-order desire to be loyal to my friend that I could say that hiring my friend is what matters the most to me, but, according to this view, after the reflective equilibrium process I should be able to recognize that this feeling is misguided, rationally reject it, and affirm that what is really most valuable is fairness.

My value pluralism, however, informs my conception of how the construction of values takes place, in two important ways, which leads me to conclude that reflective equilibrium, or any similar rationalist methodology, is inadequate as a description of the construction of values, and in this way I depart from constructivists who view some version of the reflective equilibrium process as the only legitimate procedure of construction. First of all, if some values are irreducibly different in kind and incommensurable, there won't be a single, clearly right resolution to all value conflicts. From different evaluative standpoints (whether the standpoints of different individuals, or different social groups) – including the different standpoints from which we make second-order evaluative judgments – we might prioritize different values in the case of conflicts between incommensurable values.

Secondly, because there is strong empirical evidence that most of our moral and other evaluative judgments are made through an affect-laden, intuitive process rather than a conscious reasoning process, I believe that we should recognize a plurality of ways of reaching a second-order affirmation or rejection of our initial evaluative judgments. Consistency reasoning of the sort used in a reflective equilibrium process need not be the only basis for our second-order judgments. In fact, in some cases, to engage in justificatory reasoning about a first-order evaluative judgment is to have 'one thought too many' (Williams 1981, 18) about it. Those whom we love want us to act *out* of love, not out of the thought that the action based on our love is justified even though it conflicts with an action based on some other value. We may still be said to reach second-order endorsements (or rejections) of our first-order values and thus to engage in a process of construction, even if those second-order endorsements (or rejections) are reached through an intuitive process rather than a reasoning process. If our confidence in a particular value is, even at the level of a second-order judgment, automatic and intuitive, then we might endorse that value regardless of its consistency with our other confidently held values. This is an alternative picture of how we construct values.[6]

A constructivist position that insists on pluralism in these ways will end up having to acknowledge that real – constructed – values are plural, and do not necessarily form a coherent set. What really matters might be plural and conflicting, with no uniquely right answer, in the case of conflicts between plural values, to the question of what 'really' matters the *most* and thus what should be sacrificed.

The position that I am describing exhibits something akin to what David Wong calls 'moral ambivalence', though I mean to extend the notion of ambivalence to values that may not be moral. According to Wong's pluralistic relativism, there are some universal constraints on what can count as an adequate morality, because only some moralities can, given human nature, fulfill the function of morality: to enable people to live cooperatively together by regulating and ordering their relations, both intra- and inter-personally, largely by balancing self-regarding and other-regarding concerns (Wong 2006, 43–65). Because any adequate morality must attend to both self-regarding and other-regarding interests, intra-personally a morality must shape individuals to have a good balance of egoistic and altruistic psychological traits, and inter-personally it must incorporate a norm of reciprocity. Additionally, any adequate morality will be limited by how much domination can be tolerated, and under what conditions; Wong believes that humans have strong natural tendencies to resist being dominated, and will tend to at least require justification for any norms of domination. This justification must not itself depend on falsehoods, such as the falsehood that women must be ruled by men because women are not capable of acting rationally (Wong 2006, 59–62).[7]

Within these (and several other) constraints, however, there is a plurality of adequate moralities. According to Wong, because adequate moralities tend to have a great deal of overlap in which values they encompass, much of what will differ between adequate moralities is the priority ordering of their values; for instance, if two moralities each recognize the value of both autonomy and community, one morality may tend to prioritize autonomy and the other community, in circumstances in which one of these values must be sacrificed for the sake of the other. In ambivalence, we recognize that there are other individuals, or other social groups or cultures, who – from their own evaluative standpoints – are just as qualified to make evaluative judgments as we are, and we recognize that they may very well construct their values differently than we do, largely by giving a different priority ordering to things that matter both to them and to us. For Wong, what makes someone else as qualified as we are to make evaluative judgments is that they are sufficiently knowledgeable about the non-normative facts, and sufficiently reasonable (Wong 2006, 5). As long as others meet these criteria, and as long as the morality that they construct falls within the universal constraints, we have no reason to think that our morality, rather than theirs, is uniquely right; instead, we should adopt a stance of ambivalence.

I agree with Wong that there are some very broad universal constraints on the moral (and other) values that can function to enable humans to live flourishing lives together, and I agree that these values might be given different priority orderings and that there is no neutral standpoint from which to determine that some priority ordering is the uniquely correct one. Ambivalence will often be an appropriate response to conflicts of values. For the same reasons, ambivalence will often be the appropriate response to the question of whether self-sacrifice is called for. But in conflicts in which one of the options is self-sacrifice, an *additional* reason for ambivalence may be relevant: values may differ not just in substance but also in source – there is what I value more as an individual, such as my loved ones, and there is what we as a social group value, such as fairness and other impartial values. Both individuals and groups can construct value, so it is not obvious which values are to take priority when they conflict. Because of the incommensurability of these values – in this case due to their differences in source – they cannot be measured by a common metric and ranked in some objective way. Thus whether I should sacrifice what matters the most to me as an individual when it conflicts with what matters to a social group to which I belong will sometimes be indeterminate.

But this does not mean that ambivalence will *always* be the appropriate response; sometimes it will be possible to identify ways in which the process of constructing and prioritizing values has gone wrong. Perhaps cognitive biases have been overlooked, or coercion took place, or the evaluative judgments were made by members of a social group who have been socialized to not exercise their agency fully. And perhaps the resulting set of values does not fall within something like what Wong has identified as the universal constraints on morality.

4. The self-sacrificial woman, the do-gooder, and the opportunity hoarder

I will briefly consider three paradigm cases in which there is reason to suspect that someone either undervalues or overvalues their self or something that matters to their self, and thus makes bad decisions about whether or not (or how much) to self-sacrifice. I'll call these the case of the self-

sacrificial woman, the do-
gooder and the opportunity hoarder. The self-sacrificial woman and the do-
gooder are prone to be self-sacrificing when we might want to say that they
shouldn't be (or should be less so), and the opportunity hoarder tends not
to self-sacrifice enough – but neither is there an effective social norm
according to which they *should* self-sacrifice; this suggests that we should
construct such a social norm, which at least would weigh against the
opportunity hoarder's altruistic or self-interested motives. In each case,
there is some reason to believe that something has gone wrong in the
construction of the pattern of valuing – but also some room for ambivalence. These judgments – for instance, that something has gone wrong –
might be self-critical judgments or they might be judgments that we make
about someone else. They might also be judgments that we tend to reject as
individuals but endorse as members of a social group.

4.1. *The self-sacrificial woman*

Any discussion of self-sacrifice must be informed by the awareness that – to
make a generalization to which, of course, there will be exceptions – in male
dominated societies women are socialized to be self-sacrificing or self-
abnegating. Consider the portrait of the 'Deferential Wife' that Thomas
Hill offered in 1973 as an illustration of servility:

> This is a woman who is utterly devoted to serving her husband. She buys
> the clothes *he* prefers, invites the guests *he* wants to entertain, and makes
> love whenever *he* is in the mood. She willingly moves to a new city in order
> for him to have a more attractive job, counting her own friendships and
> geographical preferences insignificant by comparison. She loves her hus-
> band, but her conduct is not simply an expression of love. She is happy, but
> she does not subordinate herself as a means to happiness. She does not
> simply defer to her husband in certain spheres as a trade-off for his
> deference in other spheres. On the contrary she tends not to form her
> own interests, values, and ideals; and when she does, she counts them as
> less important than her husband's. She readily responds to appeals from
> Women's Liberation that she agrees that women are mentally and physically
> equal, if not superior, to men. She just believes that the proper role for a
> woman is to serve her family. (Hill 1973, 89; italics in the original)

The self-sacrificial woman sacrifices what constitutes and benefits her
self for the sake of her family, and so according to my definition of 'self-
sacrifice', this counts as an instance of self-sacrifice. However, she
doesn't sacrifice what matters the most to her, because her own self, or
her own well being, is not what matters the most to her. Because self-
sacrifices may or may not be problematic, it is possible that the sacrifice
of what constitutes and benefits her self is unproblematic and even
commendable, if it is done for the sake of something that really matters

more. If we want to claim that the self-sacrificial woman's sacrifices are problematic, we need some grounds for saying that what matters the most to her is not what really matters the most. To do this, we have to turn a critical eye to the self-sacrificial woman's process of developing her values, or we have to determine that her set of values, prioritized as they are, do not meet universal constraints on morality, given human nature and given the problems of cooperative living that humans have to solve.

Obviously, gender norms have played a coercive role in shaping the self-sacrificial woman, and had it not been for the coercion, it is doubtful that she would have developed her self-sacrificial traits to the same degree. For Hill (1973, 97), servility and the self-sacrifices that it involves are in most cases evidence of 'the absence of a certain kind of self-respect' (which, in his Kantian framework, violates a duty to oneself). In Wong's language, we might want to say that the intra-personal tension between self-regarding and other-regarding concerns, or between egoistic and altruistic motivations, is not regulated well, and that a society in which one subgroup – women – tend to be constituted this way is one that will have trouble incorporating an adequate inter-personal norm of reciprocity.

Feminist theorists have suggested in various ways that something has gone wrong in the self-sacrificial woman's evaluative judgments. One line of thinking focuses on the question of whether or not someone's values have been formed autonomously. Diana Meyers takes this approach. She critiques a variety of other autonomy theories for their failure to acknowledge how internalized oppression can undermine autonomy. Amongst the theories that she critiques are those that she refers to as 'hierarchical identification theories', which take the process of making second-order evaluative judgments as sufficient for exercising autonomous agency. The problem, Meyers (2002, 13) contends, is that 'hierarchical identification theories neglect the possibility that an oppressive social context could subvert people's autonomy by imparting detrimental values that warp their second-order volitions'. The self-sacrificial woman's second-order judgment that what is most important is her husband's wishes – which overrides any conflicting first-order self-interested desires that she might have – is suspicious in this way. What we suspect is that the second-order judgments are being made from a place of compromised agency. Meyers develops a list of what she calls 'agentic skills', skills that she believes 'make self-determination possible' (20), arguing that 'autonomous people have well-developed, well-coordinated repertoires of agentic skills and call on them routinely as they reflect on themselves and their lives and as they reach decisions about how best to go on' (21).[8] This critique is entirely procedural, but it is made from an evaluative standpoint that already prioritizes autonomy, so it is not entirely clear that it releases us from ambivalence, since there may be other values that we could prioritize over autonomy.

Another feminist line of thinking that can lead us to conclude that the self-sacrificial woman does not value what she in some sense ought to value focuses on what are called adaptive preferences. Serene Khader's work on this topic is especially relevant. She defines inappropriately adaptive preferences as: 'preferences inconsistent with basic flourishing that a person developed under conditions nonconducive to basic flourishing and that we expect her to change under conditions conducive to basic flourishing' (Khader 2011, 17). The self-sacrificial woman's preferences to serve her family without reciprocation – even when reciprocation would be possible – could be inappropriately adaptive preferences; they could be inconsistent with her basic flourishing (though not necessarily with her subjectively felt happiness), and they are likely to have been developed under the strong influence of an ideology according to which servility is normative for women; we would expect the woman to change her preferences or to have developed different preferences in the first place were this ideology not in place.

What Khader calls 'the Flourishing Claim' – namely the claim that 'people tend to choose in accordance with their basic flourishing' (Khader 2011, 19) unless they are in conditions nonconducive to flourishing – plays a role similar to Wong's universal constraints. She believes that human nature limits what kinds of flourishing lives humans can lead, but these limits are very broad, so we should invoke only a general and vague conception of human flourishing when evaluating preferences that we suspect might be inappropriately adaptive. To say that someone's preferences are incompatible with their basic flourishing is similar to saying that, insofar as these preferences form part of a morality or system of values, they would violate the universal constraints on any adequate morality. We could thus say that they have gone wrong in some way rather than adopt a stance of ambivalence toward them.

Khader's critique is both procedural and substantive: procedurally, preferences are only adaptive if they have been shaped under certain conditions, and would be different under better conditions; substantively, they must fail to meet the criteria set by constraints on the ways in which humans can flourish. Khader's characterization of inappropriately adaptive preferences is compatible with thinking of values as constructed, and as contingent, but as constrained by some features of human nature and by the challenges of cooperative living that humans must find solutions to. We can critique the process of construction – by saying, for instance, that coercive norms shaped someone's ability to form evaluative judgments ('preferences'). We can also critique the resultant set of values or prioritization of values by judging them to have failed to meet minimal substantive criteria – similar to Wong's universal constraints. The self-sacrificial woman could be said to be making sacrifices that are not warranted, if they are motivated by inappropriately adaptive preferences.

Note, however, that none of this indicates that it is problematic for a parent to self-sacrifice for a child, or that a parent somehow makes a mistaken evaluative judgment if their child matters to them more than their own individual self does. I find nothing wrong with a person sacrificing what constitutes or benefits their individual self for the sake of someone whom they love, as long as their love has not been shaped coercively. If the norms of self-sacrificing for a loved one were not gendered, and involved no other forms of domination (or other similarly distorting influences), there would be no evidence that they were inappropriately adaptive preferences. Should a parent whose child matters more to them than their own self make self-sacrifices for the sake of the child? I believe there is room for ambivalence here – this is a matter of a priority ordering of two incommensurable values, with no objective way to determine a uniquely correct ordering.

4.2. The do-gooder

The do-gooder differs from the self-sacrificial woman because the do-gooder has not (necessarily) been subject to coercive gender norms, but has still formed a tendency to be exceptionally self-sacrificing – so the question is whether there have been other pernicious influences in the formation of their values. Like the self-sacrificial woman, do-gooders are eager to sacrifice what constitutes and benefits their self for the sake of others. And, like the self-sacrificial woman, do-gooders *don't* sacrifice what matters the most to them; in fact it is by pursuing what matters the most to them that they are led to sacrifice their own selves. Again, this pattern fits my definition of self-sacrifice, and the only way to show that there is something problematic about this kind of self-sacrifice is to claim that there is something wrong with the way in which the do-gooder's values have been shaped, or with the values themselves. This claim is harder to support than it is in the case of the self-sacrificial woman, because we cannot point to systemic coercion or domination as the culprit.

One way of conceiving of the do-gooder is simply as someone who, by definition, is self-sacrificing in a way that is psychologically unhealthy. Psychoanalysts and other psychologists have a number of different explanations for why someone would develop in this way, and have begun to use the term 'pathological altruism' (McWilliams 1984) to describe a wide range of phenomena. The label of 'pathological altruist' has been applied to masochists, codependents (namely supportive partners of alcoholics or drug addicts), animal hoarders (who take in animals to care for them, but tend to take in more than they can actually care for), anorexics (who feed everyone but themselves), women who stay with abusive partners, foreign aid workers, suicide bombers, people who are addicted to self-righteousness or indignation and people who experience empathic distress fatigue or suffer from survivor guilt (Oakley et al. 2011). It is hard to generalize over all of these phenomena, but in each case the act of self-sacrifice is motivated by something that can be diagnosed as a pathology or disorder.[9]

Pathological altruism may also be characterized by the altruist's failure to achieve the good for others that they are aiming to achieve. Barbara Oakley, Ariel Knafo and Michael McGrath suggest that:

> *Pathological altruism* might be thought of as any behavior or personal tendency in which either the stated aim or the implied motivation is to promote the welfare of another or others. But, instead of overall beneficial outcomes, the 'altruism' instead has irrational and substantial negative consequences to the other or even to the self. (Oakley, Knafo and Michael 2011, 4)

When the altruist fails to benefit others, their self-sacrifice is clearly indefensible, as the sacrifice of the self could only be justified by the value of that for the sake of which it is sacrificed. For instance, Guruprasad Madhavan and Barbara Oakley (2011, 237) discuss the ways in which altruistically motivated foreign aid projects may have deleterious effects on the aid recipients, pointing out that 'although external economic assistance has been helpful for many countries, a large number of altruistic, nonstrategic, foreign aid programs over the past several decades have failed – worsening the very situations they were meant to help'. Altruistic foreign aid, they argue, tends to be ineffective when it is driven by overly emotional responses, rather than by 'a balanced mix of empathy and objectivity' (240). Thus their two critical points about these sorts of aid projects are that they are pathologically driven, and that they end up hurting the intended beneficiaries: 'Staring at pictures of starving children can ... hijack the analytical portions of the brain ... [which] results in some of the ineffectual and pathologically altruistic behavior that characterizes many foreign aid policies and programs' (241). The do-gooders involved in these projects seem to have both formed their values in a problematic way, and chosen actions that do more harm than good.

While it would be difficult to justify self-sacrifice that does not even achieve its aim (especially when this can be foreseen), when the altruistic self-sacrifice does achieve its aim, the only critical point that remains is about how the do-gooder developed or constructed their values. Some psychologists (Oakley et al. 2011) seem to assume that someone who makes extraordinary sacrifices of what constitutes or benefits their self, or imposes extreme costs on those close to them such as their family, for the sake of *effective* altruism toward distant strangers, may still manifest some pathology, such as masochism, problems with intimacy or an addiction to righteousness. Because the pathological altruist most likely is not aware of the true source of their motivation to act altruistically, there is a lack of transparency in their own evaluative judgments about their first-order altruistic desires, and this calls into question whether they should really have confidence in these judgments.

Nevertheless, it is worth noting that the situations that the do-gooders are in – and, in fact, that all of us are in but tend not to notice – are situations in which values conflict in tragic ways: either choice involves a cost that no one should have to bear. Either the do-gooder makes an extreme self-sacrifice, or all of the people in dire need whom they could help will suffer or die. Thus it is hard to argue that the do-gooders are making a wrong choice, because *either* choice results in such a serious loss. What is distinctive in the case of the do-gooder, at least if they are indeed pathologically altruistic, is that they do not recognize the value of their own selves, and so may not even consider their own sacrifice to be tragic.

This is a point that is highlighted in Larissa MacFarquhar's thought-provoking book, *Strangers Drowning*, which presents detailed portraits of do-gooders, and guides the reader to respond ambivalently toward them. The do-gooders who are profiled include parents who put their children at risk by moving the family to a leprosy colony; a couple who adopted child after desperate child – a total of 22 children – until the earlier children began to resent the new ones; a young man who gave up everything to devote himself to animal rights; a couple who, after joining the effective altruism movement,[10] began to calculate all their values numerically in order to maximize their giving, justifying having a child themselves with the thought that the child would grow up to be an effective altruist; and many others. Most of the characters described by MacFarquhar would probably be considered to be pathological or disordered in some way; but many of them (particularly those involved in the effective altruism movement), from the perspective of an impartial, monistic moral system such as consequentialism, are living in exactly the right way. MacFarquhar, however, seems to hold a form of value pluralism, recognizing that other values may compete with impartial morality. Thus, her overall message is that altruism of these extreme sorts is full of tragic dilemmas: a great deal is lost – in the form of what I have been referring to as costs that no one should have to bear – for the sake of the 'good' that is done. It is precisely because of value pluralism – and the related difficulty in resolving conflicts of values – that the questions that MacFarquhar poses have, in my view, no single, uniquely right answer. She writes:

> Ambivalence toward do-gooders ... arises out of deep uncertainty about how a person ought to live. Is it good to try to live as moral a life as possible – a saintly life? Or does a life like that lack some crucial human quality? Is it right to care for strangers at the expense of your own people? Is it good to bind yourself to a severe morality that constricts spontaneity and freedom? Is it possible for a person to hold himself to unforgiving standards without becoming unforgiving? ... Should morality be the highest human court – the one whose ruling overrides all others? (MacFarquhar 2015, 6)

4.3. *The opportunity hoarder*

The opportunity hoarder is in some ways the opposite of the do-gooder, and errs on the side of not self-sacrificing enough – even when acting in this way is *unfair* – rather than self-sacrificing excessively, as the do-gooder seems to. 'Opportunity hoarding' is a term that was first introduced by Charles Tilly (1998, 10) to apply to a social group (for instance, an immigrant group) that acts so as to monopolize a valuable resource. The concept of opportunity hoarding has more recently been popularized by Richard Reeves' work on social mobility. Reeves employs a narrower account of opportunity hoarding in order to pinpoint a specific phenomenon, namely the way that the American upper middle class (defined roughly as the top fifth of society, measured in terms of income) exercises unfair advantages that allow them privileged access to the sorts of opportunities that help them pass their class status down to the next generation – that is, to their own children. In other words, the opportunity hoarder is reluctant to self-sacrifice, but it is not what constitutes or benefits their own individual self that they refuse to give up – it is instead what matters the most to them: their children's future well-being, and thus the opportunities that (they imagine) will secure this future.

According to Reeves' (2017, 100–101) definition: 'opportunity hoarding takes place when valuable, scarce opportunities are allocated in an anticompetitive manner: that is, influenced by factors unrelated to an individual's performance'. Reeves discusses three primary avenues for opportunity hoarding: 'exclusionary zoning in residential areas; unfair mechanisms influencing college admissions, including legacy preferences; and the informal allocation of internships' (12). Consider, for instance, the case of college admissions. Upper-middle-class students have a better chance than anyone else of securing a spot at a top college or university, but there are numerous causes of this inequality, some of which count as opportunity hoarding and some of which do not. Upper middle-class students are, on average, better qualified to attend a top college. This is due to a variety of inequalities that allow upper-middle-class kids to develop the qualifications: they are likely to attend a good high school; to be exposed to more books and complex spoken language; to have access to better spaces for enriching play activities; to travel, take private lessons in the arts and participate in summer programmes; to have a greater amount of time to spend studying rather than working; to enjoy higher levels of safety, and so on. All of these inequalities that contribute to upper-middle-class students becoming more qualified are unjust in their own ways, but they don't constitute opportunity hoarding. According to Reeves' specific definition, opportunity hoarding related to college admissions takes place when an upper-middle-class student is advantaged in the admissions process over an *equally qualified* but poorer applicant. This happens when the admissions process gives weight to factors that have to do with having greater wealth, or more educated parents, rather than factors indicating higher qualifications. For instance, admissions offices prioritize applicants who show a special interest in the school by visiting the campus, which requires resources. Additionally, a student who applies 'early decision' has a higher chance of being admitted than an equally qualified student who applies 'regular decision' – but typically, students who need financial aid cannot apply early decision. Reeves (2017, 107) notes that 'taken together, these processes mean that, even for two equally qualified candidates, the upper middle-class one has a better chance'. One of the most powerful mechanisms of opportunity hoarding in college admissions is the practice of legacy admissions – privileging applicants whose parents are alumni – and, even more blatantly, allowing parents to essentially buy admission for their children by making substantial financial contributions to the college. All of these practices are particularly *unfair* because they violate the rule that opportunities be awarded on the basis of merit (a rule which is *more* fair, though still quite unfair because of unequal opportunities to develop the qualities that count as merit).

Opportunity hoarding interferes with social mobility. While many members of the upper middle class are politically liberal and purport to embrace progressive values – including equality of opportunity – these values can come into conflict with what reveals itself to be of overriding importance to members of this class: the security, well-being and success of their own children. This, it appears, is what matters the most to an opportunity hoarder *as an individual*, and what they are unwilling to sacrifice. Are opportunity hoarders making a wrong decision in how to resolve the conflict between the value of fairness and the value, to them, of their own children's future prospects?

Upper-middle-class parents' sense that their own children's interests may be threatened is increasing as the gap between the upper middle class and everyone else grows, for the possibility that their own children may fall from their social class becomes more frightening when there is further to fall: 'As inequality between the upper middle-class and the rest grows, parents will become more determined to ensure their children stay near the top' (Reeves 2017, 9–10). It is perhaps this fear that compels opportunity hoarders to lose sight of their egalitarian values. Thus opportunity hoarders may act in bad faith, ignoring what Reeves points out is a 'stubborn mathematical fact':

> at any given time, the top fifth of the income distribution can accommodate only 20 percent of the population ... For one person to move up the ladder, somebody else must move down. Sometimes that will have to be one of our own children. (10)

I believe that what may go wrong in the opportunity hoarder's construction of values is that their care for their own children is tinged with anxiety about what their children's future security or well-being will require. This anxiety functions as a sort of a bias whenever the opportunity hoarder confronts a conflict between their commitment to fairness and egalitarianism, on the one hand, and the prospect of securing every possible opportunity for their own children, on the other hand. The dilemma gets decided in favor of opportunity hoarding when fear distorts the decision. Furthermore, bad faith – in which the opportunity hoarder ignores the unfairness of their actions – also taints the construction of values, for their choices lack transparency.

Reeves argues that the upper middle class must sacrifice the option of wielding their wealth and status in unfair ways, but that the size of this sacrifice tends to be exaggerated in the mind of the opportunity hoarder:

> Reducing opportunity hoarding will mean some losses for the upper middle-class. But they will be small. Our neighborhoods will be a little less upmarket – but also less boring. Our kids will rub shoulders with some poorer kids in the school corridor. They might not squeak into an Ivy League college, and they may have to be content going to an excellent public university. But if we aren't willing to entertain even these sacrifices, there is little hope. (Reeves 2017, 122)

If Reeves is right – that the sacrifices are smaller than they seem to the opportunity hoarder – then it is clear that the opportunity hoarder is wrongly refusing to make these sacrifices; in other words, opportunity hoarders are resolving the conflict of values in the wrong way, in part because they wrongly construe what sorts of losses will result. They suppose that the losses to their own children, if they forgo the mechanisms of opportunity hoarding, will be tragic, when in fact they will not be. They are not losses that no one should have to bear. And, as Reeves (2017, 98) puts it, 'our natural preference for the welfare and prospects of our own children does not automatically eclipse other moral claims'.

But there is an additional point to be made, which is that decisions about whether to hoard opportunities – or whether to sacrifice the ill-gotten goods that these opportunities really are – ought not to be in the hands of individual members of the upper middle class, where they are likely to be made badly; there should be policies that make it impossible to employ the mechanisms of opportunity hoarding. If any adequate morality must avoid domination – or at least justify any necessary domination to the dominated – then the economic domination that opportunity hoarding contributes to should be excluded. Since the mechanisms of opportunity hoarding *are* available to members of the American upper middle class, we can see, in their widespread use, how difficult it is to forfeit them on an individual, rather than collective, basis. We might even experience, ourselves, how irresistible it is to employ these mechanisms, perhaps despite knowing that we ought to sacrifice our access to them. When we adopt the standpoint of a member of the larger society, however, then, if our other values are generally egalitarian, we are likely to endorse policies that prevent opportunity hoarding. Or, if someone's egalitarian principles were thoroughly inter-nalized so that they were what mattered the most to them as indivi-duals – overriding the altruistic value of ensuring what they believe would enable their own children's flourishing – then forbearing from opportunity hoarding would not be experienced as self-sacrificial. Members of the upper-middle class experience forfeiting the mechan-isms of opportunity hoarding as self-sacrificial only if they have not internalized egalitarian principles sufficiently. Nevertheless, from either a self-critical evaluative standpoint, or from the evaluative standpoint of someone who doesn't have the resources to engage in opportunity hoarding, or from a collective evaluative standpoint, we can judge that the opportunity hoarder does not make self-sacrifices that they in some sense ought to, and that the solution lies in developing policies to present opportunity hoarding.

Self-interest provides a strong motivation for an individual to refuse to make a self-sacrifice, even when the moral values of the larger society suggest that some particular self-sacrifice is required. But as revealed by the three paradigm cases – the self-sacrificial woman, the do-gooder and the opportunity hoarder – self-interest is not the only factor that can motivate an inappropriate tendency to self-sacrifice either too much or not enough. We can go wrong in what we value, valuing our own self too much *or too little*, and we can go wrong in balancing the rest of what matters to us. Identifying such missteps, however, is not simple for those who reject both value monism and value realism. In many cases, when there are plural and conflicting values, there will be no uniquely right answer about how to resolve the conflict. Some conflicts warrant ambivalence. And some conflicts – regardless of whether ambivalence is warranted – are such that whatever sacrifice is made will constitute a tragic loss.

Notes

1. For a comparison with other ways of treating this point, see Rosati (2009), who remarks that 'the key to understanding self-sacrifice is, so to speak, to put the self back into the sacrifice' (313); and Carbonell (2015), who responds to Rosati's remark by noting that we can distinguish between what is traditionally called 'self-sacrifice' and what she dubs 'sacrifices of self', a term that she uses to refer to cases in which what is sacrificed is 'our identity or moral agency' (55). I use the term 'self-sacrifice' to be inclusive of what Carbonell calls 'sacrifices of self'.
2. Carbonell's (2012, 2015) discussions of self-sacrifice also emphasize the implications of value pluralism, including the lack of commensurability and inter-substitutability of values.
3. I have in mind the kind of consequentialism that Tim Mulgan (2001, 38) refers to a 'simple consequentialism'.
4. For a full account of my position, see Tessman 2015.
5. See Bagnoli 2002; Lenman 2010; Lenman and Shemmer 2012; Street 2012.
6. This position is fully developed in Tessman 2015, esp. ch. 3.
7. A very similar claim is made by Margaret Urban Walker (2003, 109), who argues that when our moral understandings are made transparent and we see them for what they actually are, we will lose confidence in them if 'these understandings turn out to be driven by deception, manipulation, coercion, or violence directed at some of us by others, where all are nonetheless supposed to 'share' in this purported vision of the good'.
8. The agentic skills include: (1) Introspection skills; (2) Communication skills; (3) Memory skills; (4) Imagination skills; (5) Analytical skills and reasoning skills; (6) Self-nurturing skills; (7) Volitional skills; and 8; Interpersonal skills. (Meyers 2002, 20; see also1989; for an earlier version).
9. Thus the 'do-gooder' differs from the 'moral saints' discussed in Carbonell 2012, for she stipulates that they are not pathological (228).
10. See https://www.effectivealtruism.org/ and http://www.givewell.org/.

Disclosure Statement

No potential conflict of interest was reported by the author.

References

Bagnoli, C. 2002. "Moral Constructivism: A Phenomenological Argument." *Topoi* 1-2: 125–138. doi:10.1023/A:1014805104487.

Carbonell, V. 2012. "The Ratcheting-Up Effect." *Pacific Philosophical Quarterly* 93: 228–254. doi:10.1111/papq.2012.93.issue-2.

Carbonell, V. 2015. "Sacrifices of Self." *The Journal of Ethics* 19: 53–72. doi:10.1007/s10892-014-9186-x.

Frankfurt, H. 1988a. "Freedom of the Will and the Concept of a Person." In *The Importance of What We Care About*, 11-94-25. New York: Cambridge University Press.

Frankfurt, H. 1988b. "The Importance of What We Care About." In *The Importance of What We Care About*, 80–94. New York: Cambridge University Press.

Hill, T., Jr. 1973. "Servility and Self-Respect." *The Monist* 57 (1): 87–104. doi:10.5840/monist197357135.

Khader, S. J. 2011. *Adaptive Preferences and Women's Empowerment.* New York: Oxford University Press.

Lenman, J. 2010. "Humean Constructivism in Moral Theory." *Oxford Studies in Metaethics* V: 175–193.

Lenman, J., and Y. Shemmer. 2012. *Introduction to Constructivism in Practical Philosophy*, 1–17. edited by James Lenman and Yonatan Shemmer. Oxford: Oxford University Press.

MacFarquhar, L. 2015. *Strangers Drowning: Grappling with Impossible Idealism, Drastic Choices, and the Overpowering Urge to Help.* New York: Penguin Press.

Madhavan, G., and B. Oakley. 2011. "Too Much of a Good Thing? Foreign Aid and Pathological Altruism." In *Pathological Altruism*, edited by B. Oakley, A. Knafo, G. Madhavan, and D. S. Wilson, 237–244. New York: Oxford University Press.

McWilliams, N. 1984. "The Psychology of the Altruist." *Psychoanalytic Psychology* I (3): 193–213. doi:10.1037/h0085103.

Meyers, D. T. 1989. *Self, Society, and Personal Choice.* New York: Columbia University Press.

Meyers, D. T. 2002. *Gender in the Mirror: Cultural Imagery and Women's Agency.* New York: Oxford University Press.

Mulgan, T. 2001. *The Demands of Consequentialism.* New York: Oxford University Press.

Nussbaum, M. 2000. "The Costs of Tragedy: Some Moral Limits of Cost-Benefit Analysis." *Journal of Legal Studies* 29 (2): 1005–1036. doi:10.1086/468103.

Oakley, B., A. Knafo, G. Madhavan, and D. S. Wilson, eds. 2011. *Pathological Altruism.* New York: Oxford University Press.

Oakley, B., A. Knafo, and M. Michael. 2011. "Pathological Altruism—An Introduction." In *Pathological Altruism*, edited by B. Oakley, A. Knafo, G. Madhavan, and D. S. Wilson, 3–9. New York: Oxford University Press.

Reeves, R. V. 2017. *Dream Hoarders: How the American Upper Middle Class Is Leaving Everyone Else in the Dust, Why that Is a Problem, and What to Do about It.* Washington, DC: Brookings Institute Press.

Rosati, C. 2009. "Self Interest and Self Sacrifice." *Proceedings of the Aristotelian Society* 109 (1_pt_3): 311–325. October 1. doi:10.1111/j.1467-9264.2009.00269.x.

Street, S. 2012. "Coming to Terms with Contingency: Humean Constructivism about Practical Reason." In *Constructivism in Practical Philosophy*, edited by J. Lenman and Y. Shemmer, 40–59. Oxford: Oxford University Press.

Tessman, L. 2015. *Moral Failure: On the Impossible Demands of Morality.* New York: Oxford University Press.

Tilly, C. 1998. *Durable Inequality.* Berkeley: University of California Press.

Walker, M. U. 2003. *Moral Contexts.* Lanham, MD: Rowman and Littlefield.

Williams, B. 1981. "Persons, Character and Morality." In *Moral Luck*. Cambridge: Cambridge University Press.

Wong, D. 2006. *Natural Moralities.* Oxford: Oxford University Press.

The Value of Sacrifices

Jörg Löschke

ABSTRACT

Most authors who discuss the normative impact of sacrifices do so with regards to the impact that a sacrifice can have on the practical reasons of the agent who makes it. A different and underappreciated phenomenon of sacrifices is their other-regarding normative impact: the sacrifice of person A can have an impact on the practical reasons of person B, either by generating practical reasons for B to act in certain ways or by intensifying existing reasons of B for specific courses of action. This paper asks when and why sacrifices have such other-regarding normative impact and argues that sacrifices can have other-regarding normative impact because sacrifices can be intrinsically good. The intrinsic value of sacrifices is explained by the recursive account of value: sacrifices are intrinsically good if and because they are appropriate responses to intrinsic values, and appropriate responses to intrinsic values are themselves intrinsically good. Furthermore, sacrifices are difficult to make, and successful pursuit in difficult activities can also be intrinsically good.

Sacrifices are normatively relevant: whenever an agent makes a sacrifice or bears the risk of doing so, this has an impact on her practical reasons. But the sacrifices of an agent can also be normatively relevant for others: when A makes a sacrifice, then this can have an impact on the reasons of B, either by giving B new reasons for action or altering the strength of B's existing reasons for specific courses of action. For example, if A sacrifices her life in order to save B's life, then B ought not continue living his life as if nothing has happened. Rather, B has reason to respond to that sacrifice, not only through his thoughts and attitudes, but also through the way he lives his life. I will refer to this phenomenon as the other-regarding normative impact of sacrifices.[1]

Such other-regarding normative impact is an underappreciated feature of sacrifices insofar as most authors who work on sacrifices discuss what impact a sacrifice has on the normative situation of the agent who makes that sacrifice. This is especially clear in the context of demandingness in ethics.[2] Many authors assume that an act that involves great sacrifice on behalf of the agent (or that implies a significant risk of involving a great sacrifice) ceases to be obligatory. For example, if I can save another person's life by pressing a button while I sit in my comfortable armchair, it seems reasonable to suppose that I am required to do so. But if pressing the button will give me a lethal electric shock, then it plausible that I am *not* required to press the button – if I choose to sacrifice my own life for another person, then I am acting supererogatorily. There is some disagreement on whether all supererogatory acts involve a sacrifice on behalf of the agent who performs it,[3] but it seems to be widely accepted that acts that involve great sacrifices on behalf of the agent are often supererogatory. This way, a sacrifice often has an impact on the reasons of the agent who makes it, by changing the deontic status of an act and therefore the agent's reasons to perform it.

Another context in which the sacrifices of an agent are taken to be relevant is the context of wellbeing. For example, Douglas Portmore (2007, 13) thinks that '[t]he redemption of one's self-sacrifices in itself contributes to one's welfare' in that 'the closer that one's self-sacrifices come to being fully redeemed, the greater the contribution their redemption makes to one's welfare'. Thus, the fact that an agent has made sacrifices to achieve a goal has an impact on her reasons, because those sacrifices affect the agent's reasons to pursue that goal: the more sacrifices an agent has made, the more would achieving the goal contribute to her wellbeing. This might constitute an additional reason to perform acts that contribute to achieving that goal, or it might intensify the reasons that the agent has to perform such acts. Again, sacrifices have a normative impact for the agent who makes them.

While it is important to address the self-regarding normative impact of sacrifices, it is no less important to address the other-regarding normative impact of sacrifices. In particular, it is important to explain *why* sacrifices have other-regarding normative impact, and *when* they have such impact. To address these questions, I will proceed as follows. Section 1 explains how I understand sacrifices for the purposes of this paper. Section 2 presents some paradigmatic cases in which it seems plausible to suppose that the sacrifices of A have an impact on the reasons of B. Section 3 discusses possible explanations of the other-regarding normative impact of sacrifices that are wanting, and section 4 presents my positive account. To anticipate: I will argue that sacrifices can have other-regarding normative impact because they can be intrinsically good. Intrinsically good things are normatively relevant in the sense that agents have reason to respond appropriately to their value, and this can generate practical reasons for action, or it can intensify the strength of existing practical reasons.

1. The Notion of Sacrifice

What is a sacrifice? To answer this question, it is important to first draw a distinction between two ways in which the term of a sacrifice is used, namely the distinction between 'sacrifice to' and 'sacrifice for' (Halbertal 2012). In its primary use, a sacrifice is a sacrifice *to*; more specifically, sacrifices in this first sense only arise in the religious sphere, and a sacrifice is 'a gift, an offering given from humans to God'. In the second use, which emerged later, a sacrifice involves 'giving up [an] interest for a higher cause' (Halbertal 2012, 1).[4] These two usages of the term are related, since a sacrifice *for* also involves a giving, and a specific sacrifice can be both a sacrifice *for* and a sacrifice *to*, as in the case of a religious fanatic who commits a suicide bombing: she sacrifices her life for a (political) cause, but she also sacrifices her life to God, whose will she believes to be carrying out. Nevertheless, the two senses should be kept apart. In this paper, I am only concerned with sacrifices in the second usage of the term. Hence, I will only discuss cases in which agents give up something for a cause, rather than cases in which they give something to some divine entity.

While a sacrifice *for* involves giving up something that is in the interest of the person who makes the sacrifice, this definition alone does not tell us when exactly an act counts as a sacrifice. This depends on how to specify the interests that are given up when agents make sacrifices. In this article, I will follow those authors who understand sacrifices in terms of objective list theories of wellbeing.[5] Thus, an agent makes a sacrifice if he relinquishes a good that is part of the relevant list of objective goods that contribute to his wellbeing. This leads to another question: under which circumstances does the giving up of a relevant interest count as a sacrifice? Two views are possible here. The first view holds that a sacrifice involves a *net loss* of wellbeing: an agent makes a sacrifice if the act makes him worse off, all things considered (Heathwood 2011). The second view understands sacrifices as *gross losses* on wellbeing (Rosati 2009, 319; Carbonell 2012, 234, 2015, 54): an act can count as a sacrifice even if performing the act benefits the agent in the long term, because an agent can give up a relevant good without being fully compensated for that loss – the good that he relinquishes and the goods that he receives in return might be incommensurable. The second view seems to be more plausible. It seems quite natural to say that a person who wins a gold medal in figure skating at the Olympics made a lot of sacrifices (she gave up the normal pleasures of childhood), even if we think that she gained more than she gave up, all things considered.[6] For the purposes of this paper, I will understand sacrifices as gross losses of wellbeing, but as far as I can see, nothing that follows depends crucially on this.

In any case, calling an act a sacrifice requires specifying a relevant object of comparison. A sacrifice consists in a (gross or net) loss of wellbeing – but compared to what? There are two possibilities here. First, one might hold that a sacrifice implies a loss of wellbeing in comparison to the agent's situation before the act; second, one might hold that a sacrifice implies a loss of wellbeing in comparison to at least one other act that is open to the agent (Archer 2016, 336). The second option seems to be the more plausible one. Cutting one's losses in a situation in which all of the alternatives open to an agent are costly usually does not count as a sacrifice, but forgoing a greater benefit for oneself in favor of a lesser benefit for oneself and greater benefits for others does count as a sacrifice (Archer 2016, 336). Sacrifices thus have a counterfactual nature.

Finally, I will assume that an act only counts as a sacrifice if the agent acted with the knowledge that her act will result in the loss of a relevant good. If I am ignorant that my act will lead to a gross loss of wellbeing, then performing that act does not count as a sacrifice. An agent makes a sacrifice for some cause if she knows that she gives up an interest for that cause, not if she coincidentally happens to do so.

With these brief remarks about the concept of sacrifice in the background, I will now turn to some cases that give us reason to assume that the sacrifices of a person can have other-regarding normative impact. These are the cases that I will work with for the remainder of the paper.

2. Sacrifices with Other-Regarding Normative Impact

Suppose that Al is about to drown in a river, and that Beth jumps into the river to save him. Beth succeeds in carrying Al to the riverbank. Just when other helpers pull Al out of the water, Beth is caught by a powerful wave and drowns. It seems reasonable to suppose that Beth's sacrifice gives Al an extra reason to make something out of his life, or that it increases the strength of Al's existing reason to make something out of his life: if Al throws his life away, becomes a heroin addict, and dies 10 years later from heavy usage, then he wastes not only his life, but also Beth's life and her sacrifice.

Here is another example. Suppose that Christine is a single mother who makes great sacrifices in order to enable her daughter Doris to go to college and get a good education. Again, it seems reasonable to suppose that Christine's sacrifices have an impact on Doris's reasons. Doris has extra reasons or maybe weightier reasons to go to college and get a good education, rather than doing nothing but playing video games and living off welfare for the rest of her life.

Finally, suppose that Eric and Fred have made great sacrifices to establish a small neighborhood café that serves organic food for reasonable prices.

They went without holidays for several years, they worked so much that they had to give up several friendships and they put all the money they earned into their business to keep it from getting taken over by a large fast-food company. This forced them to live in a small and uncomfortable apartment for a couple of years. It seems reasonable to suppose that their sacrifices have an impact on the practical reasons of their son George: after the passing of Eric and Fred, George has a special reason not to sell the café to the fast-food company (or a weightier reason than he would have had without those sacrifices), and the fact that Eric and Fred have made so many sacrifices to establish their business and resist the offers by the fast-food company seems to be a major part of the explanation.

It is important to emphasize that in neither case we would want to say that the sacrifice of one person generates a moral *duty* on behalf of another person. Some sacrifices might generate duties, but it would certainly be implausible to claim that they necessarily do. If the sacrifice of A would necessarily generate a moral duty for B, then B would be severely limited in how he is permitted to live his life simply because A has made a sacrifice. A could then blackmail B into acting in a certain way by making a sacrifice simply for the sake of giving B the relevant duty. Thus, we would not want to say that George is morally *required* to keep the café going – after all, he might have a life plan that differs significantly from being the manager of a neighborhood café, and we would not want to say that he acts morally wrongly by pursuing his different life plan. And we would not even want to say that he acts wrongly if he sells the café to the highest bidder if this is necessary to pursue his life plan, even if that highest bidder happens to be the fast-food company. Morality should not require George to abandon his life plan simply because his parents have made significant sacrifices to establish the café. But even if sacrifices do not always generate duties, the weaker claim – that they often generate defeasible moral reasons on part of other agents, or that they intensify the weight of existing reasons – seems less controversial, and it seems to be supported by intuition.[7] The question is what explains this intuition. This is what I will discuss in the next section.

3. Possible Explanations

One possible explanation for the other-regarding normative impact of sacrifices refers to the notion of gratitude. Call this the gratitude view. On this view, an agent has a moral reason (and possibly a duty) to be grateful to a person who benefitted her and to express her gratitude through her actions, especially in cases in which the benefactor has made great sacrifices to benefit the agent. This explanation might appear plausible in many cases – if your mother has made great sacrifices to enable you to receive a good education, or if a stranger sacrificed her life to rescue yours, you might very well have a reason (and possibly a duty) to be grateful and to express your gratitude through your actions. However, while gratitude might be called for in many cases in which an agent makes a sacrifice on the behalf of another person, the gratitude view does not fully explain why sacrifices can have other-regarding normative impact.

The reason to be skeptical here is that reasons or duties of gratitude only arise if certain conditions are met, and these conditions are not always met in cases in which we intuitively judge that the sacrifices of a person have other-regarding normative impact. For example, gratitude is a response not merely to the fact that a person benefitted you, but to your benefactor's benevolence, and benevolence is a (successful or unsuccessful) attempt to benefit a person that is motivated by the desire to help that person. Hence, gratitude is called for when the benefactor *intended* to benefit the grateful agent (Berger 1975, 299; Jecker 1989, 74). But the sacrifices of one person can have other-regarding normative impact when this condition is not met. Suppose that Eric and Fred made their sacrifices to establish the café long before George was born, and long before they ever thought of adopting a child. In this case, their sacrifices might have benefitted George because the existence of the café might have had some positive impact on his life, but Eric and Fred did not intend to benefit George – after all, George did not exist yet. And neither did Eric and Fred intend to benefit their future child, because they made the sacrifices before they even thought of adopting a child. We can also imagine that Eric and Fred were motivated to make the sacrifice because they wanted to advance the organic lifestyle. In this case, they made the sacrifices for a cause without intending to benefit anyone, not even themselves. Nevertheless, it seems plausible to suppose that their sacrifices have an impact on George's reasons. Thus, gratitude cannot be the whole story.

An alternative explanation of the other-regarding normative impact of sacrifices has been put forward by Mosheh Halbertal (2012). He argues that sacrifices can have an impact on the practical reasons of others if those others are members of the same political or cultural form of life and if the sacrifices contributed to reiterate those forms of life. 'Such forms include political institutions, religious practices, and linguistic and artistic traditions – all of which provide the fabric for a rich, specific life. Members of such structures can conceivably be obligated to the past in a manner that is not overriding but still powerful. One central way in which membership in a particular tradition is expressed is through people assuming responsibility for the sacrifices of previous generations' (Halbertal 2012, 101). Call this the membership view. The membership view seems to explain George's reason not to sell the neighborhood café to the fast-food company better than the gratitude view. Families are specific forms of life, and one might think that they generate obligations to assume responsibility for the sacrifices of previous generations, especially in cases in which a family has a group identity that is shaped by collective endeavors such as maintaining a family business. If this is correct, then it explains why the sacrifices of Eric and Fred have an impact on George's reasons even if they did not make those sacrifices in order to benefit George.

However, even if we think that the membership view explains George's case, it does not seem to be the whole story either. Consider the case of Al and Beth. Beth's sacrifice has an impact on Al's reasons, but it is not clear in what sense membership in a political or cultural form of life should be relevant here. Suppose that Al and Beth are complete strangers – in what sense do they constitute a group whose members are obligated to assume responsibility for the sacrifices of other members? Of course, Al and Beth might be co-nationals, in which case they are members of the same political form of life, and one might argue that this explains why Beth's sacrifice has an impact on Al's reasons. I don't think that this possible response is particularly convincing, given that the sacrifice does nothing to reiterate a common form of life, but even if we grant the relevance of co-nationality for the sake of the argument, the membership view still fails to convince. Suppose that Beth does not save Al from drowning, but Hiroshi, during her vacation in Japan. Beth and Hiroshi are not members of the same political or cultural form of life, but nevertheless it seems plausible to suppose that Beth's sacrifice has an impact on Hiroshi's reasons – just like Al, Hiroshi has a special reason to make something out of his life.

Another possible explanation is disjunctive: a sacrifice has other-regarding normative impact if an agent has reason to be grateful for the sacrifice, or if the agent belongs to the same form of life as the person who makes the sacrifice (and possibly if other conditions are met). I do not have a knockdown argument against such a disjunctive view, but I think that, while the disjunctive explanation might cover all cases, a unified explanation of this seemingly unified phenomenon would be preferable. And as I will argue in the remainder of this paper, it is possible to give such a unified explanation that applies to all cases in which it seems reasonable to suppose that sacrifices have other-regarding normative impact.

In my view, the best explanation for the other-regarding normative impact of sacrifices is that sacrifices can be intrinsically valuable.[8] Intrinsically valuable entities are normatively relevant in that agents have reason to act in ways that are appropriate responses to their value, either because the intrinsic value generates reasons for action, or because the existence of an intrinsically valuable object introduces a dimension of value that intensifies the strength of an existing practical reason of an agent. And intrinsically good objects do so not only for the agent in whose life the value occurs, or who is responsible for the existence of the valuable entity, but for other agents as well. If sacrifices can be shown to be intrinsically good, then this explains the other-regarding normative impact of sacrifices: the reasons of a person can be affected because that person has reason to respond appropriately to the sacrifice's intrinsic value.[9]

This claim might appear prima facie implausible. Sacrifices are gross losses of wellbeing, and they are therefore bad for the person who makes them (at least in one regard). How can they be intrinsically good if they are bad for the agent? The answer is that 'good' and 'good for' are distinct concepts. I cannot discuss the relation between these concepts here,[10] but I would like to point out that from the fact that a sacrifice is bad for the agent who makes it, it does not follow that the sacrifice cannot be intrinsically good. And neither does the claim that a sacrifice is intrinsically good entail that the sacrifice is good for somebody. Suppose that a Buddhist monk burns himself to protest against the Chinese oppression of Tibet. In this case, his sacrifice might be intrinsically good: it might express the conviction that injustice is not to be tolerated, and that might be good in itself, independently of any further good consequences that it brings about. However, the sacrifice is not good for any specific person, especially if it does not lead to an end of the Chinese oppression of Tibet. Hence, the fact that a sacrifice is bad for the person who makes it does not mean that the sacrifice cannot be intrinsically good.

However, the question remains why and under which circumstances sacrifices are intrinsically good. This is what I will discuss in the following section.

4. The Intrinsic Value of Sacrifices

Two observations help to spell out the intrinsic value of sacrifices. First, only some sacrifices are intrinsically good. If Ingo made great sacrifices to advance his career in the Gestapo, then this does not give his grandson Jan a practical reason to respond positively to those sacrifices. If anything, it gives Jan a reason to be ashamed. This suggests that the evaluative status of a sacrifice depends on its objective: a sacrifice is intrinsically good if it is made for a good cause, and it is intrinsically bad if it is made for a bad cause.[11] This, of course, is a pretty commonsensical claim, and it does not yet explain why sacrifices for a good cause are *intrinsically* valuable – if sacrifices are only good as long as their objective is good, their value could be merely instrumental value. Nevertheless, it is an observation that should be kept in mind.

The second observation is that an intrinsically valuable sacrifice must not only be done for a good cause, but it must also meet a proportionality requirement. For example, it is plausible to assume that it is intrinsically good to sacrifice one's life in order to rescue another person's life, but it is less plausible to think that it is intrinsically good to sacrifice one's life in order to spare another person from a minor inconvenience. For a sacrifice to be intrinsically good, there must be some kind of match between the goodness of its objective and the magnitude of the loss of wellbeing. The greater the value of the objective, the greater a sacrifice is appropriate. If the mismatch between the value of the objective and the sacrifice is too crass, then the sacrifice is not intrinsically good.

Taken together, these observations suggest an explanation of the intrinsic value of sacrifices in terms of the so-called *recursive account of value.* The recursive account, in its most basic form, says that responses to intrinsic values can themselves be intrinsically good or bad. More specifically, it claims that it is intrinsically good to hold pro-attitudes toward intrinsically good objects, and that it is intrinsically good to hold contra-attitudes toward intrinsically bad objects. Furthermore, it claims that is intrinsically bad to hold pro-attitudes toward intrinsically bad objects, and it is intrinsically bad to hold contra-attitudes toward intrinsically good objects (Hurka 2001). If we plausibly assume that pro-attitudes towards good objects are appropriate responses to their value, and that contra-attitudes towards bad objects are appropriate responses to their disvalue, then we can summarize the recursive account as the claim that appropriate responses to intrinsic values are themselves intrinsically good.

The recursive account seems intuitively quite plausible.[12] Compare two worlds, W1 and W2.[13] W1 contains suffering, but no compassion, whereas W2 contains the same amount of suffering, but also compassion with those who are suffering. If we compare and evaluate W1 and W2, it seems that W2 is the better world. Since the only difference between W1 and W2 is the fact that W2 contains compassion, it follows that the compassion in W2 is valuable: after all, the occurrence of compassion makes W2 the better world. And the compassion is not merely instrumentally valuable, since it does not reduce the suffering in W2. The mere existence of compassion in W2 makes W2 the better world, and this means that the compassion must be intrinsically good. And on the plausible assumption that compassion is an appropriate response to disvalue, namely to the disvalue of the suffering, this in turn suggests that appropriate responses to values (or disvalues) are intrinsically good.

The recursive account of value helps to explain the intrinsic value of sacrifices. Making a sacrifice for the sake of some valuable entity is an appropriate response to that value. After all, it is plausible to suppose that to be intrinsically valuable just is (among other things) to be worthy of sacrifice (Halbertal 2012, 99). If the recursive account is correct, then it follows that as appropriate value responses, sacrifices are intrinsically good. So, for example, if persons have intrinsic value, then it is an appropriate response to a person's value to make a sacrifice on her behalf, and such a sacrifice is intrinsically good qua appropriate value response. Similarly, if a good education is intrinsically valuable, then it is appropriate to make sacrifices for the sake of receiving a good education, and such sacrifices are intrinsically good. And if it is a valuable achievement to establish a small neighborhood café that serves organic food, then it is appropriate to make sacrifices to achieve that goal, and these sacrifices are intrinsically good.[14] By contrast, becoming a Gestapo leader is not a valuable goal. Rather, it is quite immoral to aim at becoming a Gestapo leader, and it is thus not appropriate to make sacrifices in order to achieve this immoral goal. To the contrary, it is an inappropriate value response to make such sacrifices. Such sacrifices are therefore intrinsically bad, and Jan has no reason to honor Ingo's sacrifices to become a Gestapo leader. Rather, he has reason to respond with contra-attitudes to those sacrifices.

Understanding the intrinsic value of sacrifices in terms of the recursive account gains further support by the fact that it offers a coherent explanation why intrinsically good sacrifices must be done from the right motivation, and why this precludes cases of moral blackmailing in which an agent makes a sacrifice in order to influence the normative situation of another person. If I jump into a river to save another person's life merely for the sake of imposing a duty of gratitude on her, I do not respond to that person's value. Rather, I respond to the prudential value of having another person indebted to me. I am not directed towards an intrinsically good object, and hence, my sacrifice is not intrinsically good.

Not only does the recursive account explain why and under which conditions sacrifices are intrinsically good (they are intrinsically good if and because they are appropriate responses to value), it is also in line with the aforementioned proportionality requirement. The recursive account itself includes a proportionality requirement (Hurka 2001): the strength of a pro-attitude must correspond to how good its object is. The better the object, the stronger the appropriate pro-attitude. For example, it is appropriate to be slightly delighted when another person receives a small benefit, and it is appropriate to be greatly saddened by the death of a loved one. The proportionality requirement therefore supports the idea that the intrinsic value of sacrifices can be spelled out in terms of the recursive account, but it is necessary to be careful here. There are important differences between the recursive account and the intrinsic value of sacrifices: sacrifices are actions, not pro-attitudes, and there is no 'strength' of an action that could correspond to the value of the object of the response in the same way as the strength of a pro-attitude can. The question is therefore how to understand the proportionality requirement in the case of sacrifices. As far as I can see, there are two options.

The first option is to analyze value responses that include practical reasons (such as reasons to make sacrifices) in terms of desires. Desires are pro-attitudes, and we might be able to understand the (proportional) appropriateness of a sacrifice by the (proportional) appropriateness of the strength of the desire that is associated with the sacrifice. For example, it is appropriate to desire greatly that another person is rescued from drowning, and it is appropriate to desire rather weakly that a person is spared from a minor inconvenience. To understand the proportionality requirement in the case of sacrifices, one would then have to make the further claim that the appropriateness of a sacrifice is a function of the appropriateness of the desire that is promoted by making the sacrifice. On this view, it is appropriate to make a great sacrifice to promote a strong appropriate desire, and it is appropriate to make a small sacrifice to promote a weak appropriate desire.

The second option is to understand the proportionality requirement directly as a relation between a sacrifice and the value of the objective that the sacrifice promotes. On this view, proportionality is warranted between the amount of wellbeing that is lost by making the sacrifice on the one hand and the gain in wellbeing (or in some other kind of value) that is brought about by the sacrifice on the other hand. For example, it might be proportionate to sacrifice one's own life in order to rescue some other person because the loss in wellbeing and the gain in wellbeing are roughly equal, but it is disproportionate to sacrifice one's own life in order to spare some other person from a minor inconvenience, since the gap between the loss in wellbeing and the potential gain is too large.

The first option appears *prima facie* preferable. It gives a unified picture of the recursive account: rather than posing one version in terms of pro-attitudes and another version in terms of actions, it explains the goodness of actions (understood as appropriate responses to value) in terms of the goodness of pro-attitudes (understood as appropriate responses to value). Furthermore, it can explain cases that the second option has difficulties to make sense of. Consider again the case of a Buddhist monk who burns himself to protest against the Chinese oppression of Tibet. It seems plausible to suppose that this act is intrinsically valuable, given that it is plausible to suppose that agents have reason to honor this sacrifice and that honoring is one way to respond appropriately to intrinsic value. The first account of the proportionality requirement can explain the intrinsic value of the monk's sacrifice: the oppression of Tibet is a very bad thing, and it is appropriate for the monk to desire very strongly the freedom of his people. It is therefore appropriate for him to make a great sacrifice for this cause. The second option has more difficulties to explain the intrinsic value of the monk's sacrifice, because the gap between what is lost (a human life) and what is gained (there is no immediate gain, as the protest does not alleviate the oppression of Tibet) is very large. Thus, on the second view, the monk's sacrifice appears to violate the proportionality requirement, and the sacrifice therefore ceases to be intrinsically good. But the fact that we have reason to honor the monk's sacrifice suggests otherwise: it suggests that the sacrifice *is* intrinsically good.

110 SACRIFICE AND MORAL PHILOSOPHY

Proponents of the recursive account have argumentative resources to explain the proportionality requirement in the context of sacrifices. Since the proportionality requirement is intuitively plausible when taken in isolation, but also an important feature of the recursive account, this is some evidence that the recursive account helps to explain the intrinsic value of (some) sacrifices.

However, there is one important difference between sacrifices as appropriate responses to value on the one hand and pro-attitudes on the other hand. In the case of pro-attitudes, the value of the appropriate response cannot surpass or outweigh the goodness or badness of the object of the response (Hurka 2001). For example, while compassion is an appropriate response to the disvalue of the suffering of another person, the intrinsic goodness of compassion does not outweigh the intrinsic badness of the suffering. Otherwise, we would get the counterintuitive result that a world that contains suffering as well as compassion is better than a world that contains no suffering at all.[15] But in the case of sacrifices, it seems that the value of the response can outweigh the value of its object. Consider again the case of George. When George refuses to sell the café to the fast-food company, he either does so because he regards the café as intrinsically valuable and he thinks that refusing to sell is an appropriate response to the intrinsic value of the café, or he considers his refusal to sell as a way to honor (and thus respond appropriately to) Eric and Fred's sacrifices. In the first case, George takes the value of the sacrifices' objective as having an impact on his reasons. In the second case, the value that is more salient to George as having an impact on his reasons is the value of Eric and Fred's sacrifices.

Now, suppose that George does not want to become manager of the café, but that he neither wants to sell the café to the fast-food company. What value does George respond to when he refuses to sell? The plausible explanation is that George refuses to sell because he thinks that he has to honor Eric and Fred's sacrifices that were necessary to establish the café, rather than that he refuses to sell because he thinks that the café has great intrinsic value.[16] He therefore considers the value of an appropriate value response (the sacrifices of Eric and Fred) as a reason-giving entity, rather than the value of the object of that response (the café). But this might appear problematic for proponents of the recursive account: after all, that account claims that appropriate responses to value are *less* valuable than the object of the response. Thus, proponents of the recursive account seem to have to claim that George is making a mistake in his evaluation, and that he should be concerned with the value of the café, rather than with the value of his parents' sacrifices, since the café has greater value than Eric and Fred's appropriate response to that value. But that is not a particularly attractive position. Agents can certainly err in their evaluations, but it is implausible to assume that agents do so in a great and systematic way as the claim seems to assume. And more importantly, George does not seem to make a mistake. It seems quite reasonable for George to honor his parents' sacrifices, rather than the café that they established.

I think that the solution to this problem is to acknowledge that appropriate responses to intrinsic values that take the form of actions can have more intrinsic value than their objects. In the case of attitudes, the appropriate value response just is the attitude, and it is plausible to assume that appropriate attitudes are less valuable than their object. But in the case of actions, the response can realize further value that can increase the overall value of the response to the point that it surpasses the value of its object.

Here is how this might work. When determining the value of an action as an appropriate response to value, the first thing to consider is the value of the desire that motivates (or is part of the motivation of) the relevant action. That desire is a pro-attitude, and it has value like any other pro-attitude that is an appropriate response to an intrinsic value. It therefore has less value than its object. However, the action that accompanies the desire can constitute additional value that must be added to the value of the corresponding desire. The action as a whole can then have more value than the original object of the corresponding desire. The question, of course, is: which aspects of an action might constitute such additional value?

A plausible candidate is the *difficulty* of the sacrifice. As several authors have argued, success in difficult activities is intrinsically valuable (Suits 2005; Hurka 2006; Bradford 2013b), over and above the value of the goal that is achieved. For example, there is not much intrinsic value in standing on top of Mt Everest, but there seems to be much intrinsic value in standing on top of Mt Everest as a result of having climbed Mt Everest (Bradford 2013b). And a plausible explanation for this is that it is quite difficult to do so. The difficulty of a successful activity can therefore constitute value over and beyond the value of the activity's goal. And this might help to explain why sacrifices can have more intrinsic value than the causes for which they are done, because it is one typical feature of sacrifices that they are difficult to make.

The difficulty of sacrifices can take several forms. Sacrifices are not necessarily difficult in the sense that they require a lot of physical strength or coordination – jumping into a river is not in the same way difficult as climbing Mt Everest is. But making a sacrifice is often difficult from a psychological or motivational point of view: it is certainly difficult (at least for the average person) to motivate herself to risk her life to save the life of another person.[17] Of course, a person who makes a sacrifice might have no difficulty to motivate herself – being Doris's mother, Christine might have made her sacrifices willingly and without motivational difficulty. But even in such a case, there is another way in which her sacrifice could be regarded as difficult. As Dana Nelkin has pointed out, difficulty is a disjunctive category: performing an act is difficult if it requires a great deal of effort, or if it requires a great sacrifice of one's interests (Nelkin 2016). Even if Christine's sacrifices required no motivational effort, it could still be the case that it required great effort to actually enable Doris to get the college education, which would imply that achieving that goal was difficult. Furthermore, the mere fact that that achievement required sacrifices on Christine's part also implies that it was difficult to achieve that goal. Whenever an agent makes a sacrifice, this by itself suggests that she engages in difficult activity, and making the sacrifice might itself be difficult. To the extent that success in difficult activities is valuable over and beyond the value of the goal of those activities, this explains why sacrifices can have intrinsic value over and beyond the value of the goal that they aim at.[18]

At this point, one might object that I have given no explanation *why* success in difficult activities is intrinsically valuable, and that sacrifices are therefore not shown to be intrinsically valuable yet. I cannot discuss this question in detail here, but one explanation has been offered in the literature that is both independently plausible and provides further support for the claim that sacrifices can be intrinsically valuable. This explanation is perfectionist: the will is among our fundamental human capacities, and the excellent exercise of fundamental human capacities is intrinsically good. Since engaging in difficult activities *just is* the excellent exercise of the will, engaging in difficult activities is intrinsically good (Bradford 2013b). This perfectionist view fits well with the claim that sacrifices can be intrinsically good: if a person manages to motivate herself to make a significant sacrifice for the sake of another person or for some valuable cause, or if she makes a sacrifice for a valuable cause that is difficult to make because it is demanding, then this can be plausibly be seen as an instance of exercising her will in an excellent manner. And the same applies to sacrifices that a person makes for her long-term personal projects, especially if her projects involve series of actions that are unpleasant. If the perfectionist explanation of the intrinsic value of difficult activities is plausible, then it also seems to offer a convincing explanation of the intrinsic values of (some) sacrifices.

However, at this point, one question remains. The value of sacrifices seems to be agent-neutral value, but the reasons to respond appropriately to the sacrifices of other agents are agent-relative. The question is how this is possible, and I will turn to this question in the next section.

5. Sacrifices and Agent-Relative Reasons

Here is the problem. The value of appropriate value responses is agent-neutral value in that its goodness does not depend on the identity of any particular person. My appropriate response to a value depends on me in the sense that it only exists because *I* respond appropriately to that value, but that does not make that value agent-relative, because the fact that my appropriate response to that value is intrinsically good has nothing to do with me in particular. The value of my appropriate value response exists because of me, but my appropriate value response is not good because of me. And the same applies to the value of engaging in difficult activities. I create value by engaging in difficult activities, and in this sense, that value depends on me for its realization. But the value is agent-neutral value, because the fact that it is *me* who engages in such activities is not the explanation for why engaging in difficult activities is intrinsically good.

By contrast, the reasons that agents have to respond appropriately to the value of sacrifices of other agents are often agent-relative reasons. Everybody has reason to admire Beth's sacrifice: that reason is agent-neutral. But Al has agent-relative reason to respond to Beth's sacrifice because Beth saved *his* life. *Al* has special reason not to become a drug addict that other agents do not have in the same way. Similarly, George has special reason not to sell the café to the fast-food company because of the sacrifices that *his* parents made. If, for some reason, a person inherits the café who has no relationship to Eric and Fred, it is not obvious that that other person has similar reason not to sell the café to the fast-food company.

This seems to pose a puzzle. If practical reasons are reasons to respond appropriately to agent-neutral values, how can these reasons be agent-relative? If the value includes no reference to any particular agent, why do some reasons to respond to the value include such a reference? *Prima facie*, it seems plausible to suppose that agent-neutral values generate agent-neutral reasons, not agent-relative reasons. And some authors raise doubts about the possibility of explaining agent-relative reasons in terms of agent-neutral values (Jeske 2008; Goldman 2009; Wallace 2010; McFadden 2015). Does this speak against the explanation of the reason-affecting force of sacrifices as outlined in this paper?

It will not be possible to provide a full account of how agent-neutral values give rise to agent-relative reasons, but I want to outline a possible explanation. To say that a sacrifice generates agent-relative reasons for a specific person is to say that the sacrifice has an impact on that particular agent's reasons, and a plausible explanation for this phenomenon is that the sacrifice has had an impact on that person's life. To use a somewhat metaphorical way of speaking, the claim would then be that the sacrifices of another person give me agent-relative reasons for responses if and because those intrinsically valuable sacrifices have left traces in my life. If a value has left traces in a person's life, then that person cannot ignore the value; rather, she has to take the value differently into account than a person who knows about the value without being affected by it. Different agents might therefore have different reasons to respond to the same value, depending on what traces the value has left in their lives.

It is important to emphasize that, if a sacrifice has left traces in a person's life, it is not necessarily the case that the sacrifice has been good for that particular person. The sacrifice of one person can have left traces in another person's life even if that sacrifice has not been good for that other person. For example, George has a reason to respond to Eric and Fred's sacrifices even if it would have been better for George if Eric and Fred's would not have made those sacrifices: without those sacrifices, Eric and Fred might not have established the café and might have taken jobs that would have been better for their family overall, or for George in particular. In such a case, Eric and Fred's sacrifices have not been good for George, all things considered, but they still have left traces in his life. Of course, if the traces that a sacrifice has left in another person's life are thoroughly negative, then that person might have no reason to respond to that sacrifice in a positive way. But in other cases, a person can have such reasons even if the sacrifice has not been good for that person, all things considered.

Admittedly, this proposal is very sketchy and raises more questions than it answers. I do not claim to give a full account of how agent-neutral values generate agent-relative reasons; I am merely suggesting that it is possible to tell some story about how agent-neutral values generate agent-relative reasons. And as long as it is possible to tell such a story, it is no objection against the explanation of the intrinsic value of sacrifices in terms of the recursive account that reasons to respond to the value of sacrifices are often agent-relative reasons.

6. Conclusion

In this paper, I have argued that the sacrifices of one person can have an impact on another person's reasons, and I have suggested that the best explanation for this phenomenon is that sacrifices can be intrinsically valuable. Moreover, I have argued that the intrinsic value of sacrifices can be explained by the recursive account of value: sacrifices are intrinsically valuable if and because they are appropriate responses to intrinsic values. This requires extending the recursive account to actions as appropriate value responses, and it requires acknowledging that in some cases, an appropriate value response can be more valuable than its object: actions can realize value in addition to their goodness as appropriate value responses, such as the value that is realized by engaging in difficult activities.

It is important to emphasize again that I have not claimed that sacrifices have overriding value, or that agents ought to make as many sacrifices as possible. I merely claim that sacrifices can be intrinsically valuable. What agents have overall reason to do is a different question. Nevertheless, the discussion of the intrinsic value of sacrifices might have interesting repercussions for other questions in moral philosophy, such as the discussion about the status of supererogatory acts. Supererogatory acts are often considered to be particularly good, and to the extent that they include sacrifices, the view sketched here might help to explain the goodness of supererogatory acts: they gain value merely by involving sacrifices, in addition to the value that they help to realize, or to the value of the motivation from which they are done, etc. To be sure, more needs to be said here. What I hope to have shown is that sacrifices are an underappreciated phenomenon of our moral practice, and that it is inappropriate to think about them merely in terms of the reduction of wellbeing that they imply. Sacrifices can also be intrinsically valuable.

Notes

1. It would take another paper to discuss adequately whether this other-regarding normative impact consists in creating new reasons to perform an act, or whether it consists in altering the strength of existing reasons (or possibly both). What I am about to say is consistent with both of these options.
2. There are some exceptions. For example, David Sobel 2007 rejects the Demandingness Objection against consequentialism on the grounds that it presupposes a distinction between morally relevant cost that an act imposes on the agent and morally irrelevant cost that failing to perform that act imposes on the potential beneficiary. Sobel argues that a theory that does not require agents to give up significant goods in order to benefit others can be thought of as being demanding as well – but it is demanding on the person who does not receive the help that she needs. For a criticism of Sobel's arguments, see Woollard 2016. I thank Marcel van Ackeren for drawing my attention to Sobel's paper.
3. Authors who think that all supererogatory acts involve sacrifice include Mellema 1991 and Dancy 1993. Dorsey 2013 also seems to be at least sympathetic to the view. For criticism, see Archer 2016.
4. Halbertal thinks that a sacrifice *for* involves giving up a *vital* interest, but that claim seems to be too strong. We usually speak of sacrifices even if the interest that the agent gives up is not a vital one.
5. Objective list theories of wellbeing can be found in Parfit 1984 and Nussbaum 1999. For an understanding of sacrifices in terms of such theories, see Carbonell 2012, 2015.
6. For a similar example, see Carbonell 2012.
7. I do not claim that the other-regarding normative impact of sacrifices is necessarily an impact on the moral reasons of a person. Some sacrifices might have an impact on her non-moral reasons. I will not discuss other-regarding non-moral normative impact of sacrifices in this paper, but I believe that most of what I am going to say also applies to such non-moral cases.

8. In what follows, I will use the term 'intrinsic value' in the sense of non-instrumental value, or value as an end, rather than in the sense of value that an object has solely in terms of its intrinsic properties. For a discussion of these two ways of using the notion of intrinsic value, see Kagan 1998.

9. For a different view of the relation between sacrifices and value, see Axinn 2010. Axinn claims that sacrifices *create* value, rather than being intrinsically valuable themselves.

10. For discussions on the relation between 'good' and 'good for', see, among others, Regan 2004; Zimmerman 2009; Tenenbaum 2010; Fletcher 2012; Hurka 2014.

11. For the purposes of this paper, I am mostly concerned with moral value, but this claim is not limited to moral cases. For example, Eric and Fred's sacrifices are intrinsically good, but establishing the café is not necessarily morally good. And sacrifices might also be intrinsically good if they are made for, say, aesthetically valuable objectives. This raises complex questions about the evaluative status of sacrifices that are made for non-moral goods and that also involve moral wrongdoing – think of Gauguin's case. I do not have the space to discuss such complex cases here, but I hope to discuss such complexities that arise when sacrifices are made for morally neutral, morally mixed or non-moral goods in another paper. I thank an anonymous reviewer for pressing me on this point.

12. Other authors who accept the recursive account include Nozick 1981; Way 2013; Bradford 2013a.

13. I take this example from Hurka 2001.

14. For a general account of the value of achievements, see Bradford 2015.

15. Some Christian theists might hold that this result is far from counterintuitive, and that it explains why evil exists if God is both omnipotent and good. For a critical discussion of this solution to the problem of evil, see Mackie 1955. I thank an anonymous reviewer for pointing this out and drawing my attention to Mackie's paper.

16. One might think that George does not sell the café because he thinks that he has to honor Eric and Fred's wishes, rather than because he thinks that he responds to any kind of value. This is certainly a possibility, and I do not deny that Eric and Fred's wish can play some role in the explanation of why George refuses to sell. However, I do not think that this possibility shows that Eric and Fred's sacrifices have no impact on George's reasons. It seems to me that even if Eric and Fred tell George before their death that they do not care what George does with the café after their death, George might very well take himself to have reason not to sell the café, given that he knows what sacrifices were necessary to establish it.

17. For a detailed discussion how motivational difficulty contributes to the demandingness of acts, see McElwee 2016.

18. Note that this does not imply that we should make our activities as difficult as possible. If I write a book on Kantian Ethics, it would be pointless for me to tie one arm behind my back simply because that makes it more difficult to write the book. After all, our time and energy is limited, and making all of our activities absurdly difficult will keep us from realizing many other dimensions of value in our lives. For more on this, see Bradford 2013b.

Acknowledgments

For valuable feedback and discusssion, I thank Marcel van Ackeren, Alfred Archer, Christian Budnik, Anna Goppel, Simon Keller, Andreas Müller, Jutta Schmidt, Meinhard Schmidt, Markus Stepanians and an anonymous referee.

Disclosure Statement

No potential conflict of interest was reported by the author.

References

Archer, A. 2016. "Supererogation, Sacrifice, and the Limits of Duty." *The Southern Journal of Philosophy* 54 (3): 333–354. doi:10.1111/sjp.2016.54.issue-3.

Axinn, S. 2010. *Sacrifice and Value. A Kantian Interpretation.* Lanham: Lexington Books.

Berger, F. 1975. "Gratitude." *Ethics* 85: 298–309. doi:10.1086/291969.

Bradford, G. 2013a. "Evil Achievements and the Principle of Recursion." *Oxford Studies in Normative Ethics* 3: 79–97.

Bradford, G. 2013b. "The Value of Achievements." *Pacific Philosophical Quarterly* 94: 204–224. doi:10.1111/j.1468-0114.2012.01452.x.

Bradford, G. 2015. *Achievement.* Oxford: Oxford University Press.

Carbonell, V. 2012. "The Ratcheting-Up Effect." *Pacific Philosophical Quarterly* 93: 228–254. doi:10.1111/papq.2012.93.issue-2.

Carbonell, V. 2015. "Sacrifices of Self." *The Journal of Ethics* 19: 53–72. doi:10.1007/s10892-014-9186-x.

Dancy, J. 1993. *Moral Reasons.* Oxford: Blackwell.

Dorsey, D. 2013. "The Supererogatory, and How to Accommodate It." *Utilitas* 25: 355–382. doi:10.1017/S095382081200060X.

Fletcher, G. 2012. "The Locative Analysis of Good for Formulated and Defended." *Journal of Ethics and Social Philosophy* 6 (1): 1–26. doi: 10.26556/jesp.v6i1.

Goldman, A. 2009. *Reasons from Within.* Oxford: Oxford University Press.

Halbertal, M. 2012. *On Sacrifice.* Princeton: Princeton University Press.

Heathwood, C. 2011. "Preferentism and Self-Sacrifice." *Pacific Philosophical Quarterly* 92: 18–38. doi:10.1111/j.1468-0114.2010.01384.x.

Hurka, T. 2001. *Virtue, Vice, and Value.* Oxford: Oxford University Press.

Hurka, T. 2006. "Games and the Good." *Proceedings of the Aristotelian Society Supplementary Volume* 80: 217–235. doi:10.1111/j.1467-8349.2006.00143.x.

Hurka, T. 2014. *British Ethical Theorists from Sidgwick to Ewing.* Oxford: Oxford University Press.

Jecker, N. 1989. "Are Filial Duties Unfounded?" *American Philosophical Quarterly* 26: 73–80.

Jeske, D. 2008. *Rationality and Moral Theory. How Intimacy Generates Reasons.* London: Routledge.

Kagan, S. 1998. "Rethinking Intrinsic Value." *The Journal of Ethics* 2: 277–297. doi:10.1023/A:1009782403793.

Mackie, J. L. 1955. "Evil and Omnipotence." *Mind; a Quarterly Review of Psychology and Philosophy* 64: 200–212. doi:10.1093/mind/LXIV.254.200.

McElwee, B. 2016. "What Is Demandingness?" In *The Limits of Moral Obligation: Moral Demandingness and Ought Implies Can*, edited by M. van Ackeren and M. Kühler, 19–35. London: Routledge.

McFadden, M. 2015. "Reasons, Value, Valuing: Teleology and Explanation." *Kriterion – Journal of Philosophy* 29: 45–62.

Mellema, G. 1991. *Beyond the Call of Duty: Supererogation, Obligation, and Offence.* New York: SUNY Press.

Nelkin, D. K. 2016. "Difficulty and Degrees of Moral Praiseworthiness and Blameworthiness." *Nous* 50: 356–378. doi:10.1111/nous.12079.

Nozick, R. 1981. *Philosophical Explanations.* Cambridge: Harvard University Press.

Nussbaum, M. 1999. *Sex and Social Justice.* Oxford: Oxford University Press.

Parfit, D. 1984. *Reasons and Persons.* Oxford: Oxford University Press.

Portmore, D. 2007. "Welfare, Achievement, and Self-Sacrifice." *Journal of Ethics and Social Philosophy* 2 (2): 1–28. doi:10.26556/jesp.v2i2.22.

Regan, D. 2004. "Why Am I My Brother's Keeper?" In *Reason and Value. Themes from the Philosophy of Joseph Raz*, edited by R. Jay Wallace, P. Pettit, S. Scheffler, and M. Smith, 202–230. Oxford: Oxford University Press.

Rosati, C. 2009. "Self-Interest and Self-Sacrifice." *Proceedings of the Aristotelian Society* 109: 311–325. doi:10.1111/j.1467-9264.2009.00269.x.

Sobel, D. 2007. "The Impotence of the Demandingness Objection." *Philosophers' Imprint* 7: 1–17.

Suits, B. 2005. *The Grasshopper. Games, Life, and Utopia.* Peterborough: Broadview.

Tenenbaum, S. 2010. "Good and Good For." In *Desire, Practical Reason, and the Good*, edited by S. Tenenbaum, 202–233. Oxford: Oxford University Press.

Wallace, R. J. 2010. "Reasons, Values and Agent-Relativity." *Dialectica* 64: 503–528. doi:10.1111/dltc.2010.64.issue-4.

Way, J. 2013. "Value and Reasons to Favour." *Oxford Studies in Metaethics* 8: 27–49.

Woollard, F. 2016. "Dimensions of Demandingness." *Proceedings of the Aristotelian Society* 116: 89–106. doi:10.1093/arisoc/aow003.

Zimmerman, M. 2009. "Understanding What's Good for Us." *Ethical Theory and Moral Practice* 12: 429–439. doi:10.1007/s10677-009-9184-4.

Sentimentalist Practical Reason and Self-Sacrifice

Michael Slote

ABSTRACT

For obvious reasons sentimentalists have been hesitant to offer accounts of moral reasons for action: the whole idea at least initially smacks of rationalist notions of morality. But the sentimentalist can seek to *reduce* practical to sentimentalist considerations and that is what the present paper attempts to do. Prudential reasons can be identified with the normal emotional/motivational responses people feel in situations that threaten them or offer them opportunities to attain what they need. And in the most basic cases altruistic/moral reasons involve the empathic transfer of one person's prudential reasons and emotions to another person or persons who can help them. Practical/moral reasons for self-sacrifice also depend on empathic transfer and can vary in strength with the strength of the transfer.

1.

In my opinion, self-sacrifice occupies the center of morality: I wouldn't be inclined to call someone a morally good or decent individual if they were totally unwilling ever to make any sacrifice of their own welfare for the sake of others. So in all consistency I hold that a full and adequate account of morality needs to be able to find a place for self-sacrifice. This is something I shall try to accomplish here, but rather than run through and criticize or borrow from more familiar accounts of the ethics of self-sacrifice, I am going to approach the issue from my own distinctive standpoint as a moral sentimentalist. I am going to try to show you how a sentimentalist can allow for reasons to sacrifice oneself, but I think I need to embed that account within a general sentimentalist framework for understanding practical reasons. And it is not obvious how a sentimentalist can really do such a thing. After all, sentimentalists think that moral virtue and moral claims about right and wrong, virtue and vice, are based in sentiment, not reason, and previous sentimentalists have been reluctant to connect, or have been at least ambivalent about connecting, morality with reasons for action.

For example, Hume in the *Treatise of Human Nature* claims that calm passions are often 'confounded' with reason (Book II, Part III, Section III), but almost immediately afterwards (Book II, Part III, Section VIII) he says that 'by *reason* we mean affections ... such as operate more calmly...'. Similarly, in Book III, Part I, Section I, Hume argues that there is no such thing as practical, as opposed to theoretical, reason; but he later goes on to claim that we can regard certain mild emotions or calm passions as instances of (practical) reason (Book III, Part III, Section I). So Hume is at the very least ambivalent about the possibility of practical reason(s), and I can think of no (theoretical) reason why a moral sentimentalist can't choose to be *either* an eliminativist *or* a reductionist about practical rationality/reasons. They can say there is no such thing, or, as sentimentalists, they can hold that practical reasons/rationality are in general understandable in emotional terms.

In the present essay, I am going to take the latter course and will then apply what I have said about practical rationality to the issue of self-sacrifice. In previous work, I have avoided saying that we have practical reasons to help others or sacrifice ourselves for others because I regarded the most serious work of moral philosophy as capable of being accomplished without committing oneself to such claims. In my book *Moral Sentimentalism* (Slote 2010), I used Saul Kripke's (1980) notion of reference fixing to argue that moral judgments can be based in empathy and yet be capable of being completely objective (and true), and I attempted to show that anyone who makes a moral judgment will automatically have motivation to act in accordance with that judgment. This gives one most of what rationalists have wanted from or believed present in morality and moral judgments – except for the issue of reasons for action. I never said (or denied) that the person who is motivated by moral considerations to help others has a reason to do so. But I am now going to show you how a sentimentalist can make sense of the idea of practical reason(s), and this general approach will then be applied to the issue of self-sacrifice. (I have elsewhere [Slote 2014] argued that recent efforts to revive psychological egoism and deny the possibility of genuine self-sacrifice involve various forms of conceptual confusion.) Overall, I believe it will add to the plausibility of moral sentimentalism if we can show, as against rationalist doubts, that it can give a broad and plausible philosophical account of reasons for action.

Hume's later remarks in the *Treatise* relating calm passions to reason seem to be a conciliatory effort, in relation to the rationalism he was familiar with, to make room for practical reasons or rationality. But Hume, who was the first person ever to discuss empathy in any kind of systematic way (of course, he lacked that term and used 'sympathy' instead), never related empathy to practical reason(s); and if we bring in empathy, I think we can offer a sentimentalist account of practical rationality/reason that is more nuanced and has more explanatory power than

SACRIFICE AND MORAL PHILOSOPHY 121

anything Hume's remarks about calm passions make available to us. I think both prudential reasons and altruistic (or moral) reasons emerge out of certain emotions and, at least in the latter case, via mechanisms of empathy, and if we can spell this out, we may be then be in a position to say something useful about the rational justification of self-sacrifice.

2.

I want to begin by talking about prudential reasons, the reasons we have to pursue (or not undercut) our own overall or future well-being or happiness; but then I hope later to connect what I have said about prudential reasons with the kinds of altruistic reasons that are so often thought to be characteristic of and necessary to the moral life. And I don't propose at this point to argue against other views of prudence so much as to frame, in sentimentalist terms, an intuitively plausible and theoretically useful conception of prudential reasons that can then also help us understand the altruistic reasons of morality. Let's begin with an example.

Imagine a man trapped in a burning house. There are no accessible windows and only one accessible door, but he finds that that door is stuck. The distress and fear he initially felt on realizing the house was on fire then turns into a kind of desperation. He continues pushing on the door to see if he can make it open before the fire engulfs him, but he also starts banging on the door in order to attract the attention of anyone outside who might be able to help him open it (it is too late for anyone to quickly put out the fire).

The man clearly has (a) reason, (a) prudential reason, to try to escape through that door, but I want to add that that reason has to do with the emotions he feels while trying to escape. It is rational from the standpoint of prudence for someone trying to escape a raging fire to feel distress, fear and alarm at his situation, and if he finds the only possible avenue of escape to be blocked, it is entirely understandable that his distress and fear should turn into a kind of desperation. But one can go further with and by means of this initial example. It is an essential part of his being practically or prudentially rational in this situation that he should feel the kind of distress and/or fear we are attributing to him. (We are not talking about someone who wants or is trying to commit suicide.) He isn't indifferent to what is happening to him, and neither does he merely *prefer* to open the door and save his own life – that is, he doesn't treat the issue of life and (painful) death as if it were like choosing which of his two favorite flavors of ice cream he preferred on a given occasion. Rather, his attitude toward living, freedom from pain/suffering, and good health involves *caring* about these things, and caring about something means thinking it is important – which in turn involves emotion or at least a disposition to feel negative emotion when what one considers important is threatened or at risk and also positive emotion when the threat or risk doesn't eventuate.

I want to say that a normal, e.g. non-suicidal, rational person has or is disposed to have emotions like fear and distress when their (long-term) welfare or happiness is threatened in certain significant ways and like relief and joy if and when the threat doesn't materialize or is evaded. In my view, their overall prudential rationality *consists* in their having or being disposed to have such situationally based emotions: in other words, consists in their *caring* about such things.[1] But what can one then say about the particular situational reasons such a prudent person has? They have reason or a reason to promote or preserve their own present and future welfare, but in particular circumstances that reason is informed by, well, information about what the circumstances require of one in order to further the goal of one's own well-being. So the man in the burning house has prudential reason in general to try to promote, to care about promoting, his own future welfare, and in the circumstances that means trying to escape through the one door that seems to allow for an escape from the fire that is burning all around him. He has reason to try to escape through that door, but I think we can also say that his eagerness or strong desire to escape through that door is the *locus* of that reason.

Reasons for action, reasons to do one thing rather than another, are commonly supposed (by philosophers) to have motivational force. If one recognizes that one has a reason to do something – and the man in the burning house may at some level think that he has reason to try to escape through the one door – then one is at least to some extent motivated to act accordingly. The man is afraid of the fire, fears for his life, and in the circumstances as he knows them, that makes him want to escape through the one accessible door. But he doesn't merely *prefer* to escape through that door. In the circumstances he cares a great deal about getting through that door, and the caring, of course, leads to distress and perhaps even desperation as the door continually fails to yield to his pushing. And those emotional reactions are expressions of his caring, of his eagerness or strongly felt desire to get through that door. But I want to say that it is the emotional caring itself that constitutes his reason to try to escape through the given door.

Now what I am calling the caring is not some generalized state or disposition that is exemplified in all sort of different circumstances. A woman can feel hope, for example, at many times of her life but the hopes she has as a newly-wed are not the same hopes the feels when she later gets divorced and hopes to be able to salvage something good out of the remainder of her life. Similarly, when the man of our example cares strongly, even desperately, about getting through that door, he has a strongly felt desire to get through that door, and that desire, that state of caring, is not identical with any earlier episode of desire or caring. But as a particular psychological state that exists only in the given circumstances, the man's state of caring or strongly felt desire can be construed, in sentimentalist terms, as (the locus of) his situationally specific reason to try to get out through the one door. But these conclusions rest, at least partly, on the earlier-mentioned thesis that prudential rationality requires and rests on the disposition to have various sorts of emotions in various kinds of circumstances. The sentimentalist can, therefore, understand prudential rationality and reasons (reductively, if you will) in terms of emotion or sentiment.

3.

I would like now to use what we have just been saying about prudential rationality and prudential reasons to give an account of altruistic reasons that, as with prudential reasons, sees them as grounded in or constituted by various sentiments. But in order to extend our sentimentalist account in this way, empathy has to be brought into our discussion. The picture of moral rationality we arrive at is going to be more complex – but also, I think, somewhat more philosophically interesting and rewarding – than what we have just been saying about prudential rationality because it will intersect with widely influential present-day rationalist views about our reasons for action in a way that redounds, I believe, to the disadvantage of the latter – and I believe nothing I have just said about prudential rationality/reasons cuts as sharply and as significantly against ideas that have great currency in Western moral philosophy. I want to begin our discussion by saying some general things about how empathy is supposed to work here.

The kind of empathy I am going to focus on is what has been variously called emotional, associative or receptive empathy. There is also such a thing as projective empathy, or simulation, which involves putting oneself into the shoes or the head of another person. But emotional/receptive empathy, as the name implies, involves taking in the feelings of others in a way that one is very often unaware of: hence all the talk of empathic contagion or even osmosis. Whatever else associative/emotional empathy involves, it also is or contains a psychological mechanism (often said to be underlain by the functioning of mirror neurons), and I want to say that that mechanism allows not only for the interpersonal transmission of emotions, but for the interpersonal transmission of reasons to the extent they are grounded in relevant emotions. Just as (other things being equal) empathy transmits emotions more strongly when the person on the receiving end is (physically or personally) closer to the person whose emotions are being transmitted, it more strongly transmits the reasons for action of someone who needs help if they are closer to the person on the receiving end, thus giving the latter *more or stronger* reason to act helpfully the more strongly the first person's reason is transmitted by empathy. Bradford Cokelet once said to me in passing that empathy as such might give us reasons, but what I want to say is a bit different and more specific. It is not that having empathy for someone's fears or anxieties is itself automatically or obviously a reason to help them avoid what they fear because the fears could, after all, be irrational. Rather, empathy *transmits reasons* from one person to another and does so by reflecting and registering the emotions that accompany and/or constitute situationally prudential rationality, the fears that it is rational for someone to have if, as per our previous example, they seem to be trapped in a burning house and the strong concern such a person will have to get out of that house through what seems to be the only possible exit. But let me now embed these inchoate ideas in something more structured and definite.

Most philosophies and philosophers have been willing to grant that being prudent on one's own behalf is a condition of rational desire, choice and action. And that is how common sense views the matter too. If someone doesn't care about or act to protect their future health (or freedom from severe pain), we think and most philosophers have thought that they count as practically irrational: they have strong practical reasons to desire and act differently. Of course, on a sheer desire-based view of rationality, there might be nothing irrational in all of this: after all the person who doesn't act to ensure their later health or freedom from pain presumably doesn't *care* about these things, doesn't desire things to be any different, and such theories also typically presuppose that such a person needn't be under any strictly cognitive misapprehensions. But I am just going to set desire-based theories aside during our further discussion. Most of them end up being qualified to include a condition of rational consideration of one's desires that makes them approach or even extensionally coincide with the kind of prudential theory of self-interested rationality I have been and am going to be working with, and in any event I am trying to be commonsensical here, and prudential theories seem to conform to our antecedent ordinary intuitions about practical reasons and rationality better than other sorts of approaches. (This point is explained further and somewhat qualified in footnote 1.) It seems practically and prudentially irrational not to be concerned with one's future health or freedom from pain even if, or perhaps especially if, one has no present desire for future health or freedom from pain.

What is really controversial, however, is the frequently-made assumption that morality or moral considerations as such give all of us practical reasons for desiring things to be a certain way and for choosing or acting accordingly. Now you may say that the idea that morality offers practical reasons

SACRIFICE AND MORAL PHILOSOPHY

really isn't controversial because almost all philosophers think it does. And indeed most Western ethicists – Aristotelians, Kantians and even many utilitarians – are rationalists about morality and think that morally relevant considerations and explicit (valid) moral conclusions are automatically reason-giving. But I such rationalism doesn't in fact fit our ordinary commonsense thinking about reasons and rationality. The rationalist has to say that a psychopath who doesn't care about anyone else has (some non-egoistic) reason nonetheless to help someone who they know needs their help and may also have to say that there is something practically irrational about such a person if they lack any motivation to help others. But ordinary folk don't think in this way about psychopaths. They tend to regard the psychopath who doesn't care about anyone other than themselves as cold-hearted or even heartless, and they certainly think of them as morally criticizable or deficient (their actions reflect a lack of concern for and even malice toward others). But ordinary folk don't usually think of or criticize such a person as irrational, and to ordinary ways of seeing things it seems quite a stretch to claim that the psychopath has a (strong) reason to help others that they don't recognize and are never motivated to act on, as strong a reason as those of us who care about others (who we don't personally know) have for helping them.

In what follows I shall mention a line of response to this point that is available to the ethical rationalist, but also indicate how that response doesn't completely answer the objection I have just made to ethical rationalism. However, for the moment, I just want to emphasize that ethical or moral rationalism is far from self-evident or even commonsensically intuitive. And as we shall see, there are theoretical/philosophical reasons for doubting ethical rationalism and for recognizing a previously unsuspected foundational role for the emotions within practical reason(s) as directed toward other people. I believe that that foundational role operates through or by means of empathy, so let me spell out why I think such a view of emotion's role makes better theoretical or philosophical sense of the phenomena of ethics than any rationalistic approach. And my argument will be strictly a priori, even though it will refer to the empirical phenomenon/ concept of empathy.

Many people have said that empathy is an emotion, but we philosophers think we know better. We think that sympathy is an emotion, but that associative empathy is a *mechanism* whereby emotions like sympathy or fear or joy are transmitted 'osmotically' or 'contagiously' from one person to another. So the gist of what I am going to argue for now is that empathy is not only a mechanism for the transmission of emotions but also a mechanism for the transmission of reasons for action, where the transmission of the reasons of necessity and on a priori grounds operates *via the empathic transmission of emotions.*

Let me begin here by returning to the example of the man in the burning house and complicating it by bringing in the point of view of an observer who happens to be outside that house. As you are passing by a house one afternoon, you notice that it is on fire and that someone, trying desperately to escape the fire raging inside, is screamingly loudly and banging repeatedly on a stuck door that won't allow them to leave the house. So you go to help and pull on the door from the outside, and let's say that your combined strenuous efforts make the door come unstuck and that the person inside finally escapes through that door. We have previously assumed that the person inside the house has or had a pretty strong prudential reason to want to escape through that particular door. Perhaps there were no windows in that room, the person found himself there, and the fire was coming on fast. And, as I have mentioned, in such a situation the person facing such a fire will feel fear and some desperation if their most immediate means of escape seems blocked. That fear and perhaps even the desperation are in the circumstances rational from a practical point of view; they are what a rationally prudent person with a desire for self-preservation would or easily could feel in those circumstances. The person has reason to be afraid at the very least and to care strongly about getting through that one door.

Now the person outside (if I may switch from a second-person to a third-person reference) hears screams and violent banging from inside the house and recognizes the fear and desperation that are causing all that activity. They recognize the danger to the person inside and empathically register how the person inside is feeling about his situation, and they act on that basis. And I want to say that the reason the person inside the house has for trying to get out of that particular door is transmitted to the person outside through the latter's empathically feeling and identifying with what the other person feels, wants and cares about at that point. The fear and practical concern of the one are empathically conveyed to and felt by the other, and if the first has prudential reason to fear for his life and try to get through the door, then the latter has what we can call an empathic, moral or altruistic reason to help that person get through that door on the basis of the focused fear and concern that have been empathically conveyed to them.

But remember that this doesn't have to mean that empathy with someone automatically or always gives an empathizer reason to act on behalf of that other person or their desires. If someone's fear is irrational and bears no relation to actual prudence, if it is the fear of flying, for example, and is based on an irrational belief that flying is dangerous, then that fear may be conveyed empathically to an observer, but be validly discounted or qualified as a reason for helping them make a train reservation instead. The reason if any for helping them make such a reservation is not the danger of flying, but the fear itself as a state so unpleasant that one wouldn't want to prolong it for someone unnecessarily. And of course there will sometimes be reason not to help the person escape their fears but to want them to fly in a state of fear because if they don't, they are going to miss, say, their granddaughter's wedding.

So I am suggesting that it is only reasons, only emotions that make rational sense in prudential terms, that transmit rational force to those who empathically register the feelings of another. When I go along with the irrational fear of someone who wants to take a train instead of a plane, I am perhaps registering their present state of fear, but (according to the present view) that is not what gives me a non-prudential and moral or empathic reason to help them take the train, if I have it. What gives me such a reason, rather, is my registering of or sensitivity to the unpleasant feelings they will or would have *in the future* if they have or had to take a plane.

This (arguably *a priori*) philosophical picture of how reasons are transmitted and acquired roots such processes in epistemically-based emotion and so views (altruistic) practical reason as in important respects intrinsically involving emotion rather than as separate from, opposed to, or merely causally connected to emotion. And we have to now ask why we should accept such a theory when we already have available to us what looks like a much more straightforward rationalist/cognitivist approach to (altruistic) practical reasons that views them as transmitted to us through the non-emotional cognitive apprehension or recognition of other people's reasons. The origin of such an approach lies, I think, in Thomas Nagel's (1970) *The Possibility of Altruism*, though something like it can be found in the work of other recent ethical rationalists. Why should we bring in emotion when we already have this more familiar way of viewing things? I think we have to answer this question if the sentimentalist approach to reason transmission is to make any philosophical headway. But answer it I think we can, and our answer, by showing what the sentimentalist approach allows us to better explain, will give us good reason to accept our sentimentalist approach.

Nagel (1970) argues (roughly) that reasons transmit both across time within a given person and simultaneously between different individuals once they are correctly apprehended. Someone, for example, who says they recognize that they later will have a reason to do something, but who (in the absence of conflicting reasons) makes none of the known necessary preparations for doing that thing, shows himself not to have fully *apprehended* or *recognized* the future reason they claim to recognize or the reason they presently have to make preparations for later rational action. According to Nagel, they are cognitively dissociated from their future selves and in effect don't clearly see what will happen to them in the future as part of the same one life they are now leading. And similar points apply, for Nagel, to the recognition, apprehension or appreciation of reasons across persons. Someone who doesn't see the pain of another person as giving them some reason to help relieve that pain doesn't (on Nagel's view) fully acknowledge, apprehend or appreciate the reality of the other('s pain) or of the reason the other has for wanting to relieve their own pain.

Now I think there are some important aspects of the transmission of reasons for action that this rationalistic theory cannot account for, and this is something that Nagel himself actually seems to acknowledge at one point in his book. But before I get into this problematic aspect of this rationalist account and explain why the sentimentalist approach doesn't face similar problems, I would like to consider a more immediate objection that someone might make to Nagel's view.

The immediate objection is that it seems implausible to suppose, as Nagel's view must, that a psychopath doesn't really or fully grasp the reality of those whom they are motivationally indifferent or hostile to and the reality of what such people actually feel. Psychopathic or sociopathic con artists are notoriously capable of 'getting inside the heads' of their intended victims, so how can the rationalist say that they lack a reason or motivation to help rather than hurt such people only because they don't grasp the reality of what or whom they are meeting and/or dealing with? Nagel and other rationalists assume that the normal person who grasps the reality, say, of another person's pain will automatically have a reason to help that person that translates into their having at least some motivation to do so. And I have no desire to question that assumption. But, then, if the con artist doesn't have a reason or motivation of this kind and if that lack of reason and/or motivation reflects, as Nagel might claim, the con artist's failure to grasp or appreciate the reality, say, of the other person's pain, what makes the difference here? Why, to put things as John McDowell (1997) does, isn't the pain of the other salient for the con artist the way it is for the normal person?

Well, let me suggest that empathy may make the difference here between a psychopathic con artist and a normal or moral person. Psychopaths may be able to get into the heads of others, but, as I have already pointed out, this is or may be what in the literature of psychology is called projective empathy, and they characteristically lack the ability to empathically feel what others are feeling. That is, they lack the capacity for associative or receptive empathy and feel joy at the other's pain rather than feeling the other's pain. So if a psychopath fails to appreciate certain facts about another's suffering, fails to see those facts as salient in a way that would motivate them toward helping the other person, that may be precisely because they lack the capacity for a kind of empathy that involves sharing or sharing in others' feelings. But if one has to bring in the absence of empathy to explain the difference between what the normal person (cognitively) appreciates and has reason/motivation to do and what the psychopath or sociopath fails to (cognitively) appreciate and fails to have a reason/motivation to do, then one's account of reasons has to bring in a sentimentalist element that undercuts the strictly rationalistic character of what Nagel initially proposed. It can no longer separate the cognitive and the motivational from the emotional in the way rationalism essentially seeks to do. (This is not, again, to question the tight connection the rationalist seeks to draw between the full cognitive apprehension of certain facts and relevant motivation to act.)

In that case, the view we end up with when we press Nagel's rationalism in the above manner is very close to and may eventually force one toward the sentimentalist ideas about the transmission of reasons I outlined earlier. But now I want to mention some further considerations that favor the sentimental view of transmission over any kind of pure rationalism about such transmission *in regard to normal non-sociopathic personalities*. Nagel's view as it stands has a hard time dealing with the psychopath's lack of moral motivation or reasons, but it also cannot account for differences in the strength/force of the interpersonal transmission of reasons in various cases involving very normal people.

For example, we typically empathize more with family members than with strangers, and that means that the pain distress of family members empathically transmits itself to us more strongly than the pain distress of mere strangers does. Because of the way empathy operates on our relations with others, therefore, we tend to feel more sympathetic, altruistic concern for family members than for strangers who may have similar problems. *And there is reason to infer from this that we have more reason to be concerned with family members than with strangers we meet or people we only know about second hand.* That, at least, is what naturally follows out of our earlier view that traces interpersonally transmitted reasons to processes of empathy, and in itself such a view doesn't seem at all implausible. But a purely rationalist theory of reason transmission à la Nagel has no way of explaining such differences in the strength of the altruistic reasons we have. For all it says, the reason I have to relieve the evident pain of a family member is no stronger than the reason I have to relieve the evident pain of a stranger I have just met. So such a theory doesn't in itself tell us that when we have to choose between helping a suffering family member and helping a suffering stranger, we typically have more reason to help the family member, and this last assumption is something we certainly should want to be able to support and justify with a theory of practical reasons.[2]

At the very least, therefore, Nagel's rationalism seems radically incomplete as a theory of (altruistic) reasons and of reason transmission. It can explain the fact that reasons are transmitted, but not the difference we would tend to assume there is between the strength of the reason we have to help a family member and that of the reason we have to help a total stranger. And Nagel himself seems to recognize this problem: he allows

that there may be reasons more specific or specialized than any he has dealt
with that differentiate self and other and different classes of others, but
claims that 'the acknowledgement of prima facie reasons to help others [in
general] is a significant result' (1970, 127f). And he goes on to say (1970,
133) that his theory of the objective (i.e. agent-neutral or impartial) reasons
everyone has to help everyone else doesn't explain why 'an individual is
justified in paying more attention ... to the needs of those close to him than
to the problems of humanity at large'.

So there are differences in the strengths of our reasons vis-à-vis others
that Nagel's *The Possibility of Altruism* doesn't explain at all, much less
explain in terms of his theory of how objective reasons are transmitted. But
the view I outlined above does both of those things at the same time. It
explains the difference in force or strength between our reasons to help
family members or friends and our reasons to help others in terms of the
difference in the force or strength with which, say, the distraught pain of a
family member and the distraught pain of a stranger are empathically
transmitted to us. And similar arguments can be applied to all the other
areas where empathy underlies differences in our moral reactions (and
judgments).

Thus when such a view of the central and foundational moral role of
empathy is applied to the transmission of reasons for action, it can tell us
plausible things about our altruistic/moral reasons that Nagel's account in
The Possibility of Altruism doesn't tell us, and although Nagel (1986) later
sought to say more about how and why we have, say, more reason to help
family members than to help strangers (and about other sorts of moral
distinctions we make in and about our lives), the resultant picture was
much more impressionistic and less systematic, organized and explanatory
than what one gets from tracing interpersonal reasons back to empathy and
empathically transmitted feeling. I don't think any other ethical rationalist
has done any better with this specific issue so on the whole our sentimentalist account of (the) reasons (that pertain to morality) has much to
recommend it and is more useful, I think, for understanding the actual
altruistic/moral reasons people have than anything that comes out of ethical
rationalism. For it not only takes in our reasons to prefer family and a
whole host of similar, familiar empathically-based moral reasons, but even
explains the psychopath's failure to have *any reason* to help others.

I know that we would like to think we can give the psychopath or egoist
a rational argument to show them that they have reason to behave better
than they do, if only they could recognize what philosophy has to teach
them. But I don't think psychopaths are going to respond motivationally to
any of our philosophical arguments, and that may be in part because they
simply lack any (non-egoistic) reason to care about or help others and
because one simply cannot argue people into having reasons of this sort. As

I mentioned earlier, it is commonsensically plausible to suppose that psychopaths simply lack the reasons we think we have for helping others, and the difference here – and this too is a point of common sense – seems to lie in the fact that the psychopath is incapable of associative empathy with others, never feels what others feel, and for that (causal-explanatory) reason never really cares about anyone else. The sentimentalist (i. e. emotion-based) theory of reasons I have sketched can account for these plausible facts or assumptions much better than any form of ethical rationalism can, and so, in addition to the way the transmission of reasons works in ordinary people, the just-mentioned presumptive facts about psychopaths also support our sentimentalist theory of altruistic reasons. In other words, what we have said about the (differential) transmission of reasons between normal people supports our account, but so too does what it can say in intuitively plausible terms about psychopaths.

Alternatively, and reversing engines, we can say that our ability to account plausibly for the fact and *variable strength* of the 'normal' interpersonal transmission of reasons for action in empathic/sentimentalist terms also gives us a philosophical reason to believe that psychopaths altogether lack such altruistic reasons. It therefore gives us reason to strongly resist the general rationalist tendency to believe that *everyone* has reason to help others. Sentimentalism supports a more nuanced and less universalistic conception of altruistic reasons, once the sheer reality of psychopathy is taken into account, and that conception ties (certain aspects of) practical reason, emotion and empathy together much more tightly than the traditionally-understood dualism of reason and emotion would regard as possible or plausible. And within that tighter, conceptual relationship, it is emotion and empathy that have the foundational, grounding role.[3]

4.

However, before we conclude our general discussion of practical reasons, I think I should say just a bit more about the practical reasons of conscientiousness. Most of us take it that a situationally conscientious person, a person who is concerned to do what is morally required in a given situation, has some reason on that basis to actually do what is or what they take to be required of them. And I put things in this way because I don't want to assume that a psychopath is capable of having such reasons. Arguably, the psychopath is never morally conscientious and never feels guilt if they do what is considered wrong. And it is not even clear that they have the moral concepts that would allow them to speak meaningfully of what is right or wrong or morally required. I have offered (philosophical) reasons (in Slote 2010) for considering the psychopath to lack moral concepts precisely because they lack the capacity for emotional/associative empathy, but (again) I do not

132 SACRIFICE AND MORAL PHILOSOPHY

think we need to go into that particular issue here. The more interesting point, from the perspective of the present essay, concerns the reasons a conscientious non-psychopathic person has to do what they (let us assume correctly) take to be morally required of them. Do these represent a basically new kind of practical reason we have not yet considered?

But first a point about terminology. The reader may wonder why I am distinguishing reasons of conscience from altruistic reasons and I think I owe them at least a brief explanation. Altruism, as it is commonly understood, involves an intrinsic desire to help other people, and such desire is commonly regarded as involving an emotional connection to or involvement with others. But some rationalists, e.g. Kant, hold that the commitment to doing what is morally required of one doesn't entail that one have any feeling toward those whom a sense of duty impels one to help; and Kant never mentions empathy as in any way involved in moral conscientiousness. In any event, contemporary Kantians hold that altruistic reasons (e.g. reasons of or based in the 'natural virtue' of compassion) are quite different from reasons of conscience. But this difference is less plausible if one assumes a sentimentalist picture of what is involved in our moral concepts and thus in anyone's desire to do what is morally required of them. If (as I argued at length in 2010), moral concepts involve empathy, then altruistic reasons and reasons of conscience that involve thinking about moral right and wrong are not all that far apart. Indeed, and I hope you can see this without further argument, if moral concepts involve empathy, then reasons of conscientiousness cannot exist apart from altruistic reasons.

My argument (in 2010) claims that our capacity for making moral judgments depends on our having second-order empathy with the first-order empathy moral agents feel toward those they want to help. Such second-order empathy cannot exist in someone who lacks first-order empathy, and that means that when I feel it would be wrong for me to do something and have a reason of conscience not to do that thing, my having such a reason rests on my ability to have first-order reasons to help based on first-order empathy. So although I hold (Slote 2010) that there is something second-order about considerations of conscience, those considerations depend on the kind of first-order empathy with the feelings of others that I earlier argued is fundamental to our emotion-laden reasons to help others. Altruistic reasons and conscientious ones are more closely or deeply related than rationalism allows for.

So sentimentalism can offer an account of prudential, altruistic and conscientious reasons for action in contemporary terms and has very specific and marked advantages over ethical rationalism not only (as I have argued in Slote 2010) as an account of right and wrong and of moral semantics, but also within rationalism's home territory, as a general

5.

But now it is time to apply all of the above to the notion of self-sacrifice. Self-sacrifice can occur at the behest of conscience, but in many cases, indeed the most central ones for our moral imagination, self-sacrifice occurs because what we feel for another person and what they need motivationally overrides or preempts certain concerns of self-interest. What we have said above can give us a model of how this could occur. We said earlier that we tend to feel the suffering of another more strongly if they are someone we know and love rather than a total stranger, and empathy, of course, can help us explain this sort of phenomenon. But what was assumed in that discussion and is presupposed in every discussion of empathy I know of is that empathy tends to be more strongly aroused the *greater* the suffering or danger that is at issue; and this holds true whether the person arousing our empathy is someone close to us or is some distant person we only know *about*. This can give us a basic model of how to understand the possibility and reality of self-sacrifice.

To begin with, the quantity or size of suffering can make a difference even as between someone we know and love and someone we are merely acquainted with or only know about. For example, if I come home from work early in order to take my child out for an ice cream treat, my plans will probably change if I learn that my neighbor's house is in danger of being internally flooded as a result of a leak and I am in a position to help them out. My empathy with my neighbor's plight can empathically outweigh my child's likely disappointment at not being able to eat ice cream, and it is characteristic of the empathy of morally good or (as we sentimentalists and many people in general nowadays like to say) caring people that it can move one toward helping a mere acquaintance or relative stranger in great need of help in preference to providing some nice thing for someone one is more intimate with or generally cares more about.

Why shouldn't the same thing be possible with regard to a choice between helping or not hurting oneself and helping some stranger whose need at some moment is obviously greater than one's own? For example, in the case described earlier in which someone hears a person trapped in a house trying to escape via a certain door, it is possible that the person who hears the trapped person's attempts to escape is wearing a suit, a suit that will need cleaning if they go and help the trapped individual by pulling hard on the stuck door from the outside. But a good person, a caring person, won't pay heed to such self-interested considerations if the other person's need, what is at stake for the other person, is so much greater than any aversion one might have to having to pay for one's suit to be cleaned. A person trapped inside a burning house cares much more about escaping that they ever could about keeping a suit of theirs clean and neat, and even if empathy typically cannot make us care as much about another person's escaping as that person cares about his own escape, it can have enough force for us to overwhelm or obliterate any concern for our being inconvenienced by having to get a suit cleaned. We can through empathy feel someone's large or powerful reason to want to escape a burning house more strongly than we register our own smaller reason or concern to keep our suit neat and clean.

If someone is not like this, if they hesitate or more than hesitate to help a trapped person escape a fire because they don't want to get their suit dirty, then they are less caring as individuals than what we would expect most individuals to be like, and we can say that empathy operates less strongly in them than it arguably operates in good people. They are closer to a psychopath than most of us think we are, and they do not therefore share the altruistic reasons most of us have to help others in situations like the one of the man trapped in a burning house. This doesn't prevent us from condemning them morally, however. A good person's empathy operates in the stronger fashion, and if, as in the just-mentioned case, empathy doesn't operate in that fashion, then that shows the person in question not to be a caring individual. *Moral Sentimentalism* argued that actions that show us as lacking in empathy and/or caringness are morally wrong, so we can morally criticize the person who doesn't want to get their suit dirty, even while holding them to lack the altruistic reason or reasons most of us would have when faced with a man trapped in a burning building. (Similar criticism applies to those who refuse to help people of different race, religion, ethnicity or sexual orientation.)[4]

Only one more point then needs to be added. I have suggested that in most cases someone feels their own need more strongly than an empathic observer would, but does this have to be the case? It seems possible to me that a parent might feel a child's (present) need more strongly than the child herself does, and this opens up at least the possibility that a parent, friend or lover might sacrifice their own greater need to the lesser need of another person. All that would be necessary is that the parent or other would feel that lesser need more strongly than they feel their own greater self-interested need. Why couldn't empathy sometimes be so powerful as to make our concern for another stronger than what that person feels for herself or what we would feel if we were in their situation? I see no reason to rule out such possibilities, and if we don't then the way is clear for there to be cases of extreme self-sacrifice understandable in terms of extraordinary strengths of empathy. I cannot now prove to you that such cases exist, but in the light of what we have been arguing here, this possibility seems ripe for further moral-theoretic exploration.

Moreover, if such hyper-empathy *is* possible, it wouldn't necessarily follow that the person who felt another's distress more strongly than that other person would have reason or be rational to make some extraordinary sacrifice that was motivated by their extraordinary empathy. For one might question whether one person's reasons can be *magnified as reasons* through unusual empathic receptivity. This is another question whose further exploration is suggested by what we have been saying here. But in fact sentimentalists and rationalists (see Nagel 1986) alike need to be able to say more both about how or whether *enormous self-sacrifice* is possible and about how or whether such self-sacrifice can be rational if and when it occurs.

Notes

1. The issue of what to say about suicidal or depressed people who don't care about going on living or even, perhaps, about avoiding extreme pain, is a complex one. Where the impulse to suicide realistically reflects the facts of a given person's situation, there is probably no reason to describe them as irrational or imprudent; so perhaps we can say that where they aren't being realistic, their error or failing is more cognitive than practical. If they count as irrational and/or imprudent, it is because they don't or can't register or carefully enough learn the relevant facts. Similar points can be made about people who are depressed. The idea that putative instances of purely practical irrationality (*à la* Kant) are better conceived as defects of cognitive rationality is a major implication of Thomas Nagel's (1970) *The Possibility of Altruism* – though Nagel himself doesn't explicitly emphasize this point in the book itself. And in effect what I have just been saying about the suicidal and depressed represents a sentimentalist borrowing from what Nagel was saying on behalf of rationalism. The sentimentalist tends to see what are historically regarded as forms of pure practical irrationality as actually instancing some sort of cognitive defect (as well), and not just in the instances mentioned earlier in this footnote. For example and as we shall see later in this essay, the sentimentalist (or *this* sentimentalist) thinks it makes more sense to see the empathically deficient psychopath as cognitively out of touch with certain aspects of others than as failing to respond adequately to practical reasons they in fact possess. But such a view of things, as taken either by the rationalist or by the sentimentalist, runs up against the objection, initially launched by J. L. Mackie (1977) that it posits a kind of 'objective prescriptivity' in our relations with value matters, i.e. that it treats certain cognitive apprehensions of objective realities as intrinsically capable of also motivating us. Mackie thinks such a notion is 'queer', and people like Nagel and myself need to be able to answer this objection. I have given such an answer elsewhere (see Slote 2018; published in side-by-side English-language and Chinese-language versions). However, this is not the time or place to pursue this issue further.

2. Nor would it help Nagel here to point out that common-sense (rational) intuition tells us that we *ceteris paribus* have more reason to help family members than to help strangers or distant others. This still wouldn't explain *why* such a difference exists, and that is precisely what the appeal to empathic transmission allows us to explain.

3. We in the West have conceived of reason as separate or separable from emotion, and this has been thought not only about theoretical reason but about practical reason as well. The present essay gives us (theoretical) reason to doubt or deny that practical rationality is separable from emotion. Rather, as we have seen, it involves and is grounded in emotion. But then there is the other side of rationality, epistemic or theoretical rationality, and the question can naturally arise whether this important dimension or kind of rationality can be as conceptually separate from emotion as we have standardly and traditionally supposed. For reasons given elsewhere, I think the answer to this question has to be in the negative. All theoretical reasons and all theoretical reasoning are tied to belief, and I have argued at length in *A Sentimentalist Theory of the Mind* (Slote 2014) that belief, *all* belief, intrinsically involves emotional dispositions. If that is so, then both the main forms of rationality cannot be separated from and necessarily involve emotion(s). This totally undermines the received Western view that reason and emotion are separate and/or separable. (Confucian philosophy, by the way, doesn't make this assumption.) For the same (theoretical) reasons it also turns out that *there is no such thing as pure reason*. What I have just been telling you therefore adumbrates a critique of pure reason quite opposite to what Kant meant by the title of his most famous book.

4. Even when someone is unconscious or too ill to feel any relevant reason-constituting emotions, we can empathize with their (in many cases obvious) previous emotion-involving desires, fears and aspirations and have reason to help them on that basis.

Disclosure Statement

No potential conflict of interest was reported by the author.

References

Kripke, S. 1980. *Naming and Necessity*. Oxford: Blackwell.
Mackie, J. L. 1977. *Ethics: Inventing Right and Wrong*. Harmondsworth: Penguin.
McDowell, J. 1997. "Virtue and Reason." In *Virtue Ethics*, edited by R. Crisp and M. Slote. Oxford: Oxford University Press.
Nagel, T. 1970. *The Possibility of Altruism*. Oxford: Oxford University Press.
Nagel, T. 1986. *The View From Nowhere*. New York: Oxford University Press.
Slote, M. 2010. *Moral Sentimentalism*. New York: Oxford University Press.
Slote, M. 2014. *A Sentimentalist Theory of the Mind*. New York: Oxford University Press.
Slote, M. 2018. *The Philosophy of Yin and Yang*. Beijing: Commercial Press.

Demandingness and Boundaries Between Persons

Edward Harcourt

ABSTRACT

Demandingness objections to consequentialism often claim that consequentialism underestimates the moral significance of the stranger/special other distinction, mistakenly extending to strangers demands it is proper for special others to make on us, and concluding that strangers may properly demand anything of us if it increases aggregate goodness. This argument relies on false assumptions about our relations with special others. Boundaries between ourselves and special others are both a common and a good-making feature of our relations with them. Hence, demandingness objections that rely on the argument in question fail. But the same observations about our relations with special others show that there are many demands special others may not properly make, and since we cannot be *more* guilty of unjustified partiality in insisting on boundaries between ourselves and strangers than on boundaries between ourselves and special others, there are – as demandingness objections maintain – some demands strangers may not properly make on us.

1. Introduction

It's likely that after several decades of philosophical discussion, there is no longer such a thing as *the* demandingness objection to an ethical theory, but rather a family of related objections. I shall call a demandingness objection to an ethical theory an objection that says that there is some demand such that (a) the theory makes it and (b) it is not the case that we are obliged to fulfil it.

I hope this formulation makes it clear why I'm going to make nothing here of the distinction between demandingness and overdemandingness (Van Ackeren and Kühler 2015; Benn 2015; Murphy 2000), since it is possible to characterize a demandingness *objection* without using the word 'overdemanding'. The argument also proceeds independently of the characterization (Van Ackeren, forthcoming) of a demandingness objection as a type of objection that appeals distinctively to costs of the demanded action to the agent. This is partly for the theoretical reason that, at least as far as consequentialism is concerned, demandingness objections framed in terms of costs to the agent look as if they treat agents as victims of their own actions, so they look set to inherit the weakness of 'victim-based' objections (Scheffler 1982) generally. But it is also because the argument of the paper is supposed to go through (if it goes through at all) independently of any theoretical account of the basis on which a demand is alleged to be improper. To anticipate, my thought is rather that if we can agree that certain demands are improper – for whatever reason – even when they arise from special others, then it should be easier to concede that they are also improper when they arise from strangers, and these are generally the demands that most trouble those who wish to press demandingness objections.

Demandingness was originally flagged as a type of objection – whether or not it's successful – to act-consequentialism (Scheffler 1982; cf. Williams 1977). It has been argued more recently that other ethical theories may be open to a similar type of objection (Swanton 2009; Hills 2010; Van Ackeren and Sticker 2015; Pinheiro Walla 2015); but also that demandingness is to be expected of morality generally, so if according to a particular theoretical reconstruction of it, morality is demanding, then that is a virtue not a defect of the theory (Chappell 2009). I want to focus here solely on act-consequentialism, though the demandingness – such as it is – of morality generally will come back at the end. The strategic focus is on what I take to be the common core of any demandingness objection to act-consequentialism, namely that act-consequentialism implies that there is no demand strangers may not properly make on us if it increases aggregate goodness, and that *pace* act-consequentialism there is at least some such demand. (This formulation is just a substitution-instance of the schematic demandingness objection in the previous paragraph.) This also helps me to circumscribe the type of act-consequentialist I have in mind for the rest of the paper: concessive act-consequentialists – who agree that there are some demands strangers may not properly make on us even if they increase aggregate goodness – are not in the frame, so the phrase 'consequentialism' (etc.) should also be understood henceforth as an abbreviation for the non-concessive variety of act-consequentialism.

I want to focus for much of the paper, however, not on the common core of any demandingness objection to consequentialism, but on a particular type of demandingness objection to consequentialism, which is distinguished not just by the conclusion it tries to reach (which is common to them all), but by an argument it relies on and which (I argue) is fallacious. If some people think the particular type of objection I have in mind is *not* a demandingness objection, but better labelled in some other way, I am fine with that: although as the 'demandingness' label gets baggier over time so the risk of mislabelling decreases, it is the substance of the objection rather than the labelling that I am interested in.[1]

First I am going to characterize the particular type of objection I have in mind, and sketch some points of overlap between it and certain other objections to consequentialism which are sometimes labelled 'the demandingness objection' and sometimes distinguished from it. Next I am going to draw attention to some very ordinary features of relationships with special others, which are familiar from ordinary life but not (in my view) made enough of in discussions of demandingness. Then I shall argue that these phenomena undermine the force of the particular argument relied on by the demandingness objection to consequentialism I characterize, though they also help us to diagnose what some people have found disturbing about the demandingness of consequentialism itself. Finally I argue that these same phenomena can be used to revive a version of the demandingness objection which preserves the 'common core' without relying on the fallacious argument. But I remain neutral as to how far these considerations block the force of non-consequentialist, or pre-theoretical, demands which the suffering of others makes upon us.

2. Self, Strangers and Special Others: A Common Version of the Demandingness Objection Characterized

The particular objection I have in mind, roughly characterized, is that in its account of what we are obliged to do, consequentialism makes too little of the difference between, on the one hand, myself and my special others and, on the other, strangers. There is more than one way in which it might be said to do this. Thus, consequentialism requires that I maximize aggregate goodness, impartially conceived. (For variations on what consequentialism requires, but which are irrelevant to the general point, see Hooker 2009.) Compliance with this requirement may be consistent with what I pre-theoretically take to be my obligations towards my special others. For example, my children benefit from receiving birthday presents from me not only in so far as these objects are pleasant or useful (etc.) but in so far as they are from me. Were I on the other hand to send birthday presents to children I have never met, they would (presumably) benefit from them only in so far as they were pleasant, useful (etc.), so plausibly my children would benefit more, so personal obligation and impartial utility-maximization converge. But they might very easily not converge – for instance if my children already have a lot more pleasant and useful stuff than most other people. So, according to consequentialism (and of course making many other assumptions), I ought to send the presents to the people who need it more, while 'intuition' says I should at least sometimes give them to my children.

This objection locates consequentialism's indifference to the stranger/special other distinction at the beneficiary end of things. Prior to theory, it looks as if my children's claims on me as beneficiaries of my actions are at least often greater than those of strangers because of their special relation to me; whereas consequentialism, because it sees no moral significance in that special relation *per se*, sees strangers' claims on me as beneficiaries only in the light of the size of the benefits. Though related to it in some way, this is *not* the particular objection I am interested in.

The particular objection I am interested in locates consequentialism's indifference to the stranger/special other distinction in what it is proper for (on the one hand) special others and, on the other, strangers to demand *from* me – if you like, in the difference in the *sacrifices* it is proper to ask me to make for strangers versus those it is proper to ask me to make for special others. Obviously there is a correlation with the previous objection, in so far as my benefit to another may be a cost (*sc.* sacrifice) to me. But the correlation is imperfect, since in the case of special others more often (I think) than in the case of strangers, benefits to them are *benefits* to me, not costs (e.g. I like giving my children presents they like). Be that as it may, I am interested in cases where compliance with obligation *is* a cost (sc. sacrifice) to me, which it can be where both strangers and special others are concerned, though very possibly in different types of situation in each case. The objection is that consequentialism is indifferent to the stranger/special other distinction in so far as (according to consequentialism) the fact that someone bears no special relation to me makes no difference to the propriety of the demands they can make on me. But, the objection runs, the demands – prior to theory – which it is proper for special others to make on me are of quite a different order to the demands it is proper for strangers to make. So consequentialism's indifference to the stranger/ special other distinction in respect of the propriety of the demands they can make on me is a fault in the theory.

Before I move on, the term 'obligation' requires a gloss. It is often observed that consequentialism finds moral obligations in obscure corners of human experience where prior to theory none are visible. Thus if I am morally obliged to maximize aggregate happiness and the only choice on offer is to brush my hair or comb my hair, then if combing is more comfortable and nothing else is relevant, I am morally obliged to comb my hair not brush it. Though there may well be material in this odd result for an objection to consequentialism, I am going to set that aside. The point for now is that in comparing consequentialism with untheorized practical thought on the importance of the stranger/special other distinction, what we have on the consequentialist side will always be claims made upon me by my *moral* obligations, whereas pretheoretically others' claims on me may not so readily be classifiable as moral (though sometimes they will be). I simply want to flag this asymmetry in order to say that it ought not to matter.

This particular demandingness objection – if that's the right label for it – is closely related to certain other objections to consequentialism that are often made by invoking the idea of 'personal commitments' or 'projects'.

Indeed these latter are what Mulgan (2001, 4) calls *the* demandingness objection: 'The common objection that Consequentialism is too demanding, as it leaves the agent too little room (time, resources, energy) for her own projects or interests ... I ... call ... the Demandingness Objection'. (These same objections are also made – less happily – under the heading of 'integrity': Williams 1977; Hooker 2009.) One reason why it is said, rightly or wrongly, that consequentialism is at fault in setting no limits (consistently with aggregate utility-maximization) to the demands which it is proper for strangers to make on me is that these demands are liable to interfere with my projects or commitments. (This point is so familiar I hope I don't need to spell it out.) Special others, by contrast, *are* commitments of mine (though they may not be my only commitments). Williams (1977), for example, uses the word 'commitment' in just this elastic way so their possible objects include (rightly) persons, countries, causes, activities and more besides, and the aptness of placing persons on this list is underscored by the fact that one of the things consequentialist demands are so often said to interfere with are precisely close relationships with other persons. But of course if persons, or our special relationships with particular persons, are among my commitments and commitments (by definition) contribute centrally to the goodness or worthwhileness of my life, the demands these make on me cannot interfere with the goodness or worthwhileness of my life in anything like the same way as consequentialist moral obligation. As Mulgan (2007, 97) puts it, consequentialism (allegedly) is at fault because 'it does not allow you to give special weight to your own interests and projects, and to those of people who are close to you': that is, the objection goes, consequentialism wrongly blurs the line between special others and strangers in a way that it is quite right to blur the line between special others and oneself.

Another affinity is with the so-called 'separateness of persons' objection (or objections) to consequentialism (Rawls 1971, 27; Mulgan 2001, 17 ff). For various reasons, but basically because consequentialism is interested only in aggregate utility, not in whose utility it is, consequentialism is accused of paying insufficient regard to the 'separateness of persons': it is inclined to a view of the world not as composed of distinct persons, but as a 'sea of preferences' (Williams 1985, 88). Thus it (rightly or wrongly) thinks one person's benefit can compensate another's harm, overlooking the pretheoretical point that compensation must be *to* the person harmed.

3. The Objection Developed: 'no demand is improper where we are one with the other'

Indeed, it would not be putting too fine a point on it to say that, according to the 'projects and commitments' version of the demandingness objection, consequentialism *gets it right* about the demands it is proper for special others to make on me, because they are indeed limitless, and errs – as of course it would do, because it regards the stranger/special other distinction as having no moral significance on its own – just in so far as it generalizes the propriety of demands of that sort *beyond* special others to strangers. This point can be made over again in relation to the separateness of persons objection. What is *especially* objectionable about consequentialism, the thought runs, is that it treats as an inseparable mass the utility of persons who are strangers to one another: as Mulgan (2007, 103) puts it, 'the boundaries between one life and another are not as morally significant as we [pretheoretically] think ... [T]there is no reason why I should be more concerned for my own future experiences than for anyone else's'. But where persons are my special others – where I am bound to them by special ties of whatsoever sort – then perhaps it is realistic to imagine that a harm to me can be compensated by a benefit to someone close to me, for I and my special others really aren not as separate as I am from strangers. Once again, a diagnosis of the consequentialist mistake could be expressed as the thought that consequentialism gets it right in relation to special others – there are indeed *some* people, i.e. my special others, such that my own future experiences are no more valuable to me than theirs – but goes wrong in generalizing its demands to strangers as well.

This diagnosis joins hands with yet another current of thought which is often not explicitly anti-consequentialist, but fuels my analysis of the particular demandingness objection I'm examining – namely that 'I am not an island', that my own interests extend beyond the boundaries of me to my special others (Bradley [1876] 2012, 254; Sidgwick 1907, 501). This is explicit for example in Aristotle (1984). It could be described as the moral of Anthony Price's *Love and Friendship in Plato and Aristotle (1989)* but the Epilogue may stand for the current of thought as a whole:

> It is necessary that individual life should diffuse itself for another, in another, and, if need be, give itself ... [T]his diffusion is not contrary to nature ... [L]iving nature does not halt at this cut-and-dried, and logically inflexible division [of mine and thine] ... It is our whole nature that is sociable... it cannot be completely egoistic even if it wished to be. We are everywhere open, everywhere invading and invaded. (Price 1989, 206, citing Guyau [1885] 2008)

David Brink (1997, 129) also expresses the view, whether or not he is speaking accurately for Aristotle:

> Aristotle thinks that the way in which a (decent) parent nurtures, educates, and provides opportunities for her child establishes psychological relations between them that justify us in claiming that the child's well-being extends the well-being of the parent (1161b 17-29). It is this same sort of psychological interdependence that exists between friends who share thought and discussion that justifies each in seeing the other as extending his interests

SACRIFICE AND MORAL PHILOSOPHY

and, hence, as another-self. But then we can see how Aristotle can think that friendship involves concern for the friend's own sake and yet admits of eudaimonist justification. If B extends A's interests, then B's interests are a part of A's. This is true when A and B are the same person and when they are different people. My friend's good is a part of my own overall good in just the way that the well-being of my future self is part of my overall good.

However, while some writers have followed Plato and Aristotle in emphasizing *friendship* or *love* – i.e. relations in which we stand to some (small) subset of others – as the route by which self-interest expands, others have stressed routes of expansion which are capable of taking in *all* others. As an example of this tendency, Brink cites T. H. Green and F. H. Bradley, who claim that we are all one, thus giving a psychological or metaphysical justification for their view:

> Like other idealists, such as F. H. Bradley, Green thinks that the proper conception of self-realization involves the good of others as a constituent part. For Bradley, this kind of reconciliation is a direct consequence of a fundamentally anti-individualist metaphysics that treats persons as aspects of an interpersonal organic unity ... I must view others as my "alter egos" ... and [in order to realize myself] aim at a common good. (Brink 1997, 133-135)

In contemporary philosophy, the leading representative of this type of view – not arguing via identification with others or via sociability, but rather via the supposed metaphysical feebleness of the distinction between persons – is surely Derek Parfit (1984).

Obviously the stronger the premiss in these theories of the extension of self-interest, the further such a theory could go towards showing that we should indeed make nothing of the stranger/special other distinction. But at the same time the more likely it is that the premiss – at least if it rests on the idea of a psychological *bond* between myself and all persons, to say nothing of the supposed non-existence of persons as basic individuals – is false. The problem is just that not very many others *are* (to any given person) special. As for example Sidgwick (1907, 501) emphasizes, there does not seem to be a bond of the requisite kind between myself and everybody, so although my self-interest extends beyond me, typically it does not extend very far. Pressing that point into the service of a demandingness objection to consequentialism, one would stress the bonds between myself and my special others, the feebleness of the distinction between my interest and theirs, the benefits (e.g. pleasure) rather than the costs of transferring goods from me to them, and so on, and then locate the demandingness objection in the differences in all those respects between my relations to those special others and my relations to strangers. This particular version of the demandingness objection thus says that consequentialism goes wrong because it underrates the moral significance of the difference between strangers and special others, because a boundary which it is quite proper not to draw between oneself and special others thanks to the bonds between oneself and them – the phenomena emphasized by e.g. Plato, Aristotle and Sidgwick – consequentialism *also* refuses to draw between special others and strangers. Otherwise put, consequentialism underrates the moral significance of the difference between strangers and special others by modelling its incorrect conception of our relation to strangers on a *correct* conception of our relation to special others, because special others are special in so far as they are 'parts of us', and so are not – in the relevant sense – separate from us, or (in an alternative vocabulary) they constitute 'commitments' of ours; whereas strangers are separate, and do not constitute commitments.

4. An Assumption Challenged: Boundaries between Ourselves and Our Special Others

The strategy I want to pursue in this paper is almost the reverse to that of the demandingness objection I have just characterized. Of course I do not want to deny that sacrifices for special others can sometimes be pleasant, that the interests of special others are sometimes my own interest, and so on. However, I want rather to emphasize the multiple boundaries – in the shape of a sharp if inexplicit sense of the distinction between mine and thine – that characterize our relations with special others, and indeed characterize them not because in this world nothing is perfect, but as good-making features of these relations. In overlooking these (I think) common phenomena, *both* those critics of consequentialism who have emphasized the gap between special others and strangers, and those consequentialists who have claimed there is no such gap, are missing a very important feature of relations to special others. Since they both miss it, they are obviously both at fault in some respect. Interestingly, it also follows that the particular demandingness objection I have characterized fails. So at least as far as *that particular* demandingness objection is concerned, consequentialism is in the clear.

I shall return to the critique of consequentialism in the final section, but I want now to spell out why there is something amiss with the particular version of the demandingness objection I have characterized.

The reply to that version of the demandingness objection is that it misrepresents relations with special others. That version of the objection represents relations with special others as the proper but distinctive locus of potentially limitless demands, on the grounds that special others are special precisely in so far as they – unlike strangers – are indeed parts or extensions of us, and thus (and quite properly: that's what makes them special) not 'separate persons'. But, I shall argue, that is a mistake. The Platonic/ Aristotelian/neo-Hegelian authors whose view of special others lies behind

SACRIFICE AND MORAL PHILOSOPHY | 145

the demandingness objection I've characterized are very good at stressing how others' interests are also my interests, so as to emphasize the psychological possibility of (limited) altruism, but also, sometimes, to emphasize the difference between special others and strangers. I don't think the phenomena to which I am about to draw attention are at all unfamiliar, but for some reason they have tended to escape philosophers' attention. Just because philosophers of the Platonic/Aristotelian/neo-Hegelian cast of mind have been on the whole preoccupied with trying to make special others look more like ourselves – with obliterating the differences between self and special others in the interests of showing the possibility of altruism – they are not very good at stressing the *boundaries* between self and special others, to the detriment of the demandingness objection I've characterized. But, as I shall go on to argue, the problem the Platonic/Aristotelian/neo-Hegelian view has with special others is just a more local version of a problem that consequentialism has with *all* others: Plato (*et al.*) say you and I are one; Green or Bradley (or, in a different way, Parfit) say we are all one; I want to say that however special even you are, you and I are separate. So the reply to the demandingness objection I've characterized does not help consequentialism in the end.

Parents, spouses, lovers, close friends and so on often say they would give up their lives or their liberty or their wealth for their special others – there is 'no sacrifice they are not prepared to make' – and I assume they mean what they say. However, it is important to be careful in interpreting what they mean. We would indeed, let us suppose, be prepared to give up our lives for our special others if *their* lives were at stake. But it does not follow that we would be prepared to give up our lives if their next trip to the cinema, or some other trivial thing, were at stake.[2] What is more, though I would often willingly give a special other an extra bite of food rather than have it myself, and indeed it is pleasant for me to do so – this is meant of course just as a stand-in for a great many acts of a similar kind – it is no less true that there is much that I would *not* give up for special others. What exactly these things are will vary considerably among persons, among families and across cultures, and – within cultures – depending on whether the special other is a spouse, a child, a sibling, a friend or whatever it might be. Some parents for example will not give up space in the marital bed to a small child; others, who think this is a foolish thing to insist on, will not give their children money and insist that if the children want money they must go out and earn it. In some families, certain items of clothing – sweaters, say – are regarded more or less as common property and there is a culture of mutual borrowing; in others, these items are jealously guarded. Mothers (or indeed fathers) who are 'unstintingly generous' – as we say – with the time and effort they devote to caring for their young children nonetheless typically set aside certain times of the day which are inviolably theirs (that is, inviolably if there is no emergency), whether this is to have a rest, talk to a friend, or (in almost forgotten past ages) have a cigarette. Siblings share, and enjoyably share, a huge range of things but also have a strong sense of mine and thine: they can share a bath or a bed or hand-me-down clothes but may regard it as 'unthinkable' to share an ice cream or a Christmas present; all the more so, sometimes, for sharing a friend. Some friends and siblings ask and offer one another financial help of various sorts; in other friendships this would be regarded as overstepping a boundary, or as challenging the self-esteem of the friend or sibling in implying they could not fend for themselves. Of course boundaries of this sort are not always adhered to, but they are widely acknowledged even when they are not adhered to (in the form of blame, silent resentment, protest, apology and so on). These examples, which I assume are part of everyone's experience, could be multiplied endlessly. My point is not to defend any particular set of views about where, in relationships with special others, the boundaries between mine and thine should lie, and therefore about where to locate the limits to the demands – often very trivial – which one person may properly make on another. It is rather that it is a generally accepted part of relationships with special others that there *are* boundaries of this kind, never mind where exactly they lie.

Nor, however, do I see these facts as a counterexample to, say, Bradley or Aristotle – as it were as proving, against them, that the 'boundaries of the self' really do end at the boundaries of each human being, and that after all the *only* morally interesting contrast is between self and *all* others. For insisting on the boundaries I have been trying to exemplify is only very misleadingly described as mere selfishness. The reason for this is that these boundaries do not, or at least need not, *compromise* the closeness of the relationships with special others that might otherwise be available. On the contrary, the existence of these boundaries is a good-making feature of these relationships, and sometimes indeed a good-making feature of them because it enhances their closeness. Here I don't have in mind – though equally I do not wish to dissent from – David Velleman's (1999, 353) observation that one can very easily 'love someone whom one cannot stand to be with', such as the 'meddlesome aunt' or the 'cranky grandfather' (ibid.). Supposing that the fact that a relationship is a love-relationship is itself a good, cases such as these show that the good of love can be realized without closeness – that is, without the parties to the relationship seeing anything much of each other, being involved in one another's daily lives and so on. We could call the fact that I don't share my mobile phone number with my meddlesome aunt, for example, an instance of a boundary between us so here, this boundary (and others like it) keep our relationship from being close, and yet (following Velleman) it can still be love. What I have in mind is the (common) type of case where the love-relationship *is* close. Precisely what that means will also be subject to considerable inter-personal and intercultural variation but it might include – for example – that we see each other enjoyably and often, we are relatively uninhibited in our emotional expressions with each other, share with one another thoughts, plans, games, ways of behaving which we share with few others. But there are boundaries nonetheless. Where these boundaries lie helps to determine the kind of love-relationship it is – a sibling relationship or parent–child relationship or a friendship or a marriage. And within each of these, their observance helps to make the love-relationship a good instance of the close relationship it is. In sum, there are boundaries designed to decrease closeness, but which are consistent with love (the cases which interest Velleman); but there are also boundaries the specific nature of which constitute a love-relationship as a closeness of this kind rather than that, and which make the close love-relationship a *good* close love-relationship of its kind.

It may be objected that though a close love-relationship can survive the existence of boundaries, any boundary nonetheless limits its closeness, and thereby the good realized by closeness. So, on this view, boundaried close relationships belong on a continuum with Velleman's case of the meddle-some aunt. Just as in that case, various boundaries (e.g. on how often we see each other) destroy closeness though without destroying love, so in (e.g.) a relationship between spouses or parents and their small children, though boundaries do not *destroy* closeness (because the boundaries are less absolute than not sharing phone numbers, or never seeing one another), nonetheless there is always a trade-off between boundaries and closeness. In the back-ground of this objection might be the thought that insofar as a boundary between two people is a matter of one or both persons holding themselves in reserve, or of their being some part or aspect of themselves that they fail to share, it must derogate from closeness. But if insisting on a boundary is *for the sake of* the relationship, it is not for the sake of one party to it alone, and therefore should not be described as selfish. To illustrate this point, it will perhaps be easiest to examine the case of parents and their small children, since here it is easy to illustrate the ways in which the non-observing of boundaries of the kind I have described, far from constituting a still better version of the same close relationship, partly constitutes the relationship going badly, i.e. being bad of its kind. But if the good foregone is the good of closeness, this seems like good evidence that there is not – or needn't be – a trade-off between closeness and boundaries.

Parents' capacity (or, alternatively, incapacity) to put themselves first and to say 'no' to their small children is a staple of the psychotherapy literature, since this is a kind of problem which often brings parents and children to psychotherapists. Some of this literature reports parents' retrospective reports on their children made in the consulting room,

148   SACRIFICE AND MORAL PHILOSOPHY

some of it directly reports baby observations in the home, which are part of the child psychotherapist's training. Although this literature is not explicitly focused on ethical questions, it assumes – and for that reason also helpfully illustrates – the fact that the caregiver putting her- or himself first, in everyday non-emergency contexts whose outer limits are not explored, is a good thing for the caregiver/child relationship, because it is something the therapy aims to get caregiver and child to do (or to accept). So, here are some examples.

> [Peter, aged 6] had never succeeded in sleeping on his own and slept permanently in his parents' bed. He had a variety of fears that kept him there, such as the sound of the rain on the roof ... which apparently could never be challenged. During the day, Peter was described as a monster who would become violently out of control when he did not get his way. His physical attacks were ... reserved for his mother. (Schmidt Neven 2005, 200–202)

> [Kate, aged 1 year] used her mother as a kind of portable breast available at any time and in any place ... [She took] half-hourly 'sips' to gain reassurance [and would not let the mother go far away without protest. Though the mother was exhausted, she] seemed helpless to refuse; [as Kate's father was in prison, she also] seemed to rely on Kate to give her own life some sort of routine, security and meaning. This meant being at Kate's beck and call, and mother's growing exhaustion was ... the result of allowing herself to be used in this way. (Lubbe 1996, 201–202)

> Sarah, aged 15 months, 'completely refused to be weaned', as her parents put it. She 'had almost never been separated from her mother, day or night'; she clung to her mother and wanted the breast every ten minutes or so. Moreover, 'Sarah was too anxious to play and was completely silent'. In the therapist's view, both parents 'subscribed to the phantasy [sic] which unconsciously told them that the heavens would open if anyone said 'no' to Sarah'. However, in part by forming an alliance against the therapist and agreeing she (the therapist) was 'useless', the parents experienced a new solidarity with one another. Apparently because the mother could thenceforth rely on her husband for closeness as well as on her child, the parents found the strength to lay down the law – and discovered that the price of physical separation was not the loss of their emotional connection with their child. Three weeks later, 'Sarah was in her room, in her bed at night, and breastfeeding had diminished to an unremarkable level ... [There emerged] a small girl who began to take a lively interest in the toys [the therapist] provided, ... and to talk'. 'Sarah's rage [which her parents had so feared] was a paper tiger because Sarah it seems ... [gladly] complied with her parents' requests once they had made up their combined mind.' (Miller 2004, 40; cf. Daws 1993, 77)[3]

Examples of this kind could be multiplied *ad infinitum*. Whether about sleeping arrangements or about weaning or some other thing, they all revolve around the distinction between those of the child's demands which it is proper for the parent to yield to, and those it is not, and the topic of the demands is

SACRIFICE AND MORAL PHILOSOPHY

always something – a space in the bed, time together without the child, access to the mother's body –that the child wants, and that the parents (or one of them) would otherwise reserve to themselves. In other words they are all about the boundaries between mine and thine which, as I have said, are central to relations with special others. Moreover, the parents (initially) act as if these demands are proper and give in to them – for example because they think that not yielding would be selfish, for it would be to deny the child something it ought to have; or because it would compromise the closeness of their relationship with the child, because they would be withholding something from it; or because it would cause some nameless catastrophe. If that were the right way to see things, one would imagine that whatever its instrumental disadvantages (e.g. Kate's mother's exhaustion), at least the parents' *relationship* with the child would be maintained or enhanced by the parents' failure to say 'no'. But the opposite is the case: the relationships are conflictual (Peter's violence), or insecure (Kate's feeding 'to gain reassurance'; Sarah was silent and didn't play). Of course some of the badness in the relationship is instrumentally bad – exhaustion compromises parents' ability to do various *further* things for their children that need doing. But it is non-instrumentally bad too. The vignettes above are all miniature portrayals of parents and children *getting on badly*. Conversely, when the parents become able not to give in to the child's demands (that is, to insist on a boundary), things start to go better – for the child, but also between them and the child. But if insisting on reserving various things to themselves (space in the bed, their bodies, time etc.) were a case of mere selfishness on the parent's part, one would expect the reverse to be the case, since selfishness compromises the goodness of a relationship. What the parents in the vignettes find it hard to learn (but eventually do learn) is precisely the theoretical point I made in answer to the objection above: that observing boundaries is not a case of selfishness.

As to why insisting on a boundary is not a case of selfishness, because it is withheld for the sake of the relationship, we can compare games which involve turn-taking. In any such game, a player may have occasion to say 'now it's my turn'. That is of course an instance of insisting on what's theirs rather than the other player's – the turn – i.e. of insisting on a boundary. However, if it were never proper to insist on that, the game would not be a turn-taking game, but its being a game of that kind makes it a case of reciprocity, i.e. of joint or shared endeavour: it does not destroy the joint or shared endeavour. So, in such a game, insisting on the boundary helps to constitute the game as a case of shared endeavour, so insisting on the boundary is for the sake of that endeavour, not just for the sake of one of the players. The same is true, on a larger scale, of the varieties of no-saying in the vignettes. The parent's ability to say no enables the child to come to see the parent as not just a need-satisfier but as a person with wants, interests, purposes etc. of his/her own. The child and the parent seeing one another that way is an example of a relationship going well because it is a case of turn-taking writ large.

One could – optionally – dig one level deeper. Some of the therapists suggest that it is easier to say no if the underlying state of the relationship is good, or if the mother or father trusts in their own ability to give the child love – because if they do, saying 'no' to some particular demand doesn't appear to them to be a rejection of the child, or to be a token of their inadequacy in being able to give emotionally. It is *just* saying no to their feeding, or sleeping in their bed, or sitting in the front seat of the car. That is, one could say selfish is how these parents *feel* they are being – which is why they find saying no so hard. But the therapy teaches them that they should not feel that way – the relationship gets better instrumentally and non-instrumentally when they are better able to insist on what is properly theirs and get the child to accept that. Indeed one might say that in describing the claims special others properly have on us as *not* being subject to limits of these familiar kinds, and thus describing the denial of these claims as instances of selfishness, philosophers are reproducing the parents' mistake at one remove. Of course – as the parents in the vignettes show – learning when one is not being selfish, when it is proper to say no even to a highly dependent intimate, can be very difficult. I suspect the fact that many of us have experienced difficulties of these kinds either as a normal part of growing up or as a normal part of being parents explains part – though not all – of the 'feel' of the argument around some of the consequentialist's favourite cases, i.e. when it is proper to say 'mine not yours'.

Be that as it may, in all these situations – and many others like them that do not involve parents and small children, but involve siblings, couples, friends and so on – withholding something the special other demands is not a case of selfishness because although it involves A putting their own wishes, needs etc. above those of B, it is not a case of A denying B something – time, water, food, rest, money or whatever – to which they have a proper claim, in the name of A's having that thing to herself. This is not to say that there are not hugely many ordinary situations in which we (with varying degrees of pleasure) give things up for our special others, nor that the class of situations in which it is proper to affirm the boundaries I have tried to point to are not heavily if inexplicitly circumscribed by assumptions as to what defeats them – centrally, emergencies or crises of various kinds. Still, the cases show how the relationship goes worse when the demand is treated as if it is proper, and better when it's treated as if it is not. Hence, the type of boundary between mine and thine I have described does not compromise the closeness of relationships with special others but, on the contrary, contributes to a close relationship's going well.

In the types of case typified by the vignettes, where no-saying not only enhances the relationship but also enhances its closeness, the point that boundaries are a good-making feature of relationships is perhaps most easily made. However, there are also cases where relationships are good, but less obviously modelled by the analogy of turn-taking games. Especially perhaps in the case of relations between adolescent or adult siblings, or between adolescent or adult children and their parents, it may also be proper to say, in rejecting a demand by the other, 'I have a life of my own to lead', or the like. This *may* make the relationship better, in the sense that it may enable each to relate to the other as an independent adult. But insisting on a boundary in this way may not only create distance of a kind – that is what it is designed to do – but also at least temporarily damage the relationship, so an effort of reparation is needed to restore the relationship on this new basis. In such cases it is harder to argue that insisting on one's own time, space, friends or whatever it might be is partly constitutive of the reciprocity of the relationship. And if the relationship is restored on the new basis, it may well in some sense be less close than it was, for what one has insisted is one's own entitlement to a life that is not a part of that relationship. So here again, as in Velleman's cases, being good-making and being closeness-enhancing come apart. And yet, as in the parent-infant cases, we frequently do allow and indeed encourage people to insist on boundaries of just this kind.

5. An Improved Demandingness Objection

Now, finally, let me try to relate these observations to the demandingness objection, both the particular version I singled out above and the 'common core'.

The particular demandingness objection I singled out says that consequentialism underrates the moral significance of the stranger/special other distinction. Moreover it does so because it models its conception of the demands it's proper for strangers to make on us on a conception of the demands it's proper for special others to make on us which both consequentialists and some of their usual opponents agree is correct. This conception of special others' proper demands is correct, these theorists agree, because special others are special in so far as we and they are parts of a 'single unit', and so are not – in the relevant sense – separate from us; or because they constitute 'commitments' of ours; whereas strangers are or do not do so. Consequentialists go wrong, according to the demandingness objection, only in so far as what their opponents correctly say about special others, consequentialists (and also, according to Brink, Hegelians) also say about strangers.

In my view the shared conception of relations between ourselves and special others is mistaken, at least in so far as it says that the demands which it is proper for special others to make on us are limitless – essentially, it's fine to say 'no' to a stranger, but the specialness of special others is such that that is not fine.

I spent the last section arguing that relations between us and our special others are characterized by boundaries of various sorts between ourselves and them, and moreover that when in normal circumstances these boundaries are observed, this often makes these relations go well – and even when it may not (as in the sibling or adult child/parent cases) we are often inclined to say it is proper to insist on the boundary. With special others, it is often just fine to say (or 'say') 'no, that's mine not yours'.

So far so bad for the particular demandingness objection as I have characterized it. That is, the whole argument so far has striven to show that the demandingness objection rests on a conception of relations with special others which (a) proponents of the objection share with consequentialists, and (b) is false. Hence, the demandingness objection as I have characterized it fails.

However, I now propose to use the observations in the last section to revive what I take to be the 'common core' of demandingness objections to consequentialism, and which is independent of the false common assumption – namely that there is no demand strangers may not properly make on us if it increases aggregate goodness. That is, the objection I have discussed wants to resist the conclusion that strangers' proper demands are limited only by considerations of aggregate goodness *on the grounds that* special others' demands are so limited, and consequentialists mistakenly extend that thought to strangers. The objection I wish to revive wants to resist the same conclusion, but on different grounds.

The central thought is that it would be very odd if, in non-emergency cases, we were *more* at fault – more guilty of selfishness, or of unjustified partiality – in drawing boundaries between ourselves and strangers (that is, in insisting on the difference between mine and thine where strangers are concerned) than we are in drawing them between ourselves and our special others. For if we were, wherein would the specialness of the special others consist? Thus, the propriety of drawing the boundary must either be the same whatever the degree of closeness to us of the other person or, alternatively, lessen as the degree of their closeness to us increases. Presumably consequentialists would choose the first alternative (i.e. closeness makes no moral difference), and many non-consequentialists would choose the second. So, in order to conduct the argument on assumptions maximally favourable to the consequentialist and thus to strengthen any potential case against the consequentialist, let us assume the first alternative is correct.

Now consequentialism says the propriety of drawing the boundary, including in non-emergency cases, is nil. That is, it is always improper to insist on the difference between mine and thine – for example, by not sharing some resource – simply for its own sake. (Of course if consequentialist calculation determines that aggregate goodness increases if I keep what was antecedently mine, then it is proper for me to keep it, but the fact that it was antecedently mine isn not a self-standing reason.) But as the argument of the last section

SACRIFICE AND MORAL PHILOSOPHY

shows, the propriety of drawing the boundary in non-emergency cases is *not* nil even where the others are special others. Hence, on the assumption that closeness makes no difference, the propriety of drawing the boundary in non-emergency cases is also not nil where the others are strangers. That is to say, it is proper to insist on differences between mine and thine as self-standing reasons for not sharing some resource with strangers; otherwise put, there are some demands on us which, otherwise than for reasons of aggregate utility, it is not proper for strangers to make. But consequentialism says that differences between mine and thine are *not* self-standing reasons for not sharing some resource with strangers; the proper demands on us of strangers are limited only by considerations of aggregate utility. So – as the 'common core' of the demandingness objection has it – consequentialism is mistaken on account of the demands it makes.

It is not clear, finally, how far any of this helps to smoothe away the demands which morality – as opposed to a consequentialist theorization of it – places on us. Certainly the phenomena to which I have drawn attention – the normality of 'boundaries between persons' when the persons are special others, and the fact that these boundaries do not detract from, but can on the contrary contribute to the specialness of the relationship – should help to explain why it feels so wrong to be told, as we frequently are, that the refusal to yield to moral demands is merely selfish. Nonetheless the overall argument above depends on a characterization of special others' proper demands on us which are circumscribed by an important but vague 'no emergencies' clause – i.e. in emergencies, much of the above does not apply. So any argument from what is true of special others to what is true of strangers that is grounded in the no-emergency case will lapse in an emergency. If the world is frequently in a state of known emergency (Ashford 2000), it will therefore lapse often. So often we may well owe to strangers what consequentialism says we owe. But if we do, then if the above argument is correct, it will at least be owed on a different basis to the basis advanced by consequentialism.

Notes

1. I do not present any argument here as to how we should treat (plausible) pre-theoretical conviction in assessing ethical theories, simply on the grounds that any view on this question will bear equally on any (plausible) pre-theoretical conviction, and I am interested in unearthing a particular conviction or set of convictions that I think has been insufficiently attended to so far. Obviously if no pre-theoretical convictions deserve any weight in evaluating ethical theories, then this one won't, but it is still worth dragging the conviction out into the open and seeing what difference it might make, prior to this general methodological issue being settled.

2. I say 'let us suppose': there are situations where we may have to inhibit the desire to give up our lives for the sake of a loved one, because we know that if we did so, other loved ones would die – see some of the accounts in Yarov (2017). But if my argument goes through on the assumption that we would always lay down our own life for that of a special other, it will presumably go through if the assumption is waived, so I do not explore these tragic cases.
3. Miller says both that Sarah's parents had been 'holding out against the paternal function' but also that 'even in the earliest stages of a baby's development there needs to be the growing intimation that there is a division between mother and infant'. That is, Miller officially subscribes to the idea that all life begins in psychic mergedness with the mother which the paternal function, if not the father in person, needs to disrupt for development to occur; but at the same time shows awareness of the limitations of this idea, in claiming that the 'division' between mother and infant *ought* to be there 'even in the earliest stages'. This is an uneasy theoretical compromise because if the latter claim is true, then healthy psychic life doesn't begin in mergedness, so if all goes well there is nothing for the 'paternal function' to do. See Harcourt, 2018. The myth of original mergedness is of course related to what I am claiming is the false picture of special relationships that underlies the particular version of the demandingness objection I'm examining – that in them, individuals are (ideally at least) not separate from one another.

Disclosure Statement

No potential conflict of interest was reported by the author.

References

Aristotle. 1984. "Nicomachean Ethics." Tr. W.D. Ross, Rev. J.O. Urmson. In *The Complete Works of Aristotle*. 2 vols. Revised Oxford Translation. edited by J. Barnes. Princeton: Princeton University Press.

Ashford, E. 2000. "Utilitarianism, Integrity and Partiality." *The Journal of Philosophy* XCVII (8): 421–439.

Benn, C. 2015. "Over-Demandingness Objections and Supererogation." In *The Limits of Moral Obligations*, edited by M. Van Ackeren and M. Kühler, 68–83. New York/London: Routledge.

Bradley, F. H. [1876] 2012. *Ethical Studies*. Cambridge: Cambridge University Press.

Brink, D. 1997. "Self-Love and Altruism." *Social Philosophy and Policy* 14: 122–157. doi:10.1017/S0265052500001709.

Chappell, T. 2009. "Introduction." In *The Problem of Moral Demandingness*, edited by T. Chappell, 1–9. New York/Basingstoke: Palgrave Macmillan.

Daws, D. 1993. "Feeding Problems and Relationship Difficulties: Therapeutic Work with Parents and Infants." *Journal of Child Psychotherapy* 19 (2): 69–83. doi:10.1080/00754179308259389.

Guyau, M. [1885] 2008. *Esquisse D'une Morale sans Obligation Ni Sanction*. Paris: Allia.

Harcourt, E. 2018. "Madness, Badness and Immaturity: Some Conceptual Issues in Psychoanalysis and Psychotherapy." *Philosophy, Psychiatry, & Psychology* 25 (2): 123–136.

Hills, A. 2010. "Utilitarianism, Contractualism and Demandingness." *The Philosophical Quarterly* 60: 225–242. doi:10.1111/phiq.2010.60.issue-239.

Hooker, B. 2009. "The Demandingness Objection." In *The Problem of Moral Demandingness*, edited by T. Chappell, 148–162. New York/Basingstoke: Palgrave Macmillan.

Lubbe, T. 1996. "Who Lets Go First? Some Observations on the Struggles around Weaning." *Journal of Child Psychotherapy* 22 (2): 195–213. doi:10.1080/00754179608254942.

Miller, L. 2004. "The Oedipus Complex Observed in Work with Couples and Their Children." *Journal of Child Psychotherapy* 30 (1): 39–52. doi:10.1080/0075417042000205788.

Mulgan, T. 2001. *The Demands of Consequentialism*. Oxford: Oxford University Press.

Mulgan, T. 2007. *Understanding Utilitarianism*. Stocksfield: Acumen.

Murphy, L. 2000. *Moral Demands in Nonideal Theory*. Oxford: Oxford University Press.

Parfit, D. 1984. *Reasons and Persons*. Oxford: Oxford University Press.

Pinheiro Walla, A. 2015. "Kant's Moral Theory and Demandingness." *Ethical Theory and Moral Practice* 18: 731–743. doi:10.1007/s10677-015-9600-x.

Price, A. 1989. *Love and Friendship in Plato and Aristotle*. Oxford: Oxford University Press.

Rawls, J. 1971. *A Theory of Justice*. Cambridge MA: Harvard University Press.

Scheffler, S. 1982. *The Rejection of Consequentialism*. Oxford: Oxford University Press.

Schmidt Neven, R. 2005. "Under Fives Counselling: Opportunities for Growth, Change and Development for Children and Parents." *Journal of Child Psychotherapy* 31 (2): 189–208. doi:10.1080/00754170500221642.

Sidgwick, H. 1907. *The Methods of Ethics*. London: Macmillan.

Swanton, C. 2009. "Virtue Ethics and the Problem of Demandingness." In *The Problem of Moral Demandingness*, edited by T. Chappell, 104–122. London: Acumen.

Van Ackeren, M. forthcoming. *What Makes A Moral Obligation Demanding?*. [this issue].

Van Ackeren, M., and M. Kühler. 2015. "Ethics on (The) Edge?" In *The Limits of Moral Obligations. Moral Demandingness and Ought Implies Can*, edited by M. Van Ackeren and M. Kühler, 1–18. New York/London: Routledge.

Van Ackeren, M., and M. Sticker. 2015. "Kant and the Problem of Demandingness." *Ethical Theory Moral Practice* 18: 75–89. doi:10.1007/s10677-014-9510-3.

Velleman, J. D. 1999. "Love as a Moral Emotion." *Ethics* 109 (2): 338–374. doi:10.1086/233898.

Williams, B. 1977. "A Critique of Utilitarianism." In *Utilitarianism: For and Against*, edited by J. J. C. Smart and B. Williams, 75–150. Cambridge: Cambridge University Press.

Williams, B. 1985. *Ethics and the Limits of Philosophy*. London: Fontana.

Yarov, S. 2017. *Leningrad 1941-2: Morality in a City under Siege*. Tr. Arch Tait. Cambridge: Polity.

ꝏ OPEN ACCESS

Rehabilitating Self-Sacrifice: Care Ethics and the Politics of Resistance

Amanda Cawston and Alfred Archer

ABSTRACT
How should feminists view acts of self-sacrifice performed by women? According to a long-standing critique of care ethics such acts ought to be viewed with scepticism. Care ethics, it is claimed, celebrates acts of self-sacrifice on the part of carers and in doing so encourages women to choose caring for others over their own self-development. In doing so, care ethics frustrates attempts to liberate women from the oppression of patriarchy. Care ethicists have responded to this critique by noting limits on the level, form, or scope of self-sacrifice that work to restrict its role in their theories. While we do not here take issue with the initial feminist critiques of self-sacrifice, we suspect that the strategies offered by Care ethicists in response are importantly flawed. Specifically, these responses undervalue the positive roles that self-sacrifice can play in fighting patriarchal oppression. As a result, in attempting to restrict an oppressive norm, these responses risk foreclosing on valuable means of resistance. Our aim is to explore these positive roles for self-sacrifice and thereby rehabilitate its standing with feminists.

1. Introduction

Due to its attempts to do justice to women's moral experience, it is common to view care ethics as a feminist approach to ethics. However, some feminists have criticized care ethics for promoting an ethics of self-sacrifice among women, which they see as detrimental to the aim of helping women overcome patriarchal oppression. In response, care ethicists have proposed a number of ways in which to defend their theory against this charge. These responses seek to restrict the amount, type or scope of self-sacrifice that care ethics would prescribe. Our aim in this article is to argue that these strategies offered by care ethicists in response to the feminist critique are incomplete. Specifically, these responses undervalue the positive roles that self-sacrifice can play in fighting patriarchal oppression. As a result, in attempting to restrict an oppressive norm, these responses risk overlooking a valuable means of resistance. Our aim is to explore these positive roles for self-sacrifice and thereby rehabilitate its standing with feminists.

This is an Open Access article distributed under the terms of the Creative Commons Attribution-NonCommercial-NoDerivatives License (http://creativecommons.org/licenses/by-nc-nd/4.0/), which permits non-commercial re-use, distribution, and reproduction in any medium, provided the original work is properly cited, and is not altered, transformed, or built upon in any way.

Our discussion will proceed as follows. We start, in Section One, with an introduction to care ethics. We will then, in Section Two, explain the self-sacrifice objection that has been raised against care ethics. In Section Three we will outline the existing responses that have been made to this challenge. We will then provide a new response to this challenge by arguing that self-sacrifice has a positive role to play in the fight against patriarchy. We will first, in Section Four, outline the positive role that self-sacrifice can play generally in the fight against injustice. We do this by via exploring the *communicative, transformative* and *illustrative* roles of self-sacrifice in resistance action. Finally, in Section Five, we argue that self-sacrifice has a particularly valuable role to play in non-violently combatting gender based oppression and is thus especially important for those committed to an ethics of care.

2. Care Ethics

Care ethics developed out of a critique of traditional approaches to normative ethics, such as Kantianism and contract theory. These approaches, which assign a central role to impartial principles and justice, were claimed to ignore or belittle an approach to morality that is more prevalent among, though by no means restricted to, women. Carol Gilligan's (1982, 5–23) *In a Different Voice* argued that the existing theories of moral development, in particular the work of Sigmund Freud and Lawrence Kohlberg, placed too great an emphasis on the importance of principles to morality and subsequently wrongly classified men as possessing higher levels of moral development than women. Based on her own studies of women's moral development Gilligan claims that there is a distinctive moral outlook that is more common among women than men. Gilligan (1982, 100) describes this outlook in the following way:

> The moral imperative that emerges repeatedly in interviews with women is *an injunction to care*, a responsibility to discern and alleviate the 'real and recognized' trouble of this world. For men, the moral imperative appears rather as a injunction to respect the rights of others and thus to protect from interference the rights to life and self-fulfillment.

This moral outlook places caring for others at the heart of morality. According to Gilligan, this moral outlook is just as legitimate a form of moral reasoning as one that prioritizes rules and principles and should be given equal recognition in theories of moral development.

The contrast between a caring approach to morality and a justice focused approach is exemplified in the responses of two of the child interviewees in Gilligan's study. Both children were asked how to make a choice when their own interests conflict with the interests of others. Jake, an archetype of the justice approach, responded by saying: 'You go about one-fourth to the others

158   SACRIFICE AND MORAL PHILOSOPHY

and three-fourths to yourself (Gilligan 1982, 35–36). Amy, on the other hand, an archetype of the caring approach, provided the following answer:

> Well it really depends on the situation. If you have a responsibility with somebody else, then you should keep it to a certain extent, but to the extent that it is really going to hurt you or stop you from doing something that you really, really want, then I think that maybe you should put yourself first. But if it is your responsibility to somebody really close to you, you've just got to decide in that situation which is more important, yourself or that person, and like I said, it really depends on what kind of person you are and how you feel about the other person or persons involved. (Gilligan 1982, 35–36)

While Jake provides a principle to settle this question, Amy's response focuses on the particular relationships between the people who could be impacted by such a decision.

A number of philosophers have sought to develop this caring moral perspective into a distinct moral theory. Nel Noddings (1984/2013) developed an ethical theory in which, 'human caring and the memory of caring and being cared for [...] form the foundation of ethical response' (1). Caring, according to Noddings, involves a relationship between the one-caring and the cared-for. Caring involves, first of all, being engrossed in the situation of the person being cared for. This engrossment involves 'apprehending the others' reality, feeling what he feels as nearly as possible' (Noddings 1984/2013, 16). This in turn, motivates the one caring to act on behalf of the person they care for. According to Virginia Held (2006, 10), this view of caring for particular others as the foundation of morality is the central focus of care ethics.[1]

The initial feminist case in favour of care ethics seems relatively straightforward. Care ethics can be seen as articulating a distinctive moral viewpoint that, if Gilligan's empirical claims are correct,[2] is prevalent amongst women. Care ethics then can be seen as paying attention to the moral experience of women in a way that traditional moral theories do not (Jagger 1991, 90). Moreover, by emphasizing the importance of caring work, care ethics highlights the value of ethical reflection on these areas of labour that are disproportionately carried out by women.

3. The Self-Sacrifice Objection

Despite its feminist origins and the initial feminist case in favour of it, one of the most persistent criticisms of care ethics has come from fellow feminists. According to feminist critics, care ethics offers an ethical ideal that will entrench the oppression of women rather than challenge it. The basic criticism is that care ethics endorses an ideal of self-sacrifice that is harmful to the aims of the feminist movement. In this section, we will

SACRIFICE AND MORAL PHILOSOPHY

investigate this objection and its implications for our discussion of how feminists should view self-sacrifice.

This objection targets the caring ethical ideal that lies at the heart of care ethics. According to Catharine MacKinnon, women who promote this ideal are endorsing their own oppression. In her words:

> For women to affirm their difference, when difference means dominance, as it does with gender, means to affirm the qualities and characteristics of power-lessness [...] Woman value care because men value us according to the care we give them [...] Women think in relational terms because our existence is defined in relation to men. (MacKinnon 1987, 39)

MacKinnon's point is that the caring moral outlook is the moral outlook of a dominated group who have reconciled themselves to their own oppression.

Jean Hampton expresses a similar worry about the potential for care ethics to entrench gender-based oppression (though unlike MacKinnon she does not fully endorse these criticisms). In her discussion of Amy and Jake, the two children involved in Gilligan's study discussed above, Hampton (1993, 231) is struck by the ways in which their responses are perfectly suited for their respective places in the gender hierarchy.

> What happens when archetypal Jake and Amy grow up? If they were to marry, wouldn't Amy take it upon herself to meet the needs of Jake and do the work to maintain their relationship? [...] And wouldn't Jake naturally take it for granted that his interests should predominate [...] and be ignorant of many of the needs of others around him that might prompt a caring response? I find it striking that these children's answers betray perspectives that seem to fit them perfectly for the kind of gendered roles that prevail in our society. In their archetypal forms, I hear the voice of a child who is preparing to be a member of a dominating group and the voice of another who is preparing to be a member of the group that is dominated. Neither of these voices should be allowed to inform our moral theorizing if such theorizing is going to be successful at formulating ways of interacting that are not only morally acceptable but also attack the oppressive relationships that now hold in our society.

According to Hampton, Amy's caring approach to morality will encourage her to put other's interests ahead of her own, and is thus ideally suited for perpetuating the continued oppression of women.

There are two points worth drawing out from these criticisms. First, the caring approach to morality is a *symptom* of the oppression of women. One way in which the oppression of women manifests itself is through the expectation that women will sacrifice their own interests for the interests of men. Women reconcile themselves to this situation by internalizing this expectation into an ethical ideal. As Sarah Hoagland (1992, 157) puts the point:

> We appeal to altruism, to self-sacrifice, and in general, to feminine virtuous-ness in a desperate attempt to find grace and goodness within a system

160   SACRIFICE AND MORAL PHILOSOPHY

marked by greed and fear. Although these virtues may herald for us the possibility of ethics – the possibility of some goodness in an otherwise nasty world – they are the virtues of subservience.

The caring ethical ideal then is no more than a coping strategy that helps women to reconcile themselves to their own oppression.

Second, the caring approach to morality also *contributes* to the continued domination of women. By adopting the caring ethical ideal women are more likely to sacrifice their own interests for those of others. Take, for example Virginia Woolf's description of 'the angel of the house' in the following:

> She was intensely sympathetic. She was immensely charming. She was utterly unselfish. She excelled in the difficult art of family life. She sacrificed herself daily. If there was chicken she took the leg: if there was a draught she sat in it – in short she was so constituted that she never had a mind or a wish of her own, but preferred to sympathize always with the minds and wishes of others. (Woolf 1942/2012)

This example shows a woman sacrificing her own interests for those around her and who will fail to consider her own rights and entitlements, prioritising instead the interests of other people. In a society where women's interests are routinely given a lower priority to men's there seems good reason to think that celebrating such an ethical outlook will contribute to the continuation of men's interests being promoted at the expense of women's. It is for this reason that Hoagland (1991, 259) claims that: 'to pursue this sense of female agency, is to pursue oppression'.

In summary, according to these feminist critics, care ethics endorses a morality of self-sacrifice. This self-sacrificial ideal is both a symptom of and a contributing factor to the continued domination of women. In order to promote feminist aims then, feminists should reject the caring approach to morality.

Why is care ethics so frequently criticized by feminists in this way? After all, it is far from the only moral theory that seems to encourage acts of self-sacrifice. Consequentialism, for example, is frequently criticized for demanding excessive levels of self-sacrifice but this criticism is rarely if ever seen as one that should be of special interests to feminists. There are, at least, three reasons for feminists to be particularly concerned about the criticism that care ethics encourages a morality of self-sacrifice. First, care ethics is a view that is explicitly endorsed by many as the feminist moral viewpoint. It would be particularly damaging then if this view turned out to subvert feminist aims. Second, if Gilligan's claims about the comparative prevalence of women's caring perspective are correct, then care ethics articulates a view that many women already hold. This gives feminists special reason to worry about this view, as it is likely to be more appealing to women than other views that endorse an ethics of self-sacrifice. Finally, it might be thought that promoting an ethics of self-sacrifice ignores the ways in which feminists have successfully advanced the position of women in society. According to Ruth Groenhout (2003, 153), these gains have been made by women who reject the ideal of feminine self-sacrifice. For those who think that progress in gender equality has been made by women standing up for their interests and fighting for their rights, an ethical theory that encourages self-sacrifice is unlikely to be viewed as helping the cause.

4. Existing Responses

Care ethicists have offered three forms of response to the self-sacrifice objection. The first response is to claim that care ethics does not require problematic *levels* of self-sacrifice. The second response is to argue that care ethics does not require problematic *forms* of sacrifice. The final response is to restrict the scope of care ethics such that it does not offer a complete account of morality. We will investigate each of these responses in turn.

4.1 *Self-Sacrifice and Self-Care*

The first response is to claim that care ethics properly understood does not require problematic levels of self-sacrifice. One way to support this claim is to appeal to the relational account of human nature that care ethicists endorse. According to Groenhout (2003, 167–168), if we accept that human nature can only be understood in relational terms then the call to care will begin to look less self-sacrificial. First because the care that I give to others will strengthen the community that I am a part of. It will benefit me to be part of a stronger more caring community. Second, because I am part of a caring community, the call to care includes a demand to engage in self-care. This is because I am a member of the community like everyone else and any harm to me harms that community. Similarly, Tove Pettersen (2012) claims that a mature conception of care will recognize the need to engage in self-care. Finally, the levels of self-sacrifice required by care ethics is further limited by the need to allow others to develop the ability to care for themselves and others. Giving up too much of myself to the caring of others will impede their ability to develop the skills required for caring. A mother who does everything for her children, for example, runs the risk of raising children who are entirely dependent upon her. Appreciating these three points about our relational nature makes the call to care appear far less self-sacrificial. Caring does not require that I give up all of my interests for those of other people.

The second way to support the claim that care ethics does not require problematic levels of self-sacrifice is to provide a care ethical account of evil, as developed, for example by Noddings (1989) and Groenhout (2003, 168–170). Recognising the existence of evil draws our attention to the fact that others may not be caring. This is important as these people may exploit the benefits of the care that other people give to them in order to cause harm to others. Moreover, they may view a caring response to the harm they impose on others as justifying the infliction of further harm. If my care is going to be used in either of these ways then the care I have for myself and others ought to lead me to cease providing care for those who will exploit it.

Care ethicists need not endorse problematic levels of self-sacrifice, then, as a mature, relational account of care will not endorse this and an account of evil can explain why it can be wrong to give care to those who will exploit it.

4.2 Self-Sacrifice as Self-Donation

Kalynne Pudner (2007) offers an alternative response to the objection that distinguishes between different kinds of self-sacrifice. According to Pudner, there are a number of ways in which self-sacrifice can be understood and not all of these are problematic in the way the feminist critics of care ethics suggest.

Pudner (2007, 241) sees the problem of self-sacrifice for care ethics as a problem of autonomy. In caring for another, someone can become so engrossed in the other's needs that she both loses opportunities to pursue her own interests and threatens her autonomy.[3] According to Pudner, self-sacrifice should be understood as, 'the autonomous act, orientation or disposition to renounce one's own autonomous will' (2007, 243). On this account of self-sacrifice, it is not hard to see why self-sacrifice might be thought to violate autonomy: the decision to engage in self-sacrifice is a decision to relinquish one's own autonomy.

However, Pudner claims that this account allows for four different versions of self-sacrifice. The first version is self-immolation, which Pudner (2007, 244) describes as, 'the self's renunciation of its autonomous will by destruction'. For example, someone who chooses to undergo brain-washing. The second version is self-annunciation, which involves the giving up of one's will in deference to the will of another. This Pudner (2007, 245–246) claims is often done with the hope of gaining something in return. Unlike self-immolation, the self is not destroyed in this form of sacrifice, as autonomy will return once it ceases to be delegated to the other. However, Pudner claims that for as long as the self is given up in obedience to another it cannot be autonomous. The third version of self-sacrifice is self-effacement, the devaluation of the autonomous will. On this form of self-sacrifice, the agent's autonomous will is viewed to be defective or damaged in some way and so unworthy of consideration. While self-effacement does not prevent the self from having autonomy, it does prevent people from valuing their own needs, projects and desires. This damages the ability to act autonomously (Pudner 2007, 246–247). All three of these forms of self-sacrifice represent unacceptable loss of autonomy and so fail to respond to the objection that self-sacrifice is not always autonomy violating.

There is though, one form of self-sacrifice, namely self-donation, that Pudner (2007, 247) claims is compatible with autonomy. Self-donation involves making a gift of one's self to another and is 'purposive and self-affirming'. Someone who makes a gift of her self to another implicitly endorses her own value by deeming it worthy of being gifted. Moreover, according to Pudner, this form of sacrifice does not compromise autonomy. As Pudner (2007, 247) puts the point:

> Self-donation entails seeking to discover the other's good [...] autonomously endorsing that good, determining appropriate means for attaining the good, and effectively choosing those means. These are actions the agent avows as directed by her own autonomy, not that of the other.

Self-donation does not involve destruction or devaluing of the self nor does it involve deference to another. Rather, it involves autonomously deciding to promote the interests of another in a way that does not undermine the agent's own autonomy.

These distinctions provide a second response to the feminist critique. Care ethicists can accept that their ethical outlook is one that requires self-sacrifice whilst holding that the form of self-sacrifice required by their view is fully compatible with an agent retaining her autonomy. So long as people engage in the self-donation form of self-sacrifice, then their sacrifice will not undermine their autonomy.

4.3 Care and Justice

The final response to the self-sacrifice objection is to claim that care ethics should not be viewed as a complete moral theory but rather as articulating one important part of morality. As several philosophers have noted, an ethics of justice need not be seen as a rival to an ethics of care.[4] We might instead think that a complete moral theory requires both moral perspectives. This may be because both are equally fundamental moral viewpoints. Alternatively, we might think that one moral viewpoint is contained within the other. Either position would allow us to say that a complete view of morality would incorporate both perspectives.

If we accept that both the caring and the justice perspectives are part of morality, then a new response to the feminist critique of care ethics becomes available. The care ethicist can accept that an exclusive focus on the caring approach to ethics may lead to excessive self-sacrifice. This though, need not commit the care ethicist to endorse this level of self-sacrifice. Instead, it can be argued that the caring approach to morality must be balanced with an ethics of justice. This allows the care ethicist to say that a concern for justice can ensure that a caring person also pays attention to her rights. This will allow her to avoid engaging in excessive levels of self-sacrifice.

We have then, three strategies for restricting the role of self-sacrifice in care ethics: the Self-care, Self-donation, and Justice strategies. Each tries in its way to negotiate a perceived tension between the feminist value of celebrating care and recognition of others' needs, and the disvalue of endorsing a norm of subservience. We do not dispute the existing critiques of self-sacrifice – we agree that there are legitimate worries about its role in supporting patriarchy. We take issue, however, with how care ethicists have tried to avoid these worries. In their haste to avoid its ills, they may have forgone its benefits. In the following, we explore these benefits before revisiting the care ethicist stance on self-sacrifice.

5. The Value of Self-Sacrifice

The previous sections have introduced the feminist worry that an emphasis on care perpetuates gendered oppression through its promotion of self-sacrifice. This section aims to show that this worry reflects an overly narrow characterization of self-sacrifice as a virtue of subservience. We will argue that a more comprehensive study suggests self-sacrifice may be an essential component of effective opposition to oppression, including to gendered oppression.

The notion of self-sacrifice has a long association with political resistance. Soldiers, for instance, give their bodies (and sometimes their lives), while citizens ration resources in defence of sovereignty or to fight against tyranny and injustice. More recently, self-sacrifice has also been associated with the political violence of suicide terrorists, who inflict violence on themselves and others in pursuit of their causes. Finally, self-sacrifice also has played a central role in notable historical instances of non-violent resistance, including Gandhi's activities towards Indian independence and Martin Luther King Jr.'s actions as part of the American civil rights movement. In the following subsections, we outline three roles that self-sacrifice can. play in political resistance, including communicative, transformative and illustrative roles.

5.1 *Communicative*

One major role self-sacrifice can play in political resistance is *communicative*. In her anthropological analysis of self-sacrifice, Karin Fierke (2013, 39) notes a shift in the primary purpose of political self-sacrifice: '[c]

ontemporary self-sacrifice is not for the purpose of giving a gift to the gods [...] but, rather, is about *communicating a political message*'.[5] In particular, Fierke (2013, 37) suggests we understand political self-sacrifice as the inverse of an Austinian illocutionary speech act – that is, as a way of *saying* something by *doing* something.[6] For Fierke (2013, 37), self-sacrifice is 'an "act of speech" in which the suffering body communicates the injustice experienced by a community to a larger audience'. Moreover, she argues such acts also have *perlocutionary* force, in that they aim to persuade, convince or prompt certain emotions in their audiences.

Fierke's communicative understanding of self-sacrifice is in line with communicative theories of related acts of punishment and civil disobedience. Communicative theorists of punishment argue that the infliction of hard treatment serves to express the community's moral disapproval and aims to prompt reflection and remorse in the offender.[7] Moreover, in accepting punishment, i.e. the taking on of hard treatment, the offender engages in reparations and gives force or substance to an apology. Similarly, Kimberly Brownlee (2007) suggests that the civil disobedient's willingness to undergo punishment signals her opposition to an offending law, the sincerity of her conscience, and helps to persuade others to act to change the law. Fierke's communicative analysis of self-sacrifice seems the logical extension of these prior accounts.

While Fierke focuses on the general communicative function of political self-sacrifice, prominent theorists of non-violence, including M.K. Gandhi and Martin Luther King Jr., have focused on the particular messages and meanings that self-sacrifice can convey as part of non-violent resistance.[8] Gandhi (1920/1999, 135), for instance, insists on a fundamental connection between self-sacrifice and non-violent resistance such that, '[n]on-violence in its dynamic condition means conscious suffering'. As Joan Bondurant (1965, 27) explains, Gandhi intends this suffering to be a purposive, positive component of his theory. The sacrifice must be voluntary, without fear, and be an expression of love (*ahimsa*).

Gandhian self-sacrifice performs a number of functions, including the distinctly communicative aim of evoking sympathy and respect, and prompting cooperation. As with Brownlee's analysis of civil disobedience, Gandhi argues that a willingness to accept suffering can express the resister's commitment to her principles as well as her rejection of personal gain, and hence reflects a 'sincerity of purpose [... that] helps to persuade one's opponent that this objective is being pursued for the sake of justice and mutual benefit and not out of self-interest at their expense' (Atack 2012, 19).[9]

Gandhian self-sacrifice also has a perlocutionary dimension – i.e. a kind of *force*. Gandhi uses the term 'soul-force' to describe this phenomenon, which he argues helps overcome the limited persuasive power of rational discourse, which he takes to be a serious barrier in our fight against injustice. Our openness to reason, thinks Gandhi, is closely tied to the openness of our hearts, hence the need to pair appeals to reason with appeals to the heart.

This insight forms the theoretical core of Gandhi's particular form of non-violent resistance, *satyagraha*, which can be defined as 'truth-force, or, the [Gandian] technique for social and political change, based on truth, non-violence, and self-suffering' (Bondurant 1965, 260).[10]

When supporters of injustice refuse to listen to reason:

> The only effective way of bringing about a change in his attitude is satyagraha. It is a divine law that even the most hard-hearted man will melt if he sees his enemy suffering in innocence. The satyagrahi volunteers to suffer in this way. (Gandhi 1913/1999, 290)

And while it may be overly optimistic to claim that every individual will be sensitive to another's sacrificial suffering, Gandhi correctly identifies an important obstacle and proposes a method that takes that obstacle seriously.

Barbara Deming (1971/2002) makes a similar claim about the perlocutionary aims of non-violent resistance. For Deming (1971/2002, 149–150), the non-violent resister 'tries to shake [the enemy] out of former attitudes…'. Similarly, Emmeline Pankhurst (as quoted in Purvis 2002, 146), describing the perlocutionary power of sacrifice, says that:

> the willing endurance of suffering in order to gain the power to help the helpless, always has been, and always will be, the most powerful appeal to the sympathy and imagination of the great mass of human beings.

Self-sacrifice, then, can play a valuable communicative role in resisting oppression, especially for non-violent resistance. Moreover, it offers a potentially powerful way of prompting valuable emotional responses that could aid its uptake.

5.2 Transformative

Self-sacrifice can also play a *transformative* role in political resistance; that is, it can prompt a substantive change, in the resister or in others, and it can transform the nature of an act into an act of resistance. Gandhi, for instance, suggests that self-sacrifice is an essential component of a (non-violent) opposition to injustice. He insists that genuine social and political revolution requires individuals forgo the benefits or advantages that the existing unjust system offers them. In other words, they must sacrifice the benefits they would otherwise enjoy if they are to achieve the social transformation they seek. For example, rather than importing contemporary (for the time) British textiles, Gandhi advocated adopting *swadeshi* (home production), which included the home-spinning of a simple fabric for locally made garments (Bondurant 1965, 106, 180). Gandhi acknowledged that many felt that wearing these local garments rather than modern British fashion and fine textiles constituted a sacrifice. But the imported cloth not only financially contributed to Britain's rule over India; it also represented the adopting of British 'civilization'. Further, shifting to locally-made cloth provided socially productive employment, thereby combatting poverty. For these reasons, Gandhi argued, *swadeshi* ought to be recognized as a step towards *Swaraj* (self-rule). Continuing to buy imported clothes involved perpetuating and participating in injustice while *swadeshi* conversely marks the refusal to enjoy the benefits or the products of injustice.

For Gandhi, this is more than a temporary tactical measure – to the extent that the benefit is an integral part of an unjust system, forgoing that benefit is a step towards creating a replacement.[11] The associated sacrifice marks revolution, in the form of transitioning to a new system, which cannot be attained without giving up or forgoing the privileges and accustomed comforts of the old. This pre-figurative component of Gandhian self-sacrifice constitutes the revolutionary rejection of dominant forms of socio-political organization based on violence, and marks it, in Iain Atack's (2012, 96) terminology, as *transformative nonviolence*.[12]

There is one further sense in which self-sacrifice can be transformative and thereby assist in fighting oppression. As Gandhi notes, self-sacrifice is not always easy. While Gandhi thinks many have a natural ability to self-sacrifice, engaging in self-sacrifice when needed is not simply a matter of agency and force of will, it is also a matter of having a cultivated disposition. Engaging in self-sacrifice works to train this disposition such that you find it easier to self-sacrifice in the future. This is valuable not only for instrumental reasons, but on Gandhi's view, is also a central component of personal self-rule and wider social justice. Controlling one's desires and attachments, and reducing the boundaries of the self, bring one closer to the truth of our connected and relational condition.

Martin Luther King Jr. describes this as the 'redemptive' power of non-violence. King is explicit about the connection between non-violence and self-sacrifice, defining non-violence as the acceptance of 'suffering without retaliation' where standing for justice requires 'willingness to suffer and sacrifice' (Washington 1991, 9–10). As with Gandhi, King does not advocate suffering and sacrifice out of deference or passivity, rather it is integral component of his method of redemption through non-violence. This redeeming power is bi-directional for King, transforming both the resistor and oppressor. For the resistor, self-sacrifice restores the self-respect and sense of dignity that had been damaged by racist oppression and degradation. He claims:

> the impact of the nonviolent discipline has done a great deal toward creating in the mind of the Negro a new image of himself. It has literally exalted the

168 SACRIFICE AND MORAL PHILOSOPHY

person of the Negro in the South in the face of daily confrontations that scream at him that he is inferior or less than because of the accident of his birth. (Washington 1991, 125)

Redemption is also enabled for the oppressor, and for the wider society. In his essay on 'The Ethical Demands of Integration', King notes the limited power of law and punishment to 'bring an end to fears, prejudice, pride, and irrationality, which are the barriers to a truly integrated society' (Washington 1991, 124). Rather, the requisite change in social attitudes needed to support genuine emancipation must be initiated another way, namely, through love and a willingness to suffer. Barry Gan (1990/2002) argues that this attitudinal conversion is tied to the ability of self-sacrifice to elicit feelings of shame and embarrassment in one's opponent, without the express *intent* to provoke these emotions. Shame and embarrassment, claims Gan, can be evoked only when one believes one's actions to be wrong which is unlikely if one attributes one's actions to provocation, i.e. if you feel someone has forced you to act a certain way. Gan claims that through her willingness to suffer, the non-violent resister is better able to avoid the perception that they have provoked shameful action, and hence reveal the oppressor's own responsibility for her choice and thus enable conversion. As King writes:

The nonviolent resister does not seek to humiliate or defeat the opponent but to win his friendship and understanding [...] It is merely a means to awaken a sense of shame within the oppressor but the end is reconciliation, the end is redemption. (Washington 1991, 12)

The above remarks identify four distinct ways in which self-sacrifice can play a transformative role in non-violent resistance. First, self-sacrifice can be instrumental in social transformation, in the sense that resources are redirected towards resistance efforts. Second, the self-sacrifice associated with forgoing the benefits of an oppressive system can be pre-figurative, and thus be constitutive of socio-political transformation. Third, one can engage in self-sacrifice as a way to transform oneself by developing dispositions and habits of self-control that are intrinsically valuable as well as instrumental in facilitating future sacrifices. As King notes, self-sacrifice as part of non-violent resistance can also help restore dignity and transform one's sense of worth. And fourth, self-sacrifice can prompt the feelings of shame and embarrassment that aid conversion, and hence provide a route to redemption.

5.3 *Illustrative*

Finally, self-sacrifice can play an *illustrative* role in fighting oppression, that is, it can help to make injustice visible and concrete. Injustice is often

SACRIFICE AND MORAL PHILOSOPHY

upheld or perpetuated via commonplace institutions or practices that appear to enjoy widespread support. That is, the violence that underpins our participation in these practices is implicit or obscured.[13] Resisting these practices thus requires making their violent enforcement visible. This can often be achieved by refusing to cooperate with the norm, accepting the resulting consequences, and thus highlighting the source of the violence.

Relatedly, Fierke argues that self-sacrifice can work to transform bodies into social artefacts that give substance to ideological conflict. It can constitute an embodied resistance to, or rejection of, the dominant regime's attempt to determine the meaning of contested immaterial concepts such as freedom, justice, or equality. As Fierke (2013, 90) argues, self-sacrifice 'allows otherwise disembodied beliefs [...] to be reconnected with the force and power of the material world'. In this way, self-sacrifice physically demonstrates the workings of power and its material significance. For example, take Pankhurst's characterization of the suffragettes' hunger-strike while in prison:

> Human life for us is sacred, but we say if any life is to be sacrificed it shall be ours; we won't do it ourselves, but we will put the enemy in the position where they will have to choose between giving us freedom or giving us death. (as quoted in Purvis [2002, 216])

Pankhurst's comments reveal the suffragettes' attempts to determine the meaning of their sacrifice, and to materialize the nature of their unfreedom. The comments also indicate that one aim of the protest was to locate the perpetrators of injustice. The suffragettes' actions demonstrate where the choice lies, or who is making the choice between freedom and death. It is not the suffragettes who are looking to 'cause trouble' or are making demands, rather their actions *point*, or direct our attention towards others as the orchestrators of conflict.

A second way in which self-sacrifice can be illustrative comes from Cheyney Ryan's (1994) interpretation of Dorothy Day's view on non-violence, and in particular, how to understand self-sacrifice as shared suffering. Ryan explores Day's position through discussion of a specific form of self-sacrifice, namely, self-immolation. According to Ryan (Ryan 1994, 32), Day takes self-immolators as trying to 'endure the sufferings' inflicted on others. In this way, their acts ought not be taken as infliction of self-harm, but rather as 'taking violence upon oneself' (25) as a form of non-violent resistance. This endurance of suffering is not an act of compassion, but rather of *identification*; that is, it is not 'suffering *for* the Vietnamese [but] *sharing* their sufferings, so that their sufferings just *are* her sufferings too' (Ryan 1994, 32). Identification for Day is not purely conceptual nor affective, but is rather an embodied 'oneness'.[14] As Ryan (1994, 34) explains, '[i]n Dorothy Day's views, [to] say that we each

170 SACRIFICE AND MORAL PHILOSOPHY

instantiate the same "body" is to say that each of our lives can exemplify the fact of human suffering'. So, by taking violence upon themselves, self-immolators *exemplify* the suffering of others, suffering that otherwise may have been overlooked or ignored. To clarify, such acts (on Day's view) do not simply convey or communicate the suffering of others, they *show* this suffering via their self-sacrifice. Thus, self-sacrifice can play at least three illustrative roles: first, suffering that results from non-cooperation with oppression can reveal injustice and how it works. Second, self-sacrifice can give concrete reality to the abstract and contested values that inform the conflict. Finally, self-sacrifice can demonstrate oneness and make others' suffering visible.

5.4 *Summary*

Our discussion has outlined a number of ways in which self-sacrifice is considered valuable with respect to non-violent resistance. These include locutionary and perlocutionary communicative functions that can supplement rational argument against injustice. Second, self-sacrifice can be an essential feature of genuinely revolutionary transformation, as old privileges are given up and new ways of living are established. Relatedly, self-sacrifice contributes to transforming the individual, grounding dignity and self-respect, and cultivating dispositions for resistance. Finally, self-sacrifice can provide a material illustration of ideological conflict and make suffering and injustice visible.

6. Self-Sacrifice and Feminist Resistance

We will now explain the ways in which the value of self-sacrifice outlined above could prove attractive to feminists, and in particular, for a feminist ethics of care.

First, while not all women are committed to non-violence, women do have a long historical association with peace and with non-violent action. Furthermore, there are numerous feminist critiques of war and violence that lend support to the idea that feminists ought to be engaged in *non-violent* resistance to injustice, including in their fight against patriarchy.[15] Many of the positions discussed above are explicitly theories of non-violent resistance and thus ought to be of interest to feminists keen to pursue non-violent resistance to various forms of oppression. Importantly, self-sacrifice played a key role in these theories of non-violent resistance. Therefore, to the extent that feminists want to non-violently oppose oppression, they should consider a role for self-sacrifice.

Second, feminists have become particularly interested in the phenomenon of implicit bias and other psychological or attitudinal factors supporting oppression.[16] There is growing recognition that rational argument against injustice or oppression has limitations, namely, it frequently fails to convince. Moreover, the feminist focus on institutional reform has proved incomplete – resolving oppression requires changing attitudes. This issue mirrors King's analysis of segregation, and the change of attitudes needed in order to achieve genuine integration rather than mere formal desegregation. Feminists then may find a valuable resource in King's transformative (or redemptive) account of self-sacrifice. Relatedly, feminists may wish to promote self-sacrifice as a practice that men, for instance, could take up as a way to give up the privileges of patriarchy as well as cultivating dispositions to self-sacrifice. Finally, feminists can look to the perlocutionary power of self-sacrifice to give emotive force to their appeals.

Relatedly, a major obstacle to combating oppression is that oppressed groups frequently lack the means to participate in dominant discourses, or their contributions are devalued. They may, for example, find their concerns are not reported in mainstream media, or are not taken seriously. That is, such groups often find themselves silenced. The communicative and illustrative potential of self-sacrifice may offer another way to voice disagreement or dissent, and to give that voice force that oppressed groups lack in other media.

Finally, while theorists such as Fierke noted the general locutionary function of self-sacrifice, the above discussion also highlighted the particular messages associated with non-violent self-sacrifice. Here, we saw connections between self-sacrifice and sincerity, but also, importantly, connections with expressions of care and solidarity. Self-sacrifice can work to communicate support for those subjected to injustice, but also communicates inclusivity towards those upholding the unjust system. This 'universal love' (King) should appeal to care ethicists in particular, as it does not require an individual to 'choose' between parties; rather, care is expressed towards all. Moreover, the perlocutionary power of self-sacrifice can evoke feelings of sympathy and solidarity in others. As Deming (1971/ 2002, 149–150) writes, non-violent struggle aims to 'shake him out of former attitudes and force him to appraise the situation now in a way that takes into consideration your needs as well as his'. In this way, self-sacrifice can enable others to care.

These are some ways in which feminists might find value in the practice of self-sacrifice. In light of these potential benefits, it is worth revisiting the initial responses care ethicists put forward in reply to feminist critiques of self-sacrifice. Do the various theories just explored give reason to evaluate one response as more promising than the others?

First, recall the self-care response, which attempts to avoid the problems noted by feminist critiques by setting limits on the extent to which someone ought to sacrifice. These limits are grounded in the imperative to care for oneself as a necessary component of caring for others. There are two problems with pursuing this approach given the noted values of self-sacrifice. First, it seems possible to understand the demand to engage in self-care as being fulfilled *precisely by engaging* in self-sacrifice rather than avoiding it. As we saw above, King argued that self-sacrifice can restore self-respect and a sense of dignity to those damaged by violence and subjugation. Moreover, caring for others may require one to sacrifice benefits or privileges of oppression as part of revolutionary change. So, rather than protecting against oppression, the self-care restrictions work to hamper one's ability to combat oppression.

The second problem stems from the relational account of human nature, where if one sacrifices too much, and hurts herself, she harms others. It is not obvious, though, that harming is always incompatible with care. Ruddick (1995, 164), for example, distinguishes between harm and damage, where harm can sometimes facilitate learning and growth, whereas damage confers no benefits. Ruddick argues that the ideal of preservative love that informs mothering is compatible with allowing harm (at times), but incompatible with allowing damage. If this is correct, then it is not clear that the self-care approach will be able to restrict self-sacrifice as intended.

This leads to a final, and related point. The self-care response suggests that it is the *level* of sacrifice that must be limited, understood in terms of sacrificed interests. However, many of the valuable roles discussed above were not tied to the *level* sacrificed, but rather to the form or substance of the sacrifice. In this sense, the self-care approach seems to impose misguided limits on self-sacrifice that may preclude its supporters from engaging in valuable forms of sacrifice.

The second response, as put forward by Pudner, distinguished four forms of self-sacrifice, rejecting three forms (immolation, deference and effacement) as incompatible with valuing autonomy. But the fourth form, self-donation, involves an agent autonomously contributing to the good of another and is therefore unproblematic on Pudner's view. Pudner's self-donation approach locates the (dis)value of sacrifice in its form rather than its level. However, as presented, there are two problems with this account. First, the account is too narrow, and excludes numerous forms of valuable self-sacrifice. For example, it is possible to autonomously engage in valuable communicative self-sacrifice without promoting another's interests (i.e. does not qualify as self-donation), but also without destroying or disvaluing the self or deferring to another (i.e. does not qualify as immolation, deference or effacement). Similarly, King's transformative account, and Day's illustrative account of exemplification are not obviously describable in terms of self-donation. It may be possible to modify Pudner's account to be more inclusive, though this likely requires significant revision of her response. In particular, it would require rethinking the central place she gives to autonomy. Autonomy may be one important consideration, but it is not the only relevant factor. So, while a Pudner-type response may be the way forward, Pudner's particular characterization is too coarse-grained for purpose.

Finally, the third response argued that care ethics is best understood as only one component of morality, and its requirements for self-sacrifice could be balanced through combining it with other components, such as justice. At first glance, this seems a promising approach given this section's focus on resistance to injustice and oppression. However, considerations of justice may not restrict or limit self-sacrifice. Given the roles self-sacrifice can play in resisting injustice, it is likely that combining care ethics with a justice perspective will *expand* opportunities for legitimate self-sacrifice. Moreover, appealing to rights may not help: Gandhi (2009, 88), for example, describes his non-violent resistance as a 'method of securing rights by personal suffering'. Furthermore, this justice response repeats the mistake of characterizing the problem of self-sacrifice as one about amounts, or excessive levels of sacrifice, rather than about its form. This perhaps reflects the contemporary focus on distributive justice, wherein a core feminist complaint about sacrifice could be read as a complaint about unequal *distribution* of sacrifice, i.e. that women sacrifice more than men do. If so, this represents only one model of justice, and pairing care ethics with alternative models of justice may result in a different approach to self-sacrifice.

This initial review suggests the existing responses on offer to reconcile care ethics and sacrifice are either misguided or underdeveloped. However, it has provided some insight into the value of self-sacrifice, particularly for pursuing non-violent resistance, and suggests promising directions for future development in this area. In particular, this review suggests care ethicists ought to focus their efforts on delimiting the *forms* of sacrifice that are valuable, rather than trying to specify permissible *levels* of sacrifice. Moreover, we ought to look beyond the value of autonomy, and distributive models of justice, when developing these future accounts.

7. Conclusion

In many ways, care ethics offers an attractive alternative to traditional moral theory. It gives weight to sentiments, concerns and practices unjustly ignored or disvalued by dominant ethical discourse. However, its celebration of care, and the related sacrifices it seems to demand, has been accused of reproducing the norms that contribute to women's subjugation. In response, care ethicists proposed three ways to limit the role that self-sacrifice plays in their theories, thereby distancing themselves from what, for women, has been an historically oppressive virtue. We outlined three such strategies, namely the Self-care, Self-donation and Justice responses, and the ways in which they attempt to limit the level, form and scope of permissible self-sacrifice in care ethics. However, the resulting restrictions give no consideration to the multiple ways in which self-sacrifice can contribute to fighting oppression. We have tried to fill this lacuna. By examining the work of exemplary non-violent resisters, including Gandhi, King, Pankhurst and Day, we distinguished three main functions that self-sacrifice can serve: communicative, transformative and illustrative. This analysis allowed us to offer a critical review of the existing attempts to restrict self-sacrifice in care ethics, concluding that all three risk rendering potentially invaluable methods of non-violent resistance, impermissible. It may be possible, however, to revise either the self-donation, or the justice strategies in light of this analysis, such that they better incorporate the positive value of self-sacrifice as political resistance. We have laid the foundations for this revision, and are optimistic that the supposed tensions between care ethics and self-sacrifice can be resolved to reveal a powerful and revolutionary moral theory that is well-equipped for the struggle against oppression.

Admittedly, revising care ethics to better incorporate the value of self-sacrifice must also acknowledge the particular obstacles that women face in employing self-sacrifice to combat oppression. As Fierke notes, the communicative and illustrative roles that self-sacrifice can play are dependent on the social meanings of particular acts. Thus, to the extent that women's self-sacrifice occurs in a patriarchal context where it is expected, it may struggle to function as resistance. This is an important obstacle, but one we suspect is resolvable, and addressing it promises to generate innovative ways to think about self-sacrifice, care ethics and non-violent resistance.

Notes

1. Held (2006, ch.1) claims that this is one of five common features of different forms of care ethics. The others include valuing emotions as an important source of moral insight, skepticism towards abstract and universal moral principles, a reconceptualization of the public/private distinction and a rejection of liberal views of personhood.
2. Though note that Walker's (1984) study shows no difference in moral development between the sexes when subjects are matched for education and profession.
3. Note that Pudner is responding to a worry about caring in general raised by Carse (2005) and Piper (1991), rather than the specific feminist objection that care ethics undermines feminism's aims.
4. See for example Flanagan and Jackson 1987, Grimshaw 1986 and Hampton 1993.
5. Fierke (2013, 34) distinguishes between suicide and self-sacrifice, arguing that while both acts involve the self-infliction of harm, suicides are frequently individual, apolitical acts, whereas self-sacrifices are performed for the 'interests of the group'.

6. J.L. Austin (1962) distinguishes between locutionary, perlocutionary and illocutionary speech acts. A locutionary act is the 'performance of an act *of* saying something', i.e. a meaningful utterance, whereas an illocutionary act is the 'performance of an act *in* saying something' i.e. utterances that themselves constitute a further action (99). A perlocutionary act is an attempt to produce certain effects via an utterance. Austin offers the following example: Consider the utterance 'Shoot her!' The locution consists in the content, or the meaning of the words expressed. The illocution is the act of urging, ordering, or advising one to shoot her. Finally, the perlocution is being persuaded to shoot her, i.e. the effect on one's thoughts, feelings, or actions (101–102).
7. For work on communicative theories of punishment, see Feinberg 1965, Von Hirsch 1993, and Duff 2001.
8. Other advocates of non-violence who extoll the virtues of self-sacrifice include Jane Addams, Cesar Chavez, Dorothy Day, Leo Tolstoy and Simone Weil.
9. Bondurant(1965, 28–29) clarifies that Gandhian self-suffering is undertaken as an act of courage and expression of dignity, not as a submission or humiliation.
10. Someone who practices *satyagraha* is called a *satyagrahi*.
11. For example, Gandhi did not intend for Indians to take up fine clothes once India had gained political independence – he wanted *swadeshi* to continue, gaining an established place in the Indian economy.
12. Atack (2012, 86–96) distinguishes between civil resistance, which aims to reinforce or restore the liberal democratic elements of the modern state, and transformative nonviolence which aims to replace state institutions.
13. See for example, Havel (1985) on post-totalitarianism, or Butler (1990) on gender norms and performance.
14. Day (as a Catholic Worker) understands this oneness in terms of the Christian 'Mystical Body of Christ' (Ryan 1994, 34).
15. For feminist critiques of war and violence, see Ruddick 1995 and Cockburn 2010. There are also a number of feminist philosophers who do not endorse theories of non-violent resistance. Examples include Peach (1994) and Eide (2008).
16. See, for example Brownstein and Saul 2016 and Vierkant and Hardt 2015.

Disclosure Statement

No potential conflict of interest was reported by the authors.

References

Atack, I. 2012. *Nonviolence in Political Theory*. Edinburgh: Edinburgh University Press.
Austin, J. L. 1962. "Lecture VIII." In *How to Do Things with Words*, edited by J. O. Urmson, 94–107. Oxford: Clarendon Press.
Bondurant, J. 1965. *Conquest of Violence: The Gandhian Philosophy of Conflict*. Berkeley: University of California Press.

Brownlee, K. 2007. "The Communicative Aspects of Civil Disobedience and Lawful Punishment." *Criminal Law and Philosophy* 1: 179–192. doi:10.1007/s11572-006-9015-9.

Brownstein, M., and J. Saul, eds. 2016. *Implicit Bias and Philosophy, Volume 2: Moral Responsibility, Structural Injustice and Ethics.* Oxford: Oxford University Press.

Butler, J. 1990. *Gender Trouble.* New York: Routledge.

Carse, A. L. 2005. "The Moral Contours of Empathy." *Ethical Theory and Moral Practice* 8 (1): 169–195.

Cockburn, C. 2010. "Gender Relations as Causal in Militarization and War." *International Feminist Journal of Politics* 12 (2): 139–157. doi:10.1080/14616741003665169.

Deming, B. 1971/2002. "On Revolution and Equilibrium." In *Nonviolence in Theory and Practice,* edited by R. Holmes and B. Gan, 138–151. 3rd ed. Long Grove: Waveland Press.

Duff, A. 2001. *Punishment, Communication, and Community.* New York: Oxford University Press.

Eide, M. 2008. "'The Stigma of Nation': Feminist Just War, Privilege, and Responsibility." *Hypatia* 23 (2): 48–60.

Feinberg, J. 1965. "The Expressive Function of Punishment." *The Monist* 49: 397–423.

Fierke, K. M. 2013. *Political Self-Sacrifice: Agency, Body and Emotion in International Relations.* Cambridge: Cambridge University Press.

Flanagan, O., and K. Jackson. 1987. "Justice, Care, and Gender: The Kohlberg-Gilligan Debate Revisited." *Ethics* 97 (3): 622–637.

Gan, B. 1990/2002. "Loving One's Enemies". In *Nonviolence in Theory and Practice,* edited by R. Holmes and B. Gan, 306–313. 3rd ed. Long Grove: Waveland Press.

Gandhi, M. K. 1913/1999. "No Settlement." In *The Collected Works of Mahatma Gandhi Vol 13,* 289–291. New Delhi: Publications Division Government of India. Accessed August 16 2017. http://gandhiserve.org/cwmg/VOL013.PDF.

Gandhi, M. K. 1920/1999. "The Doctrine of the Sword." In *The Collected Works of Mahatma Gandhi Vol 21,* 133–136. New Delhi: Publications Division Government of India. Accessed August 16 2017. http://gandhiserve.org/cwmg/VOL021.PDF.

Gandhi, M. K. 2009. "Hind Swaraj." In *Hind Swaraj and Other Writings,* edited by A. Parel, 1–123. Cambridge: Cambridge University Press.

Gilligan, C. 1982. *In a Different Voice.* Cambridge, MA: Harvard University Press.

Grimshaw, J. 1986. *Philosophy and Feminist Thinking.* Minneapolis: Minnesota university Press.

Groenhout, R. E. 2003. "I Can't Say No: Self-Sacrifice and an Ethics of Care." In *Philosophy, Feminism, and Faith,* edited by R. E. Groenhout and M. Bower, 152–174. Bloomington: Indiana University Press.

Hampton, J. 1993. "Feminist Contractarianism." In *A Mind of One's Own: Feminist Essays on Reason and Objectivity,* edited by L. M. Antony and C. Witt. Boulder: Westview Press.

Havel, V. 1985. "The Power of the Powerless." In *The Power of the Powerless: Citizens against the State in Central-Eastern Europe,* edited by J. Keane, 23–96. New York: M.E. Sharpe.

Held, V. 2006. *The Ethics of Care: Personal, Political, and Global.* Oxford: Oxford University Press.

Hoagland, S. L. 1991. "Some Thoughts About 'Caring'." In *Feminist Ethics,* edited by C. Card. Lawrence: University Press of Kansas.

Hoagland, S. L. 1992. "Lesbian Ethics and Female Agency." In *Explorations in Feminist Ethics*, edited by E. B. Cole and S. Coultrap McQuin, 156–164. Bloomington: Indiana University Press.

Jagger, A. M. 1991. "Feminist Ethics Projects, Problems, Prospects In." In *Feminist Ethics*, edited by C. Card. Lawrence: University Press of Kansas.

MacKinnon, C. 1987. *Feminism Unmodified*. Cambridge: Harvard University Press.

Noddings, N. 1984/2013. *Caring: A Relational Approach to Ethics and Moral Education*. Berkeley, CA: University of California Press.

Noddings, N. 1989. *Women and Evil*. Berkeley, CA: University of California Press.

Peach, L. 1994. "An Alternative to Pacifism? Feminism and Just-War Theory." *Hypatia* 9 (2): 152–172.

Pettersen, T. 2012. "Conceptions of Care: Altruism, Feminism, and Mature Care." *Hypatia* 27 (2): 366–389.

Piper, A. M. 1991. "Impartiality, Compassion, and Modal Imagination." *Ethics* 101 (4): 726–757.

Pudner, K. H. 2007. "What's so Bad about Self-Sacrifice? Immolation, Abnegation, Effacement, and Donation in Ethics." *Proceedings of the American Catholic Philosophical Association* 81: 241–250.

Purvis, J. 2002. *Emmeline Pankhurst: A Biography*. London: Routledge.

Ruddick, S. 1995. *Maternal Thinking: Towards a Politics of Peace*. Boston: Beacon Press.

Ryan, C. 1994. "The One Who Burns Herself for Peace." *Hypatia* 9 (2): 21–39.

Vierkant, T., and R. Hardt. 2015. "Explicit Reasons, Implicit Stereotypes and the Effortful Control of the Mind." *Ethical Theory and Moral Practice* 18 (2): 251–265.

Von Hirsch, A. 1993. *Censure and Sanctions*. Oxford: Oxford University Press.

Walker, L. J. 1984. "Sex Differences in the Development of Moral Reasoning: A Critical Review." *Child Development* 55 (3): 677–691.

Washington, J. M., ed. 1991. *A Testament of Hope: The Essential Writings and Speeches of Martin Luther King, Jr.* San Francisco: HarperOne.

Woolf, V. 1942/2012. "Professions for Women." In *The Death of the Moth and Other Essays*, edited by V. Woolf. Urbana, IL: Project Gutenberg. Accessed August 1 2017. http://gutenberg.net.au/ebooks12/1203811h.html#ch-28.

The Cross

Sophie-Grace Chappell

ABSTRACT

My aim is a philosophical understanding of sacrifice, and especially of the Christian conception of sacrifice. Initially distancing myself a little from the strictly ritual notion of sacrifice, I work with a concept of sacrifice as 1) a voluntary choice (2) to forgo or lose or give away (3) something costly, perhaps supremely costly, (4) as an expressive action, where (5) what is so expressed typically is or includes devotion or loyalty to something exalted. I consider three historical examples of political sacrifices, sacrifices made for a cause, and three literary examples of personal sacrifices, sacrifices made by one person for another. I note that in the Christian context it is very common for sacrifices either political or personal to be taken to be imitations of Jesus' sacrifice as presented in the New Testament, and ask therefore how we are to understand that. My conclusion is that Jesus' sacrifice can be seen as involving both a political and a personal aspect—but that in fact, it can only be made as intelligible as may be by understanding it, as the Letter to the Hebrews does, in ritual terms.

Applied ethics today is very often preoccupied with questions such as "Should we kill the one to save the five?" In particular, that question is central to the booming sub-discipline of trolleyology. A question that is definitely *not* central for trolleyologists is: "What if the one volunteers to die on behalf of the five?"

What moral difference might it make if the one *consented* to sacrifice herself for the five? It is not that the trolleyologists can't ask this. It just that, generally, they don't.[1] The possibility of consensual sacrifice plays no role in the numerous standard trolley scenarios. In most of them, of course, the one would have no way of communicating his consent. But that is not sufficient reason to just rule out the possibility of consent as irrelevant to the trolley scenario. For the scenario is easily and frequently modified in various other respects. Why not in this one?

Like many silences in ethics, this silence gives something away. Typical discussions of the trolley scenario are shaped by and tailored to consequentialist

SACRIFICE AND MORAL PHILOSOPHY 179

assumptions: the whole point of the trolley, we might say, is to flatten agency down to button-pushing, to bring it about that there is nothing to anyone's agency except the consequences it produces. It goes with this flattening-down to keep *other* agents out of the picture, and ensure that the scenario is exclusively about a single button-pusher alone in the face of a manipulable but to all intents and purposes inanimate world. In trolley cases the six miners on the two tracks are present as loci of value, but in no important sense are they present as *agents*. That would make things too complicated.

Well, but real life *is* complicated, and one of the most obviously objectionable features of typical trolleyology is that it ignores the complications of real life. For sure it generates complications of its own (and how); but like a lot of other efflorescences of systematic moral theory, it has the wrong sort of complexity in the wrong places to represent anything like life as actual people actually experience it. In real life sacrifice is quite a common possibility, and nearly always a morally significant one when available. Maybe we should think a bit more about this possibility.

My aim in this essay is to try and make philosophical sense of sacrifice, and especially of the conception of sacrifice that has been culturally central in the West, the Christian one. For my purposes, the kind of sacrifices that are most worth attention consist in (1) a voluntary choice (2) to forgo or lose or give away (3) something costly, perhaps supremely costly, (4) as an expressive action, where (5) what is so expressed typically is or includes devotion or loyalty to something exalted. That plenty of real or possibly real sacrifices fit this framework is clear when we consider examples. In Sections I-II, I offer six: three from history, then three from fiction. The historical examples are all political sacrifices, sacrifices made by a person for a cause, and all involve figures later recognised as saints by the Catholic Church; the fictional examples are all personal sacrifices, sacrifices made by one person on another's behalf, and all have some relation or other to Victor Hugo. My main question about these examples is: if they are expressive actions, what do they express?

I: Three historical examples: "political" sacrifice

My first three examples are Maximilian Kolbe, Edith Stein, and Father Damien. I quote from the Wikipedia articles on each of them:[2]

(a) On 28 May 1941, Maximilian Kolbe was transferred to Auschwitz as prisoner #16670. Continuing to act as a priest, Kolbe was subjected to violent harassment, including beating and lashings... At the end of July 1941, three prisoners disappeared from the camp, prompting... the deputy camp commander to pick 10 men to be starved to death in an underground bunker to deter further escape attempts. When one of the

180   SACRIFICE AND MORAL PHILOSOPHY

selected men, Franciszek Gajowniczek, cried out, "My wife! My children!", Kolbe volunteered to take his place. According to an eye witness, in his prison cell Kolbe led the prisoners in prayer to Our Lady. Each time the guards checked on him, he was standing or kneeling in the middle of the cell and looking calmly at those who entered. After two weeks of dehydration and starvation, only Kolbe remained alive. The guards wanted the bunker emptied, so they gave Kolbe a lethal injection of carbolic acid.

(b) Edith Stein was born Jewish, in Holland in 1891; she converted to Catholicism and became a Carmelite nun... on 26 July 1942 the Reichskommissar of the Netherlands, Arthur Seyss-Inquart, ordered the arrest of all Jewish converts who had previously been spared. Along with 243 baptised Jews living in the Netherlands, Stein was arrested by the SS on 2 August 1942. Stein and her sister Rosa were imprisoned at the concentration camps of Amersfoort and Westerbork before being deported to Auschwitz. A Dutch official at Westerbork was so impressed by her sense of faith and calm, he offered her an escape plan. Stein vehemently refused his assistance, stating, "If somebody intervened at this point and took away her chance to share in the fate of her brothers and sisters, that would be utter annihilation." On 7 August 1942, early in the morning, 987 Jews were deported to the Auschwitz concentration camp. It was probably on 9 August that [Stein], her sister, and many more of her people were killed in a mass gas chamber.

(c) Father Damien [French; Flemish Damiaan] (born 3 Jan. 1840) won recognition for his ministry from 1873 to 1889 in the Kingdom of Hawaii to people with leprosy, who were required to live under a government-sanctioned medical quarantine on the island of Molokai... During this time, he taught the Catholic faith to the people of Hawaii. Father Damien also cared for the patients himself and established leadership within the community to build houses, schools, roads, hospitals, and churches. He dressed residents' ulcers, built a reservoir, made coffins, dug graves, shared pipes, and ate poi from his hands with them, providing both medical and emotional support. After 16 years caring for the physical, spiritual, and emotional needs of those in the leper colony, Father Damien realised he had also contracted leprosy when he was scalded by hot water and felt no pain. He continued with his work despite the infection but finally succumbed to the disease on 15 April 1889.

What were these sacrifices expressive of? I suggest five things: solidarity, protest, defiance, hope, and imitation.

SACRIFICE AND MORAL PHILOSOPHY

The most obvious thing these three sacrifices express is **solidarity**, common identity and common cause, with an oppressed group, as in Stein's insistence, just seen, on sharing the fate of her "brothers and sisters".[3] Damiaan too is firm that he will stand on the lepers' side when they are rejected by their own government in the then Kingdom of Hawaii, which should have been providing *for* them, not, as seems to have been the case, *against* them. In Kolbe's case the expressiveness is at least quadruple. He would not sign the Deutsche Volksliste, which would have saved him persecution by preventing his classification as a Pole; he hid Jews from their Nazi persecutors; he ministered to other inmates as a priest in Auschwitz; last and most costly of all, he took on himself someone else's condemnation to death.

Because all three sacrifices express solidarity, they are also, arguably, forms of **protest**. By standing with the victims of oppression, Kolbe, Stein, and Damiaan declare and witness that those victims' cause is just. By declaring the cause of the oppressed to be just, they declare the cause of their oppressors to be *un*just.

Protest against oppressors or evil-doers, even when one is unable to resist them by any means except such drastic steps as self-sacrifice, thus also involves **defiance**. If actions of sacrifice have the kind of expressive force just mentioned, then what they declare is an order of justice in the world that no oppressor can overturn: "No matter what you do, no matter what evil you bring on me, there is good and there is justice in this world that *you* cannot touch; and I stand with it."

Not that we should assume that acts of defiance of injustice, including sacrificial ones, are always so serious. There can be acts of defiance, and of sacrifice, that have an air of *parody*, of humour, about them. They almost mock the oppressor, by not just responding to his unreasonable demands, but *over*-responding to them (see Wells 2004). To turn the other cheek, to offer one's coat as well, can be a kind of *taking the mickey* out of the oppressor, of "winding him up", perhaps even, in St Paul's phrase, of "heaping coals of fire on his head" (Romans 12.20)—that is, of making him feel thoroughly guilty about what he is doing. It can be a way of questioning whether he really has any *power* over me, the supposedly oppressed, at all. As Socrates was at pains to prove by example, not everyone who ever sacrificed her life did so in a mood of grim underdog determination. Even in martyrdom there can be an almost light-hearted assertion that, despite everything the oppressor tries to do to me, I am as free as I could possibly be: the one who is really in chains is *him*, not me. And turning the other cheek can be all this and more too: see Section III.

This is why I say that the fourth thing that these three sacrifices involve, alongside solidarity, protest, and defiance, is **hope**: an unfailing trust in the truth of the ideals that one is prepared to die for, and a belief that those ideals will be vindicated, even if they do not look like being vindicated right now. Not that the person who is prepared to undergo self-sacrifice for what she believes in necessarily expects her own miraculous deliverance from the ordeal that is before her. Kolbe and Stein were not rescued, any more than about six million other victims of the Nazi death-camps; nor was Damiaan healed, any more than the lepers he lived with. But the victim hopes and trusts for the vindication of her ideal *some* time and *some*how, simply because it is a true ideal, and she has a primitive trust in the greatness and power of the truth to win out in the end: *magna est veritas et praevalebit* (see 1 Esdras 4.41).

That said, there is of course a specific form that vindication takes in the Christian tradition, and so in specifically Christian forms of sacrifice. And this brings us to the fifth expressive element in these three examples, namely **imitation**: "if by sharing in his sufferings, we may somehow also attain to his glory" (Philippians 3.10-11). This element of imitation seems to be, pretty clearly, part of what drew Kolbe in particular towards his act of penal self-substitution; no doubt the same element was there too in Stein's and Damiaan's motivations. No doubt, indeed, many other martyrs have gone willingly to their deaths without any clear understanding of what they are doing beyond this: that they are imitating Christ.

So if we ask what Kolbe, Stein, Damiaan, and others took themselves to be doing in so offering themselves we find ourselves in a sort of (unproblematic) regress when we get to this fifth feature. To understand their deeds fully, we need to understand what Christ took himself to be doing. (Or rather, what *they thought* Christ took himself to be doing. But here I shall mostly hop over that step, and simply assume that their views about that more or less tracked the truth.) In this way the discussion of this Section I, about Kolbe's, Stein's, Damiaan's, and similar sacrifices, points us on towards Sections III-V, which will be about Christ's sacrifice.

But before that, in Section II, I turn to a different kind of sacrifice: from the political, in which the sacrifice is made for a cause, to the personal, in which the sacrifice is made for a person.

II: Three fictional examples: "personal" sacrifice

The following three examples of sacrifice—and also, I think, of Christian sacrifice: see below—happen to be fictional examples. They need be none the worse for that. Maybe their fictionality even makes them clearer and less contentious examples of sacrifice than contestable examples gleaned from history, like my first three.

(d) Sydney Carton, in Charles Dickens' Victor-Hugo-influenced novel *Tale of Two Cities* (1859), goes to the guillotine in place of someone

SACRIFICE AND MORAL PHILOSOPHY 183

who looks just like him, Charles Darnay. He does this because he loves Darnay's wife Lucie, cares about her future happiness, and regards himself as a worthless drunkard whose life does not matter as much as Charles' and Lucie's.

(e) Gilda, in Verdi's 1851 opera *Rigoletto*—which derives its plot directly from Victor Hugo's 1832 play *Le Roi s'Amuse*—is in love with the lecherous, unfaithful, and impossibly debonair Duke; her love for him gets him as close as he ever gets to becoming a better man, though that is not very close. Her father, Rigoletto, has contracted an assassin, Sparafucile, to murder the Duke before midnight in revenge for seducing Gilda. Sparafucile's sister falls for the Duke when she sees him, and prevails on Sparafucile to spare the Duke's life, if someone else can be found for him to fulfil his contract by killing before midnight. Gilda makes sure that she is the one who gets in the way of Sparafucile's knife.

(f) Jean Valjean, in Victor Hugo's 1862 novel *Les Misérables*, was once a thieving, violent convict on the run; he has been transformed by the trust and forgiveness shown to him by the saintly old Bishop Bienvenu. Since his encounter with Bienvenu, Valjean has remade himself as a man of exemplary love and justice, and also as a respectable industrialist and mayor. But now he hears of Champmathieu, whom the police have mistaken for Valjean, and put on trial as Valjean. Champmathieu's conviction seems certain, but Valjean's conscience will not let him stand by while someone else is punished for his own crimes. He insists on travelling to the court himself and disrupting the trial by declaring his own guilt and Champmathieu's innocence. The court will not admit his testimony, and he is sent away free; yet Champmathieu's trial collapses, and he is freed too.

What Sydney Carton's and Gilda's sacrifices most clearly express is not protest or defiance or hope. And it is something for which *solidarity* is too weak a name. Rather, it is love: Carton's love for Lucie, and Gilda's love for the Duke. Both act out of love; but Carton is in no sense **protesting** against the guillotine, nor Gilda against Sparafucile, evil though they may well think them to be. Both of them see nothing to be **hoped** for from the one they love—Gilda because her father makes her see that the Duke is incorrigible (*son questi i suoi costumi*), Carton because he knows that Lucie loves not him but Charles, and even thinks it better that way. Nor is there **defiance** in their attitudes. Both accept their deaths as unprotestingly as if they were part of the order of nature; there has to be a death, and in both cases the victim prefers that it be his/her own rather the beloved's.

In the third example it is not that an innocent stands in for a guilty person, but that Valjean *is* guilty (legally, if not morally), and intervenes to protect a (legal and moral) innocent. What Valjean does is certainly "personal" rather than "political"; yet while his action expresses neither protest nor defiance nor hope, it does not express love either, nor even solidarity with Champmathieu. To Valjean, that he should give himself up to the court to prevent Champmathieu's unjust punishment is simply a matter of justice, and of nothing else.

So these personal, rather than political, sacrifices have a different character from the three that I considered in Section II. Those political sacrifices could *also* have the expressive forces that I've just attributed to personal sacrifices, viz. love and/or a reverence for justice. Those elements too are part of what Kolbe, Stein, and Damiaan were expressing. So there can be overlap between personal and political sacrifices: some of their expressive force can be shared. Nonetheless, the two categories of sacrifice remain different. Political sacrifices go, as their name suggests, with a devotion to a cause; personal sacrifices, as *their* name suggests, with a devotion to a person or persons.

What about the fifth expressive element that I saw in political sacrifices—imitation? In fiction it can be difficult to tell—for there need be no fact of the matter—whether a character intends her action to imitate someone else's. Yet all three of these stories play with a notion central to at least some Christians' notion of the Cross, namely penal substitution. Whatever determinate intentions, if any, Gilda and Valjean themselves may be supposed to have had—and both are depicted as pious Catholics—it is plausible that Victor Hugo intended[4] both of their sacrifices to wear, among other things, a theological significance. As for Sydney Carton, in a *Tale of Two Cities* Dickens seems to have been deliberately trying to write a novel in the grand manner of Victor Hugo's earlier and more Christian period. (*Two Cities* came out three years before *Les Misérables*, but rumours of what Hugo was up to were rife long before its actual appearance.) It is hardly accidental that Carton spends his last night pacing the streets of Paris and meditating on John 11.25, "I am the resurrection and the life".

The one kind of expressive content that all of my three political and three personal examples of Christian sacrifice seem to share, is *imitation*; imitation of Christ. That brings us back to the question that I first raised at the end of Section I: the question what it is that someone takes herself to be imitating, when she takes herself to be imitating Christ's sacrifice. In Section III, I ask what Jesus thought was the expressive force of his action in his own sacrifice.

III: The Cross as a political sacrifice

One caveat here: my question is "What did Christ take himself to be doing in his sacrifice?", but I intend this as an *exegetical* and not as a *historical* question. I am not here engaged in a subtask of "the quest of the historical Jesus": I am not asking what we today can know, as indisputable secular history, about the intentions of the mendicant rabbi and thaumaturge Yehoshua of Nazareth in 26-27 AD. Rather, I am asking what the New Testament (NT) tells us the Jesus of the Gospels thought he was doing in allowing himself to get crucified, and what those writers, and the Christian tradition since, took and have taken him to be doing.

Another caveat: while understanding a position and criticising it go hand in hand, my main task here is understanding, not critique. My subject in Sections III-V is the Christian account of Christ's crucifixion (for short: the Cross). I will aim to be suitably critical and reasonably sceptical in my discussion of the account. Still, before we try to say whether or not it is *true*, we need to get clear what it *is*.

"What is the meaning of Christ's death on the Cross? In what sense or senses is it a sacrifice?": I am aware that these are not very usual questions for a basically analytic philosopher like myself. The NT has next to nothing to say about either God's existence or the problem of evil, and is absolutely centrally concerned with the nature of Jesus' sacrifice; yet even Christian philosophers spend far more time on arguing about God's existence and on thinking about the problem of evil than they do on trying to develop a coherent philosophical account of the Cross. (In one way this is not surprising: as I know to my cost from trying to write this essay, those problems are far easier than the Cross.)

Nor is my method of addressing these questions particularly standard-philosophical. My aim is a philosophical understanding of a NT position. Since, as I've remarked, understanding a position necessarily comes before criticising it, much of what I do in the rest of this paper is exegetical: I aim to give an account of what the NT documents say by presenting a reading of them.[5] Thus my argument involves a close attention to the text of the NT. If you are unused to looking as closely at Biblical texts as you might look at Humean or Aristotelian ones, and/or allergic to "God stuff", bear with me. There is, I promise, a philosophical payoff to this exegetical exercise.

I suggest then first that the Cross has two groups of meanings. Referring back to my terminology above, we might expect these to be political and personal meanings. Let us see if that expectation is fulfilled. In this section I look for the political meaning of the Cross, and leave the question of personal or other meanings to Section IV.

I said above that political sacrifices typically have five things in their expressive content: solidarity, protest, defiance, hope, imitation. I shall argue that all five of these are visible in the Cross. So: solidarity with whom, protest at what, defiance of what, what hope, imitation of whom?

To understand that, we need first to look in some detail at Jesus' preaching and ministry as portrayed in the Gospels. For as I argue, the Cross is the

186   SACRIFICE AND MORAL PHILOSOPHY

logical conclusion of everything else that Jesus did in his public life. Politically speaking, what the Cross expresses is just a sharpened and intensified version of what Jesus' whole career expresses.

We need to look first, then, at the "gospel of Jesus" (Mark 1.1), and to ask a question that I suspect the average church-goer does not notice enough. (At any rate it took more than two decades of church-going for it to dawn on me.) The question arises, among other places, right at the beginning of the Gospel of Mark, where Mark says this (Mk 1.14):

> After the betrayal of John, Jesus came into Galilee preaching the gospel of God...

The question is simply this: What *is* the "gospel of Jesus"? What is the "good news" that Jesus is already preaching here? When ordinary church-goers hear the word "gospel", they naturally assume, and not I think just in evangelical circles, that what is meant is a story about how Jesus "died for our sins on the cross". More about that sort of story in Sections IV-V. But it should be self-evident that that can't have been what Jesus was preaching right at the beginning of his ministry, before any of it had happened; not even as a matter of prophecy. So what *was* he preaching? What was his good news?

The word *euaggelion* itself, the evangelists, and St Mark probably first among them, appear to have appropriated from the Septuagint version of Isaiah 61.1-2:[6]

> The Spirit of the Lord is upon me, because he has anointed me; he has sent me to preach glad tidings (*euaggelisesthai*) to the poor, to heal the broken in heart, to proclaim liberty to the captives, and recovery of sight to the blind ...

The word itself thus implies one sort of answer to our question. Another kind of answer, perhaps Mark's own, comes in the very next verse (Mk 1.15):

> ... [and saying] that "The fitting time is fulfilled, and the kingdom of God is very close. Repent, and put your faith in the gospel."

At the outset of his ministry, and indeed throughout it, the gospel that Jesus was preaching is, apparently, in essence just this: "the kingdom of God" (or of "heaven") is "at hand". As he variously puts it, it is very close, or is here today (Mt 4.21), or indeed it "has already overtaken you" (ἔφθασεν ἐφ' ὑμᾶς, Mt 12.28, Lk 11.20)—like an over-eager dinner-guest, it has arrived before you were ready for it; almost, "it has caught you napping".

What does Jesus mean by "the kingdom of God" or "the kingdom of heaven", and why is its coming good news, and why does it call for repentance? As Biblical scholars say, he is speaking the language of post-exilic apocalyptic. As twentieth-century German philosophers might say, he

SACRIFICE AND MORAL PHILOSOPHY 187

is speaking the language of existential urgency. Jesus talks as readily as the Old-Testament prophets Daniel and Zechariah of "the day of the Lord". And the point of such talk is to challenge human routine, human custom, human laws—and human oppressions—by declaring their utter vulnerability to the ever-present threat of the "refiner's fire" (Malachi 3.2) of God's justice. Human injustice, dishonest and deceitful living, racist outgrouping and scapegoating, greed, pride, oppression and brutality all stand, say Malachi and the other radical prophets, under this sentence: that God's judgement could fall upon them at any moment. And in his "gospel" Jesus repeatedly says the same, sometimes in a way that is all the more vivid for being said on a smaller scale and via the indirection of a parable (Luke 12.16-21):

> Jesus told them a parable, saying: "The land of a certain rich man yielded an abundant harvest. So he thought to himself, 'What shall I do, since I have no room to store my crops?' And he said, 'This is what I will do: I will pull down my barns, and build greater; and there will I store all my crops and my goods. And I will say to my soul, "Soul, you have many goods laid up for many years; take your ease, eat, drink, and be merry."' But God said to him, 'You fool, this night your soul shall be required of you: then whose shall those things be, which you have prepared?' This is what the man is like who lays up treasure for himself, and is not rich toward God."

The rich man is a fool not simply because he is rich, but because he puts his most basic existential confidence, not in God, but in his riches. He is not just rich, he "lives by" his riches, rather than by "every word that proceeds from the mouth of God" (Mt 4.4, quoting Deut 8.3). Whether or not what Jesus preached was a strict and consistent communism,[7] what is certain is that the difference between the rich man's perspective and what Jesus takes to be the true one, the perspective of our own mortality and of God's eternity, is no less than everything—all the difference there could possibly be.

So "proclaiming the kingdom of God" means seeing all human institutions and all human life as utterly impermanent—as impermanent as a sandcastle, Mt 7.27—and utterly vulnerable to God's power and God's judgement, of which human death is just the most obvious manifestation. To see God's kingdom as "near", or "at hand", or "among us", or as having "overtaken us", is to see no real power and no real force in anything else *except* God's judgement. The repentance that Jesus calls for is precisely the turn of the understanding (*metanoia*) that brings us to see things this way.

When we consider everything in the light of the idea of God's impending judgement, a different life becomes imperative for us. And that is the life that Jesus and his followers evidently tried to live, the life that he famously sketches out in the much admired, and too little imitated, words of the Sermon on the Mount (Mt.5-7). It is a life that repudiates human pride, acquisitiveness, watchful self-defensiveness, reputation-management, accumulated wealth of money or righteousness, and the rest of it. For short-lived and utterly dependent creatures like ourselves, all these—even when they do not lead us into committing serious evils—are pointless and burdensome distractions from the only things that really matter (Mt 6.25-33):

> Take no thought for your life, what you shall eat, or what you shall drink; nor yet for your body, what you shall put on. Is not life more than food, and the body than clothing? Behold the fowls of the air: for they sow not, neither do they reap, nor gather into barns; yet your heavenly Father feeds them. Are you not much better than they? Which of you by taking thought can add one cubit unto his stature? And why do you take thought for clothing? Consider the lilies of the field, how they grow; they toil not, neither do they spin: And yet I say to you, That even Solomon in all his glory was not arrayed like one of these. Therefore, if God so clothe the grass of the field, which today is, and tomorrow is cast into the oven, shall he not much more clothe you, O you of little faith? Therefore take no thought, saying, What shall we eat? or, What shall we drink? or, How shall we be clothed? (For after all these things do the Gentiles seek:) for your heavenly Father knows that you have need of all these things. But seek first the kingdom of God, and his righteousness; and all these things shall be added to you.

The life in question is also—crucially—a life that rejects all violence:

> You have heard that it was said, "An eye for an eye, and a tooth for a tooth"; but I say to you, "Do not resist evil." If anyone hits you on one cheek, offer him the other cheek too; if anyone takes you to court for your shirt, give him your coat as well; if anyone forces you to walk one mile, walk two. When someone begs from you give to him; when someone wants to borrow from you, lend to him. And you have heard that it was said, "You shall love your neighbour and hate your enemy"; but I say to you, love your enemies and pray for those who persecute you, so that you may be children of your father who is in heaven. For he makes his sun rise on the evil and the good, and sends rain on the just and the unjust alike.

The life that Jesus is teaching, by his proclamation that "The Kingdom of God is here", is a life of *complete* and *immediate* reliance on God's help: for food, for clothing, for vindication, and for protection from violence. Anything else—in his eyes—is an idolatrous denial of that central message, the message that "God's kingdom is come".

This teaching has two implications, one religious, and one strictly political. The religious implication is that we should not rely on any sort of human religion or intermediary between us and God: so not on religious systems or authorities or teachers or traditions. Jesus' sustained and repeated attacks on the "scribes and the Pharisees" (see e.g. Mt 23), and his refusal to teach the way they do ("he taught with authority, not like the scribes": Mk 1.22, Mt 7.29): all are based on precisely this thought. He sees

SACRIFICE AND MORAL PHILOSOPHY 189

"the scribes and Pharisees" as representatives and proponents of human religion, and he sees human religion not just as false, oppressive, self-righteous, and complacent, but also as *already broken and departed*. For what should replace it is the Kingdom of God; and Jesus' message is that the Kingdom of God is already here.

Likewise on the strictly-political side, what Jesus means when he says that "God's kingdom is here" is just this: that there is no power or force or vindication or protection to be had from anywhere else, *except* from God. For those that "repent", transform their understandings, to live as citizens of God's kingdom, the coming of *that* kingdom means *the departure of all other kingdoms*. His message "God's kingdom has come" might almost be understood, in our terms, as implying *So there is no more United Kingdom*. (Or United States, or Federal Republic of Germany, or Republic of Scotland, or whatever other secular polity, actual or possible, you care to name or happen to live in.)

To any contemporary ruler who picked up on what sort of "good news" Jesus's was, it must have been deeply alarming. The message that God's kingdom is coming—is already here—and by its very presence already judges and overthrows all human political systems, with all their violence, oppression, extortion, and domination: this message seems anything but good news to the agents of such systems.

Yet, given his pacifism, Jesus cannot be calling for the violent overthrow of worldly systems of government such as Herod's rule of a Roman client-kingdom in the Palestine of his day. Nor can he be calling for their replacement by what is called a theocracy, though what is usually meant is a theocratocracy. (See Iran, or Calvin's Geneva, or Jim Jones's church, or the Salem of *The Crucible*, or a hundred other sad and troubling examples.) Just as with human religion his message is not "Away with it!" but "It's already gone", so in the political case, he is not saying "All states must fall"; he is saying "They've already fallen."

Both religiously and politically, Jesus's gospel is not "We need a human revolution"; it is "We've already got a divine one." It is precisely because the kingdom of God is here *now* that people need to "repent" *now*. Where "repentance" means, to say it again, to recognise the utter contingency of all human forms of power and control and justice, whether religious or political, and the utter supremacy of *God's* power and justice; and to bring their whole way of living into line with that perspective.

With all this in place, we can now answer, about Jesus' preaching of his "gospel", the questions I asked above about the Cross. Jesus' **solidarity** is with the characters he calls *makarioi*, "blessed", in the Beatitudes (Mt 5.3-10)—a cast of characters who overlap notably with those mentioned by Isaiah in his chapter 61: the poor in spirit, the gentle, those who mourn, those who hunger and thirst for δικαιοσύνη (justice), the merciful, the pure

190   SACRIFICE AND MORAL PHILOSOPHY

in heart, the peacemakers, the persecuted. His **protest** is, correspondingly, against those who oppress them, whether religiously or politically, where "oppressing" them means imposing upon them, forcing them to live under, the perspective of kingdoms and rules, religious or political, other than the kingdom of heaven. For him to proclaim the kingdom of God is for him to **defy** all other political and religious authorities, as *idolatries*—as false gods —and to announce the dawning of a new hope for his people, the **hope** that they may come to live in the light of the perspective of the kingdom of heaven.

As for **imitation**: the question "Who if anyone is Jesus imitating?" might sound like it risks getting us into yet a further regress—from those who imitate Christ, to those whom Christ himself imitates. But the answer is straightforward. Jesus, I have said, rejects tradition in the sense of "human religion"; but in doing so, he is himself part of what we might call the anti-tradition tradition in Judaism. He sees himself as the last in a long line of radical prophetic voices all of whom had been in the business of calling Israel away from false and misleading reliance on human power and human authority, and back to the only truth and authenticity there is for human beings, which is immediate dependence and reliance on God himself.

Jesus himself repeatedly underlines his claim to stand in that anti-tradition tradition. However, Jesus goes further than mere imitation of the radical prophets. His claim is not so much that he is beholden to them as the origins of his preaching, as that they are beholden to him as the *telos* of *their* preaching. Thus he reads his home-town synagogue the lesson from Isaiah 61.1-2 already quoted above, about preaching good news to the poor, the broken-hearted, the prisoners, the blind, and the bruised— and his commentary on it, jaw-droppingly enough, is "This passage is fulfilled *in me*" (Luke 4.16-21). Jesus' proof that the "Day of the Lord is at hand" is a proof that none of the prophets before him ever dared to offer. His proof is *himself*. When he allows himself to enter Jerusalem to riotous acclamation, with cries from the crowd of "Hosanna to the son of David" (Mark 11.1-11), what it means, as he well knows, is that he is making the claim that *he himself* is the key and the unmistakable sign that God's kingdom has come: that is, the Messiah.

This then is the "gospel" that Jesus preached. So perhaps it is obvious now why I said earlier that Jesus' sacrifice is directly continuous with his preaching. From the beginning of his ministry, Jesus says that "the Kingdom of God is upon us", and means by it that there is now—perhaps there has never been—any real religious or political authority except God himself. (Not even Jesus himself is that authority—"Why do you call me good? One only is good" (Mk 10.18)—unless of course...) In the light of all this, it is simply inevitable that his preaching puts him on a collision course with both the religious and the political authorities of his day.

SACRIFICE AND MORAL PHILOSOPHY

But remember that it is essential to Jesus' teaching that he utterly rejects violence, weaponry, force of arms of every kind. (My question here is solely *what he actually taught,* and I hope to show that without the filter or distraction of *what it means today.* But one small point is irresistible: nothing looks more contrary to his teaching than contemporary US rifleolatry.) If we do not see that what he is proclaiming is the need for complete and unswerving reliance and dependence immediately on God and God alone—utterly defenceless, utterly naked, *without* all swords and guns and bombs—then we do not understand him at all.

Hence he is at all times wide open to arrest and execution by either or both of the religious authorities (who would stone him for blasphemy: the Jewish way) and the political authorities (who would crucify him for sedition: the Roman way). Indeed, despite the rather unpredictable measure of protection that comes from the crowds around him (Mt 22.2), Jesus judges it prudent to engage in deliberate elusiveness both physical (Jn 11.57) and doctrinal (Mt 13.34); to hold back the publicity about his Messianic claim as long as possible (Lk 4.41, Mk 8.27-30); and, regarding the miracle-stories that spring up around him wherever he goes, to do as little as possible to encourage them—apart, it seems, from performing lots of miracles (Mt 8.4, 8.16, 16.4). He is always far more vulnerable to the authorities than they seem to realise. On more than one occasion he is nearly captured long before Gethsemane (Jn 8.59, 10.39). As he himself almost sardonically points out to them when they finally do capture him (Mt 22.53), a Judas was nowhere near as necessary as they had supposed (Mt 22.5). Realistically speaking, given the imbalance of force between the authorities and Jesus, they were bound to get him eventually. Once they do, the question whether he dies by stoning or crucifixion is a point of detail. What matters to them is that he has been defying them, and therefore must die. Now from the first, Jesus acts in full knowledge that this is how his story is bound to turn out (Mt 16.21); which is one reason why I said above that his sacrifice and his preaching are one and the same.

This then is the sense in which Jesus' sacrifice is, as I called it, a political sacrifice. Can it also, as it so often has been, be taken as a personal sacrifice, in the sense of those words that Section II made clear? To that question I turn in Section IV.

IV: The Cross: a personal sacrifice?

I have noted the political aspects of the Cross, the sense in which it was a sacrifice that followed directly from Jesus' advocacy of a public cause. Did it also have a personal aspect? Was it an act prompted by one person's love for other persons? Jesus himself suggests as much, when he famously says to the disciples "Greater love hath no man than this, that a man lay down his life for his friends" (Jn 15.13) and, at the Last Supper, "Take and eat: this is my body" (Mt 26.26). There is probably no more familiar theme in all Christian hymnody than this idea that the Cross was an act of love shown not only to Jesus' actual friends—the small circle of his disciples, the rather larger circle of his other followers—but to all Christians everywhere, in fact to everyone who has ever lived, including *me*.

The idea that in some sense Jesus on the Cross "died for our sins", "took the punishment that was due to us", "was broken for me", is and always has been utterly central to Christian belief, practice, and preaching. But what does it mean to say that? If "he died for us", how does that actually work?

Most Christians in my own experience—including myself, quite often—are remarkably unclear about how to answer this question, and some of the commonest answers that they do give seem unworkable. I have heard a preacher expound the Cross by saying that it was like Maximilian Kolbe's self-sacrifice. Perhaps it was; but as an *explanation* of the Cross, this seems puzzlingly back-to-front. As I said in Section I, Kolbe was undoubtedly seeking to imitate Christ in his death. So if we add, in effect, that Christ was also imitating Kolbe, then we find ourselves working in a circle. Anyway, how is the analogy supposed to work? In the case of Jesus' death, who are the analogues of the SS, and how do they come to have power over his life, and what is *achieved* by their murdering him? Again, if Jesus' sacrifice really is *just* like Kolbe's, then in whose place does he die? The only plausible candidate is Barabbas. But if Jesus died for Barabbas in the way that Kolbe died for Gajowniczek, then surely Jesus died *only* for Barabbas.

Some theories of the Cross that are very popular, in both senses, say little more than that God the Father got so angry with us sinners that he just had to hit somebody, and God the Son got in the way of the blow. It does not look too edifying to see the Cross as a story of domestic abuse in heavenly places. Other familiar accounts have it that there is a price or a ransom to be paid for sin, and that Jesus pays that price or ransom; or that sin creates a gap between us and God, which the Cross bridges. These ideas get more puzzling the more one thinks about them. If the Cross pays a *ransom*, then to whom? Origen's answer, and sometimes Augustine's, was "to the Devil", and this answer, which might be scripturally founded on Hebrews 2.14-15, is echoed in the mediaeval carol's line that "Adam lay ybounden, bounden in a bond". But the idea that the Devil could be in a position to hold God's creation hostage ever since "the Fall", and require God to make payment for their release, seems to give Old Nick altogether too much power—and not just physical but juridical and fiscal power—over the Eternal One of Israel, the Lord of Hosts. The alternative answer is that the price or the ransom is paid to God, and specifically to God's *justice*, as opposed to God's *love*; or that the gap is between our sinfulness and God's goodness, and again, that Jesus' sacrifice bridges this gap.

But now the difficulty is to see why God Almighty, the God who can do anything, should not be able to bridge that gap *without* the Cross. Jesus commands his own followers to forgive, unconditionally and without demanding any kind of price for forgiveness (Mt 18.22). His followers might reason that if he commands them to do it, then they must be able to. But if they can do it, then so can God. Why then can an omnipotent God only forgive sins via the Cross? (Here one remembers Heine's marvellous death-bed quip: *Dieu pardonnera; c'est son métier.*)

Another account of the Cross, more usually found at the more "liberal" end of the theological spectrum, sees it as an act of radical identification. The meaning of the Cross is "Emmanuel, God is with us" (Mt 1.23): through it, Jesus comes where we are, enters right into the worst that can happen to us, shares with us in the darkest night that we ever go through; and in the resurrection, comes out the other side of that suffering, and shows us how we can too.

For myself, I find such an account moving and attractive. The main difficulties with this account are two. First, simply to understand it: to see *how* one person's suffering long ago and far away can help me or you when we suffer now. Secondly, to tie up any such account with the NT's clear and definite talk of sin and punishment and payment and ransom and restitution and atonement.

The answer to the first difficulty perhaps lies in religious experience: in suffering people's *experiencing* their suffering as something in which God is with them. I certainly do not have the impertinence to deny the reality of such experience—of which I know something for myself. On the other hand, neither can I shut my eyes to the equal reality of the experience of those who find themselves, in their suffering, totally lost, entirely alone, and completely comfortless—of which I also know something.

However that may be, the second difficulty remains unresolved by this account of the Cross. If the radical-identification story is *all* we have to say about the Cross, then we do have a (somewhat vague and mysterious) kind of answer to our original question, about how the Cross could be a personal sacrifice on Jesus's part, as well as a political one. But on the other hand, it is then hard to see how we can do anything very much with the NT talk of sin, punishment, payment, ransom, restitution, atonement that the "popular" accounts of the Cross, as I unkindly called them, do at least try to make sense of.

Maybe, for us today, that's how it has to be. Maybe there isn't, in all intellectual honesty, anything better we can do any more with the NT's atonement talk. Maybe the best we can make of the Cross is to combine an understanding of it as a political sacrifice in the sense outlined in Section III, with the kind of understanding of it as a personal sacrifice, such as that

194 SACRIFICE AND MORAL PHILOSOPHY

understanding is, that might be gained by treating the Cross as an act of radical identification.

Maybe; and this would not be *nothing*. And then maybe we will also be tempted by the further thought that there is something essentially *mysterious* about the Cross, something that necessarily eludes our understanding. Perhaps we will be attracted by the idea of applying to the Cross a more general suggestion that I have offered elsewhere:[8] that some of the deepest and richest sources of spiritual meaning and nourishment around us are *icons*. Great artworks are icons in the sense I mean: boundedly-polysemous subjects for contemplation, of which no single determinate explanation can ever be complete. Polysemous, because it is silly to look for *the* right reading of *King Lear* or *The Magic Flute*, as if there were exactly one, and as if the understanding of these dramas would be completed and "over" once that one right reading had been found. But boundedly polysemous, because it is not silly at all to look for *a rich and fruitful* reading of *King Lear* or *The Magic Flute*; the discipline involved in doing so is the discipline imposed by the text, which does not rule only one reading in, but does rule indefinitely many readings out. And looking for rich and fruitful readings is just what skilled interpreters do with such artworks.

Now maybe it is possible to see events that happen not in art but "in the real world" as icons too. If this *is* possible, if bounded polysemy applies to any real-world events, and if there is any truth in Christianity, then (you might think) it must be true above all of the Cross. And then there will be no single correct and complete *theory* of the Cross. So maybe this view could explain *why* the best we can do is try to give a variety of illuminating stories about the Cross, which however cannot be added up into one tidy story.

Maybe; and this would not be nothing either. Yet *for the NT writers*, there was nothing unclear or indeterminate about the meaning of the Cross. To them the whole business of the Cross was perfectly plain and clear, and they had a pretty complete and pretty precise theory of its meaning.

Moreover, as they saw it, it was this theory that explained the idea that Jesus' sacrifice was what I have called a personal sacrifice. As far as they were concerned, the only way in which Jesus *could* "lay down his life for his friends"—and hence, the only way of avoiding the riddles about the Cross that I have just briefly explored—was fully explained by this theory of the Cross.

We might put the point in a rather MacIntyrean way. Because we have lost the background intellectual framework within which the idea of the Cross was originally propounded, we are *bound* to find the Cross mysterious—and can only make it as intelligible to ourselves as it was to the generation that originally propounded it, by putting it back in that framework. In Section V, I try briefly to do just that.

V: The Cross as a ritual sacrifice

Here we come almost full-circle. The first building material that I rejected, or at least laid aside, at the outset, is actually the corner-stone of the theory of the Cross that we seek. For the NT's fullest and deepest theory of the Cross, the key notion is the Levitical notion of ritual sacrifice. And the key text is not the one that any Lutheran might expect, or any other Christian of broadly Protestant heritage, such as me. Neatly enough, given this essay's tendency in other respects to emphasise the *Jewishness* of Jesus and his gospel and sacrifice, it is not Romans; it is Hebrews.

I say "the NT's fullest and deepest theory of the Cross", which might make it sound as if there were a range of contender theories. Actually there are at most two. The only major division in the NT is—as I shall put it— between the radical-prophet theology of the Gospels and Acts, and the sacrifice theology of the Epistles and Revelation. Two very different accounts of the Cross are presented in these two divisions; not inconsistent with each other necessarily, but most certainly different.

Almost all the time in the Gospels and Acts, Jesus is portrayed in terms familiar from Section II above. He is shown as a radical prophet in the defiant, protesting tradition of the Old Testament, who makes a political sacrifice and is vindicated by God by being raised from the dead. This is the almost exclusive theme of the apostolic preaching in Acts (Acts 2.14, 3.12, 5.29, 7.1, 8.32, 9.20, 10.34, 13.38, 17.22, 26.23). To a degree that ought to disturb even the most supine pew-dweller from her not-even-dogmatic slumbers—and this too took far too long before it disturbed *me*—there is remarkably little in this preaching about the themes of atonement, propitiation, guilt, or sacrifice that are so much to the fore in the Epistles and Revelation, and so much the stock-in-trade of preaching, especially evangelical preaching, today.

The sacrifice theology of the Cross that the Epistles and Revelation depend upon is often left implicit, because it is not always directly what is being talked about; but it is always in the background. If we skim through the Epistles and Revelation, a catena of brief but suggestive allusions to the sacrifice theology can quickly be assembled: Rom 3.25, 1 Cor 11.25, Gal 3.13, Eph 2.11, 5.2, Col 1.22, 2.14, 3.1, 1 Tim 1.15, 2.5-6, 2 Tim 1.10, Titus 3.4, 1 Peter 3.18, 2 Peter 2.1, 1 Jn 2.2, Revelation 1.5, 5.6, 5.9, 8.14, 12.11, 13.8.

For something more than allusion, for a full and explicit exposition of the view, we turn to Hebrews. What Hebrews says, in brief, is just this (see especially Heb 2.17-18, 5.1-6, 7.23-27). There were many sacrifices, and now there is just one; there were many priests and many victims, and now the priest *is* the victim. What happened on the Cross is a sacrifice in something very like the way that the sacrifices laid down in Leviticus are;

196   SACRIFICE AND MORAL PHILOSOPHY

only more so. The point of a sacrifice, in Leviticus (see especially Chapters 1-7), is to take away sin, and recreate, by establishing (in blood) a new contract or "covenant", the human-divine relationship that has been disrupted. The more perfect the priest, and the more perfect the victim, the truer the sacrifice. Yet no earthly victim, and no earthly priest, can really be *completely* perfect; only God himself can be that. The ultimate sacrifice, then, the sacrifice that finally and definitively "fulfils the Law" (Mt 5.17), must be one *like* the Levitical sacrifices, and yet of an entirely different order, offered by a priest who, like the mysterious Melchizedek (Ps 110.4, Heb 6-7), is no Levite at all, and seems to have no clear human origin that anyone can trace. Since literal perfection is required both in priest and in victim, and since only God is literally perfect, this ultimate sacrifice must be *God offering God*; but since the sacrifice has to be one in which the priest represents humanity before and to God, it must also be *man-God offering man-God*. And that, says Hebrews, *is precisely what Jesus does on the Cross.*

This is the sacrifice theology's explanation of how it is possible for Jesus to "lay down his life for his friends". The required background intellectual framework, without which the idea of his laying down his life for his friends makes no clear sense, is the background laid out right here in Hebrews. And what Hebrews tells us is that Jesus can lay down his life for his friends because he is not only their friend, but also both perfect priest and perfect victim, offering to God, in his own person, the perfect sacrifice, the sacrifice to which all other sacrifices lead and in which they are all fulfilled, that stands for all time and atones for every person. In fact (Heb 9.23-26, 10.1, 10.12), if you like, the Cross is the Platonic Form of sacrifice.

VII: Sacrifice "aufgehoben"

This, then—if I am right—is the price that we have to pay to make the sacrifice of Jesus intelligible as a personal sacrifice, as Jesus' laying down of his own life for his friends, in the sense in which it was originally intended so to be understood by the authors of the NT, and in particular of the sacrifice-theology parts of the NT. The price is this: we have to see the sacrifice of Jesus in the terms of Levitical ritual sacrifice; but Levitical ritual sacrifice as transcended, consummated, perhaps even abolished, in one full and final oblation—in "the sacrifice to end all sacrifices".

We might, of course, think this a high price to pay. (We *might*: I am tracing a possible line of thought, not committing myself to it.) The reason would be, quite simply and eminently intelligibly, a cultured despising of all such barbarities. "To understand the Hebrews account of the Cross we have to buy into a bronze-age nomadic people's account of how they (putatively) get right with their (putative) God by (very much more than putatively) massacring goats and bulls and lambs and rams and pigeons? Thanks but

SACRIFICE AND MORAL PHILOSOPHY

no thanks." It is tempting to retort that, in popular religious controversialising today, the only time one is allowed to be un-PC about a primal people is when dismissing the society of Deuteronomy as "ignorant savages". With or without that retort, there remains a real question about whether we today can authentically choose to adopt, even temporarily, any such culturally remote outlook as that of Leviticus, with all its slaughterous literality, and all its magical thinking. But if we cannot inhabit or even visit that viewpoint, and if we cannot fully make sense of the Cross *without* doing so, then we cannot make full sense of the Cross. For us today, the Cross will have to be something else, and something less definite, and, to be blunt, something less thoroughly *Biblical*: an icon of political sacrifice, perhaps, or a symbol of radical identification, or both.

But perhaps that thought in turn invites a further thought. If the notion of ritual sacrifice is so unintelligible to us, how come *that* is so? Hebrews claims that Jesus' sacrifice is the sacrifice to end all other sacrifices. On the Cross, says Hebrews, he fulfils the sacrificial system by completing it; by transcending it; may we not add—by abolishing it?

But then if, *because* of the Cross, those of us who are Christians today live in an age where sacrifice is abolished, is a thing of the past—the very distant past—then perhaps it is no surprise that ritual sacrifice is no longer intelligible to us. If we have learned that God is not a remorseless cosmic policeman, like Javert only bigger, nor an angry tyrant in the sky who needs appeasing and propitiating with a drink of some victim's blood; if we have learned that there is no gap between God's justice and his mercy to be overcome, and never was; if we have learned that it makes sense to ask, of an exposition of the Levitical system, "But why can't God just *forgive*, without all this palaver?"—then one good question to ask is: "And where did we, our culture, learn all *this*?" Well, maybe one of the places we learned it is, in fact, from the Cross itself. A cross after all is a sign that can mean many things. And one of them is: cancellation.

Notes

1. I thank Fiona Woollard for alerting me to one exception to my generalisation: Thomson 2008. But in that paper Thomson only briefly considers the option of self-sacrifice, and she is against it: in the case she considers, she thinks it would be a bad thing to do. And she's right, it is bad *there*, because her case is like this. Suppose you learn that, for abstruse causal reasons, if you die now then 5 lives elsewhere, no matter where, will be saved, and you therefore resolve to die now. That, says Thomson, is a bad thing to do. She's right of course. But it's not a typical self-sacrifice case, precisely because of its complete lack of a normal moral context.
2. Articles retrieved November 2017.
   Some academics turn up their noses at Wikipedia. This seems a false

fastidiousness, especially since the same academics are often very happy to cite sources that take a great deal less trouble to tell the truth, such as newspapers. Of course Wikipedia should be treated with caution as a source. But that is a substitution-instance of a platitude. *Any* source should be treated with caution as a source.

3. Which "brothers and sisters"? Does Stein mean her fellow Jews, or her fellow Catholic-convert Jews, or her fellow Catholics? In the Wikipedia article that I quote, the context suggests her fellow Jews; but the point has been disputed, and both Stein herself and her Catholic admirers, such as Alasdair MacIntyre, have been accused, like Kolbe and his, of various forms of anti-Semitism. I have no dog in these fights.

4. Of course, Hugo's authorial intentions were not about Gilda in *Rigoletto* but about Gilda's original in *Le Roi s'Amuse*, who was called Blanche. No matter.

5. Of them and, be it noted, pretty much only them. Mostly, while writing this, I have actively avoided reading anything except the NT itself. My aim is to try and see, with as fresh eyes as possible, what *it* says about the Cross. That is quite hard enough to do on its own.

6. The letter to the Hebrews—of which more in Section V—has gospel-talk going back even further than the later prophets: "we received the gospel (*esmen eueggelismenoi*) exactly as they [the unbelieving Jews in the wilderness in Exodus] did" (Hebs 4.2).

7. While I was writing this essay, my attention was drawn by a friend to this interesting essay in the *New York Times*: David Bentley Hart, "Are Christians supposed to be communists?", Nov. 4 2017, https://www.nytimes.com/2017/11/04/opinion/sunday/christianity-communism.html.

8. In my unpublished essay "Soul Food".

Funding

This work was supported by the Leverhulme Trust [MRF 2016-100];

References

Bible: I use the Greek New Testament (London: BFBS 1977), plus the Jerusalem Bible and the Authorised Version for the Old Testament.

Charles Dickens, *A Tale of Two Cities*. London: Chapman and Hall, 1859.

Victor Hugo, *Le Roi s'Amuse*. Paris: Flammarion, [1832].

Victor Hugo, *Les Misérables*. Paris: Gallimard, [1861].

Judith Jarvis Thomson, "Turning the trolley", PPA 2008, pp.359–374.

Giuseppe Verdi, *Rigoletto*. Libretto by Francesco Maria Piave. Milan: Giulio Ricordi, 1851.

Samuel Wells, *Improvisation: the drama of Christian Ethics*. Grand Rapids, Michigan: Brazos Press, 2004.

Index

act-consequentialism 16, 32n4, 138
actions: costly action and effort 20; 'more ideal' actions 55, 56, 57; and reasons 122, 127–128; and values 111
adaptive preferences 89–90
adequate moralities 85, 89, 96
advance knowledge, of sacrifice 12
agent-neutral values 112, 113, 114
agent-relative expected value 64, 65
agent-relative reasons 112–114
agent-relative sacrifice 55, 56, 72; as opportunity cost 61
agent-relative value 63–64
aggregative value 67
altruism 79–80, 81, 85, 87–88, 90–92, 145
altruistic reasons: of morality 121, 123, 129; and reasons of conscience, distinguished 132
ambivalence, as response to conflicts of values 86
Anscombe, G. E. M. 31n1
anticipated losses 38, 40
anti-consequentialism 142
anti-realism 83
anti-tradition tradition 190
Antony, Louise 46
appropriate attitudes 111
Aristotle 142, 143
assistance duties 54–55, 59, 60, 73n4; agent-relative sacrifice 55, 56, 61, 72; and high level of sacrifice 56; ideal-relative sacrifice 55, 56, 57, 60, 68–71, 72; and interests 58; necessary condition for 66–68; recipient-relative sacrifice 55, 56, 57, 60, 70, 72
assistance principle 54, 55, 58, 59–60, 64–66, 72, 73n3; best-placed principle 56–58, 72; well-placed principle 56–57
associative/emotional empathy 123, 125, 131
Atack, Iain 167, 175n12

'at not too high a cost' 54, 55, 56, 63
Austin, J. L. 175n6
autonomy 42, 44, 46–47, 172–173; individual autonomy 46; individualistic autonomy 46; relational autonomy 44, 46, 48, 49; and self-sacrifices 162–163

bads 61, 62, 63–65
Baier, Annette 51n12
benefits 8, 11, 78–82, 87, 90–92, 93, 139–140
Benn, C. 26
best interests standard (BIS) 47–48
best-placed duties 57, 58–59, 67, 68–70, 71, 72, 73n5, 73n7
best-placed principle 56–58, 72
bond 143–144
Bondurant, Joan 165, 175n9
boundaries 142–143, 149, 151; in non-emergency cases 153; between ourselves and our special others 144–151; and selfishness 149
Bradley, F. H. 143, 145
Brandt, Richard 39, 51n5
Brink, David 142–143
Brownlee, Kimberly 165

cancellation, sacrifice 196–197
'can' implies 'ought' 54, 56
capable agent 70
capacity-bearer 55
Carbonell, V. 3, 51n2, 61–62, 63, 64, 72, 97n1, 97n2
care ethics 2, 156, 157–158, 173–174; common features 174n1; feminist resistance, and self-sacrifice 170–173; and justice 163–164; and morality 173; self-care, and self-sacrifice 161–162; self-donation 162–163; self-sacrifice objection 158–161; and self-sacrifice value 164–170
caring 122–123, 134

caring, moral perspective 158–159; and domination of women 160; and oppression of women 159–160
Carse, A. L. 174n3
causal influence 45
causal isolation 44–45, 48
change and development, possibility of 29
Chappell, R. Y. 21, 23, 25, 26
Christian forms of sacrifice 182; *see also* Cross, the
Christman, John 51n14
civil disobedience 165
civil resistance 175n12
closeness 146, 147–148, 149, 150–151, 152–153
Cohen, G. 32n7
Cokelet, Bradford 124
commitments 140, 141, 144, 151
concessive act-consequentialism 138
conditional duty 73n4
confinement *see* restriction of options
conflicts of values 76–77, 82, 95; and ambivalence 86
conscription 10, 11, 12
consensual sacrifice 178
consequentialism 82, 92, 115n2, 137–138, 139, 151, 160; and demandingness objection 26, 32n4; indifference to stranger/special other distinction 139–140; objections to 140; and overdemandingness 16
cost 2–3, 55, 78, 140; action is not too costly 60–68; action is the least costly of all agents' similar actions 68–71; 'at not too high a cost' 54, 55, 56, 63; costliness to the agent 60–64; costliness to the recipient 65–66; and demandingness 30, 31; net costs 55; 'not too costly' 57, 60–68; and restriction of options 26–27
Cross, the: as an act of love 192; Christians' notion of 184; God's forging sins via 192–193; as Jesus's personal sacrifice 193; a personal sacrifice 191–194; as a political sacrifice 184–191; as a ritual sacrifice 195–196; sacrifice cancellation 196–197
Cruz, Nikolaz 1

Damien [Damiaan], Father 179–180, 181–182
Dancy, Jonathan 2, 115n3
Darwall, Stephen 38, 46, 64
Day, Dorothy 169–170, 172, 175n14
death 9
decency, minimal 37–38

defiance 180, 181, 183, 184, 185, 190, 191
demandingness 30; and accessibility 19; and benefits 16; and costs 17, 20; and difficulty 18, 21, 24, 25–26; in ethics 100; high, and supererogation 17; hybrid view 17, 18, 19; importance of 16–17; and morality 138; and moral obligation 23; and overdemandingness 16, 17; *see also* overdemandingness
demandingness objections 23, 25–26, 115n2, 137–138, 140–141; as 'appeal to cost' 17; characterization of 139–141; common core of 138, 139, 151, 152; development of 141–144; improved 151–153; and special others 144–145
Deming, Barbara 166, 171
desire fulfilment theory 2
desires 38, 41, 42, 51n8, 104, 108–109, 111
desperation 121, 122, 126
Dickens, Charles 182–183, 184
difficult actions 111; benefits 19, 21–24; cost and difficulty 19–20
difficulty 18–26, 30, 32n8, 111, 116n18; accessibility and distance of worlds 18–19; affects of 21; degrees of 18; and demandingness 18, 21, 24, 25–26; disjunctive category 112; forms of 18, 111–112; and motivation 22–23; motivational difficulty 22–25; motivation and benefits 23–24; related to prudential demands 24
dignity 167, 168, 170, 172
distribution of sacrifice 173
distributive justice 173
do-gooder 87, 90–93
Dorsey, Dale 1, 115n3
duty-generating relations: action is not too costly 60–68; action is the least costly of all agents' similar actions 68–71; aggregative and iterative sacrifice 66–68; 'An Important Interest is Unfulfilled' 57–59; costliness to the agent 60–64; costliness to the recipient 65–66; someone is sufficiently capable of fulfilling it 59–60

economy of sacrifice 51n3
effort 18–20, 22, 25
egoism 81
emotional caring 122–123
emotional/receptive empathy 123
emotions 121–122, 125; and reasons 136n3
empathy 121, 123–124, 129, 134–135; first-order empathy 132; projective empathy 123, 128; second-order empathy 132;

INDEX 201

and transmission of emotions 125–126;
 and transmission of reasons 124
Epicurus 9
essential properties 45–46, 49, 50
evaluative judgments 82–86, 88–90, 92
excuses 13
expected value 64–68, 70–72

fairness 77, 84, 86, 94, 95
family 129–130; *see also* parental sacrifices;
 parents
family interests 47–48, 52n15
feminist resistance, and self-sacrifice
 170–173
Fierke, Karin 164–165, 169, 171, 174,
 174n5
first-order empathy 132
flourishing 80, 86, 89, 96
folklore of heroism 11
Frankfurt, Harry 79, 83
Freud, Sigmund 157
fundamentally normative notion, sacrifice
 as 37

Gan, Barry 168
Gandhi, M. K. 164, 165–167, 173, 175n11
gender-based oppression 159–160
Gilligan, Carol 157–158
'giving up' 101; of vital interest 115n4
glorification of sacrifices 52n17
God: forging sins via the Cross 192–
 193(*see also* Cross, the); judgement
 187–188; *see also* Jesus Christ
'good for' 106
good-making feature of relationships 144,
 146, 151
goods 61, 62–63, 64–65, 67, 106
gratitude 103–104, 108
great sacrifice 8–9; morally required 12;
 and motivation 13
Green, T. H. 143, 145
Groenhout, Ruth 161, 162
Groll, Daniel 48
gross benefit 55
gross cost 55
gross loses 43, 66; of well-being 39, 101,
 106

Halbertal, Mosheh 104, 115n4
Hampton, Jean 159
harming, and sacrifice 172
Haybron, Daniel 38
hedonistic theory 42
Held, Virginia 158, 174n1
hierarchical identification theories 88

Hill, Thomas 87–88
Hoagland, Sarah 159–160
hope 180, 181–182, 183, 184, 185, 190, 191
Hugo, Victor 183, 184
Hume, David 120
Humean constructivism 83
Hurka, Thomas 38

icons 194
ideal-relative sacrifice 55, 56, 57, 60, 68–71,
 72
illocutionary speech act 175n6
imitation 180, 182, 184, 185, 187, 190, 192
important interests 54–59, 63, 65–66,
 67–69, 73n4
incommensurability 63, 72, 77, 84, 86, 90
individual autonomy 44, 46
individualism: about best interests 47–48;
 about well-being 43–44; causal version
 48; properties version 48; self-concept
 version 48
individualistic autonomy 46
individual self 80, 81, 90, 93
interest-bearer 55, 65
interest-fulfilling action 55–56, 56–57, 69
interest fulfilling measure 65–66
interest-fulfilling measures 61–62, 65, 72
interest in other people's sacrifices,
 rationality of 37
interests enhancement, and sacrifice 8
interpersonal skills 86
interpersonal transmission: of emotions
 123; of reasons 123
intrapersonal skills 85, 88
intrinsically bad entities 106, 107, 108
intrinsically good entities 100, 105–109,
 112, 113, 116n12
intrinsically valuable entities 105–115
intrinsic value of sacrifices 99, 105, 106–
 112, 114–115
intuitive process 84–85
iterative value 67

Jesus Christ 182; crucifixion 185 (*see
 also* Cross, the); defiance 190; gospel
 of 185–189; hope 190; imitation 190;
 protest 190; sacrifice of 194; solidarity of
 189–190
justice, and care 163–164

Kagan, Shelly 17
Kant, Immanuel 27, 31n4, 132
Khader, Serene 89
King, Martin Luther, Jr. 164, 165, 167–168,
 171, 172

Kingdom of God 180, 181, 186–190
Knafo, Ariel 91
Kohlberg, Lawrence 157
Kolbe, Maximilian 179–180, 181–182, 184, 192
Kopelman, Loretta 47
Kripke, Saul 120

Lee, Stan 54
legal duty 10–12
Levitical sacrifices 195–196, 197
Lewis, D. 61
life, giving up of 9
life-enhancing goods 67
list theories 38, 41, 42
locutionary speech act 175n6
loss: anticipated losses 38, 40; gross loss of well-being 38; net loss 62; net losses of well-being 39–40
love: love-relationship 146–147; and reasons for action 35–36
loving sacrifices: and well-being 40–44
loyalty 84

MacFarquhar, Larissa 92–93
Mackenzie, Catriona 44–46, 51n12
Mackie, J. L. 135
MacKinnon, Catharine 159
Madhavan, Guruprasad 91
maximising, act, agent-neutral consequentialism 66
maximising, act consequentialism 82
McDowell, John 128
McElwee, B. 17, 18, 19, 20
McGrath, Michael 91
Mellema, G. 115n3
membership view 104–105
metaphysical individualism 4, 44–46
Meyers, Diana 88
Miller, David 58, 148, 154n3, L.
moderate relationalism 45–46
Mongoven, Ann 52n17
moral ambivalence 85
moral attitudes 14
moral blackmailing 108
moral demandingness 1, 4
moral demands 22, 24; roots 16
moral development 157
moral duties 103; to make serious sacrifices 10; to save other person 24; scope of 13
moralities 119, 157; adequate moralities 85, 89, 96; and practical reasons 124–125; and serious sacrifices 11; universal constraints on 86

moral judgments 120; capacity for making 132
moral life 14
moral obligations 25, 38, 140, 141; reciprocal moral obligations 37
moral outlook 157, 159
moral principle internalization 81
moral rationality 123
moral sacrifices 38, 39
moral sentimentalism 119, 120, 134
moral significance, of sacrifice 9–10
moral values 84
'more ideal' actions 55, 56, 57
motivation: and sacrifice 12–13
motivational difficulty 22–23; and beneficial actions 24–25
motivational sacrifice 39
Mulgan, Tim 97n3, 141, 142
Murphy, L. B. 26

Nagel, Thomas 127–128, 129–130, 135n1, 136n2
Narveson, Jan 72n1
necessity: and forbidden and permissible courses of action 27–28
Nelkin, Dana 112
net agent-relative sacrifice 55
net costs 55
net losses 62; of well-being 39–40, 101
New Testament (NT) 185, 193, 195
Noddings, Nel 158, 162
no-emergency case 153
non-desired options 29
non-negative values 63, 65–66, 67
non-positive values 63, 67, 68
non-violent resistance 164, 165–166, 168, 169, 173; and feminism 170–171
normatively relevant, sacrifices as 99
normative moral theories 16
no-saying 147–151
'not too costly' 57, 60–68
Nussbaum, Martha 78, 115n5

Oakley, Barbara 91
objective assessments of sacrifice 43
objective list theories 38, 42, 115n5
objective theories 106
obligations 9, 13, 140
opportunity hoarder 87, 93–97
oppression 156, 157, 158–160, 164, 166–167, 168, 170–174
options 27, 28–29, 30; restrictions of see restriction of options
other-regarding interests 85

other-regarding normative impact of sacrifices 99–100, 102–103, 115n7; disjunctive view 105; gratitude view 103–104; intrinsically valuable 105–106; membership view 104–105
ought 78, 82
ourselves and special others: boundaries between 144–151; relations between 151–153
overdemandingness 15, 16–17; acceptable and unacceptable 17; and demandingness 17; and supererogatory 17; *see also* demandingness
overdemandingness objections 16, 30, 31–32n4
Overvold, M. C. 2, 41, 51n4, 51n5, 51n6, 61

Pankhurst, Emmeline 166, 169, 174
parental sacrifices 35, 41–43, 90
parents 134; ability to say no 147–150
Parfit, Derek 115n5, 143
paternal function 154n3
pathological altruism 90–92
pediatric bioethics 47–48
penal substitution 184
perfect duties 27
perfectionism 38, 42
perlocutionary power: of sacrifice 166; of self-sacrifice 171
perlocutionary speech act 175n6
personal commitments 140
personal sacrifices 182–184; Carton (fictional example) 182–183, 184; Cross as 191–194; Gilda (fictional example) 183, 184; Valjean (fictional example) 183, 184
Pettersen, Tove 161
Piper, A. M. 174n3
Plato 143, 145
pluralism 85
pluralistic relativism 85
plural values, construction of 81–86
political sacrifice 179–182; Cross as 184–191; Damien [Damiaan], Father 179–180, 181–182; Maximilian Kolbe 179–180, 181–182, 184, 192; Edith Stein 180, 181–182
political self-sacrifice: communicative function of 164–166; self-sacrifice *see* self-sacrifice, in political resistance
polysemy 194
Portmore, Douglas 100
practical reasons 120, 129; of conscientiousness 131–132; and morality 124–125

practical sentimentalism 133
preferred difficulty 22, 23, 24; and beneficial actions 24
Price, Anthony 142
pro-attitudes 107, 108, 109–110, 111
prohibitions 18, 27, 28–29, 30
projective empathy 123, 128
proportionality requirement 106–107, 108–110
protest 180, 181, 183–184, 185, 190, 195
prudential demands 22, 23, 24
prudential reasons 18, 23–24, 26, 27, 28, 32n8, 121, 124
prudential value 108
psychic mergedness 154n3
psychological egoists 80
psychopaths 125, 128–129, 130–132, 134
publicly intelligible criteria, for sacrifice 37
Pudner, Kalynne 162, 163, 172–173, 174n3
punishment 165, 168
pure reason 136n3

Ralston, A. 20
rational desire 124
Raz, Joseph 2, 31, 31n3, 73n4
reasoning process 84, 85
reasons 99–100, 102–106, 108–114, 120, 122; for action 122; apprehension 127–128; and calm passions 120; and emotion 136n3; and psychopaths 130–131; transmission for action 127–128
recipient-relative sacrifice 55, 56, 57, 60, 70, 72
recursive account of value 107–108, 109–110, 114
redemption 167–168
Reeves, Richard 93–94
relational autonomy 44, 46, 48, 49
relational interests 48
relationalism 51n14; about interests 46–47; moderate relationalism about persons 45, 46–47, 48
relational well-being 36, 44, 46, 48–50
religious experience 193
repentance 186, 187, 189
restriction of options 17, 18, 26–30
Rosati, Connie 2, 51n4, 97n1
Ruddick, S. 172
Ryan, Cheyney 169–170

'sacrifice for' 101
'sacrifices of self' 61
sacrifice theology 195–196
'sacrifice to' 101

Salter, Erica 47
sanctions 11
satyagraha 166
Scheffler, Samuel 27
second-order empathy 132
second-order judgments 83, 84–85, 88
self 139; sacrifices of 97n1
self-annunciation 162
self-care 161–162, 164, 171–172
self-conceptions 45, 47, 48
self-donation 163, 164, 172–173, 174
self-effacement 162–163
self-fulfillment theory 38
self-immolation 162, 169
self-interest 79–80, 143
self-interested rationality 124, 133, 134
selfishness 146, 147, 149–150, 152, 153
selfless acts 42
self-regarding 85
self-regarding normative impact of
   sacrifices 100
self-sacrifice, in political resistance:
   communicative role 164–166; illustrative
   role 168–170; transformative role
   166–168
self-sacrifices 15, 17, 31n2, 37, 51n5,
   77, 78–79, 82, 119, 133, 156;
   appropriateness of 83; and care ethics
   161–162; and feminist resistance
   170–173; illustrative function of
   168–170; and motivation 91; objection
   158–161; and suicide, distinguishing
   between 174n5; value of 164; versions of
   162–163
self-sacrificial woman 87–90; adaptive
   preferences 89–90
self-standing reasons 152, 153
'sense of' self 45
sentimentalism 119, 123, 129, 132–133,
   135n1
'separateness of persons' objection 141
servility 87, 88
Sidgwick, H. 143
simulation 123
Singer, Peter 16, 31–32n4, 54
skills 18–19, 25
Sobel, David 30–31, 32n6, 115n2
social group value 86
social norm internalization 81
social self thesis 51n14
sociopaths 128–129
Socrates 181
solidarity 180, 181, 183, 184, 185, 189
'something matters to someone' 79–80

special others 138, 139; and ourselves,
   boundaries between 144–151; and
   ourselves, relations between 151–153
Stein, Edith 180, 181–182
Stoljar, Natalie 44–46, 48, 51n12
strangers 36, 138, 139–145, 151–153
Street, Sharon 83
subjective assessments of sacrifice 43
suicidal/depressed people 135n1
suicide: and self-sacrifice, distinguishing
   between 174n5
supererogation 1, 15, 17, 36, 37, 100, 115;
   and high demandingness 17
swadeshi 166–167, 175n11

Thomson, Judith Jarvis 197n1
Tilly, Charles 93
transformative function of self-sacrifice
   166–168
transformative nonviolence 167, 175n12
trolleyology 178–179
truism 13

ultimate sacrifice 196
unfairness 94–95
upper middle class 93–96
Urmson, J. O. 1, 17

value(s) 76–77, 109; and actions 111;
   agent-neutral values 112, 113, 114; of
   appropriate value responses 110,
   112–113; conflict of *see* conflicts of
   values; construction of 76–77; of fairness
   84; of loyalty 84; objective theory of
   63–64; prioritization of 77, 82, 84,
   85–86, 88, 89; of self-sacrifice 164–170;
   subjective theory 64; value monism 82,
   96; value pluralism 84, 92–93; value
   realism 82
Velleman, David 146
Verdi, Giuseppe 183
Visak, Tatiana 51n2
voluntary sacrifices 37, 38, 39

Walker, L. J. 174n2
Walker, Margaret Urban 97n7
Wang, Peter 1
well-being 2, 3, 15, 26, 36–40, 100;
   gross losses 101, 106; gross loss of 38;
   individualism about 43–44; of a loved
   one 42–43; and loving sacrifices 40–44;
   net losses of 39–40; net loss of 101;
   objective list theories 115n5; objective
   theory of 38, 41; relational well-being

36, 44, 46, 48–50; of self 42–43;
subjective theory 38
well-placed duties 57, 58, 68–69
well-placed principle 56–57,
71–72
wide interests model 48
Williams, Bernard 1, 141

willpower 17, 18–19, 20, 22, 25–26
Wolf, Susan 1
Wong, David 85, 86
Woolf, Virginia 160
Woollard, F. 32n6

Yarov, S. 154n2